D1104829

FIRES
ALL AROUND
THE
HORIZON

FIRES
ALL AROUND
THE
HORIZON

The U.N.'s Uphill Battle to Preserve the Peace

MAX HARRELSON

PRAEGER

New York
Westport, Connecticut
London

341.2309
H2964 f

Library of Congress Cataloging-in-Publication Data

Harrelson, Max.
    Fires all around the horizon.

    Bibliography: p.
    Includes index.
    1. United Nations—History. 2. Peace—History.
    I. Title.
    JX1977.H323   1989   341.23'09   88-15254
    ISBN 0-275-92997-3 (alk. paper)
    ISBN 0-275-92998-1 (pbk. : alk. paper)

Copyright © 1989 by Max Harrelson

All rights reserved. No portion of this book may
be reproduced, by any process or technique, without
the express written consent of the publisher.

Library of Congress Catalog Card Number: 88-15254
ISBN: 0-275-92997-3
        0-275-92998-1 (pbk.)

First published in 1989

Praeger Publishers, One Madison Avenue, New York, NY 10010
A division of Greenwood Press, Inc.

Printed in the United States of America

The paper used in this book complies with the
Permanent Paper Standard issued by the National
Information Standards Organization (Z39.48-1984).

10 9 8 7 6 5 4 3 2 1

Contents

Preface

As the reader will observe, I have made extensive use of official documents in this book. There is certainly a wealth of material in the verbatim reports of the Security Council and the General Assembly, in written communications to these organs, in summary reports on the various committees, in transcripts of press conferences, and in official press releases as well as in press releases from the various delegations. I have drawn liberally from a number of firsthand books, such as Trygve Lie's *In the Cause of Peace*, and from others that throw light on behind-the-scenes events. These included Arthur Schlesinger's *A Thousand Days*, Lyndon Johnson's *The Vantage Point*, Brian Urquhart's *Hammarskjöld*, and Dean Acheson's *Present at the Creation*. Naturally, another prime source has been my personal contacts with U.N. officials and delegates over more than a quarter century, and the information recorded in my own files. Also I have had the pleasure of working closely with Andrew Cordier and Wilder Foote—two respected U.N. officials—as coeditor of *The Public Papers of the Secretaries-general of the United Nations*. This eight-volume set contains valuable commentaries as well as providing easy access to pertinent documents on almost every subject. Many of the documents quoted in the book are found in these volumes. On details of military operations—such as the conflicts in the Middle East, Persian Gulf, Falkland Islands, and Grenada—I am indebted to media reports from the Associated Press, New York *Times*, Washington *Post*, *Time*, and *Newsweek*. They provided valuable information to supplement official U.N. reports. More specific references to sources will be found at the back of the book.

Introduction

Those who drafted the Charter of the United Nations during the final months of World War II reflected the dreams of the millions who yearned for a just and lasting peace. A generation later, the organization is still alive. It has survived far beyond the life span of the League of Nations, which had been born of similar dreams after World War I. Nevertheless, even the United Nations' most ardent supporters acknowledge that it has not met their hopes and expectations. One of the goals set forth in the charter was to "save succeeding generations from the scourge of war." Whatever else it may have achieved, the United Nations has obviously not attained this goal. There has been no third world war, but there has scarcely been a day since the end of World War II when there was not fighting somewhere—ranging from small skirmishes and brushfires to major conflicts such as those in the Middle East, Korea, and Southeast Asia. Former Secretary-general Dag Hammarskjöld sadly noted this in 1958, in words that are equally appropriate today. "There are fires all around the horizon," he said, "and they are not fires announcing peace. More perturbing than all these smouldering conflicts are the main underlying tendencies, which we all know too well and which are preoccupying our minds and darkening our hopes."[1]

One of the architects of the United Nations, Adlai E. Stevenson, once described its birth as being like the morning—"fresh with the hope of a new day." But a few years later he spoke regretfully of the battering that the organization had suffered at the hands of its members. "There are cracks in the walls," he said, "and inside the cold winds of war and danger and strife from every quarter of the globe rattle the doors and windows." He was referring to the abuse of the veto power, the unilateral use of force, the boycotts, and the go-it-alone policies that had undermined the prestige of the organization and tarnished its image.[2]

Even when the founders signed the charter on June 26, 1945, they recognized its imperfections. They had avoided many of the weaknesses leading to the collapse of the League of Nations, but they could go only so far in a world where governments zealously guarded their national sovereignty. The founders acknowledged that what they had created was far short of being a world government. As it turned out later, the imperfections of the charter were not so big a problem as the failure of its members to adhere to its provisions. The founders had not anticipated that the Western powers and the Soviet Union— allies during the war—would almost immediately become involved in an ideological conflict that projected itself into every meeting of every U.N. organ. Neither had they foreseen that the national interests of the member nations would so frequently cause them to ignore U.N. decisions, to defy such decisions, or to act unilaterally outside the United Nations to settle disputes.

Despite the organization's disappointing performance, its prestige remained surprisingly high during its first quarter-century. This was particularly true during the middle years, when approximately 80 percent of the U.S. public was shown by the Gallup polls to believe that the United Nations was doing a good or fair job. It was not until November 1971 that the Gallup polls reported for the first time that a majority of the people in the United States who expressed an opinion found the United Nations to be doing a poor job. The disillusionment of the U.S. public at that time was partly due to a feeling that the organization was sitting on the sidelines during the Vietnam War, rather than taking an active part in trying to end the conflict. It was also due to the fact that the United States found itself more and more frequently outvoted by a combination of the Soviet bloc and Third World nations. Outside the United States and some of its Western allies, public confidence in the United Nations remained surprisingly high. This was reflected in the phenomenal growth of its membership. One of the first acts of each newly independent country was to seek admission to the organization. Although these emerging states had not had a hand in the creation of the United Nations, they evidently believed that membership was worthwhile. For that matter, so did the original 51 members—including the great powers— for, at this writing, no country has withdrawn permanently from the organization.

When critics express disappointment with the United Nations, they almost invariably refer to the organization's performance in the political field and to its failure to establish effective peace-keeping machinery. In the following pages, the author ventures a look at some of the political disputes of the past four decades—in particular, those resulting in military conflicts—and examines the role of the United Nations. Despite the many disputes settled peacefully through quiet diplomacy, a surprisingly large number have led to the use of force. The United Nations intervened in almost all of these conflicts, in one way or another: by calling for cease-fires, by mediation, by condemning one of the parties, or—

in some cases—by sending in peace-keeping forces. These efforts were not always successful. There were other cases where the organization could not intervene at all. For example, the U.N. Charter prohibits any interference in the internal affairs of a member state. This ruled out any intervention in civil wars except in instances where outside forces have become involved. The organization also recognized that it was helpless to use enforcement measures against any of the five permanent members of the Security Council because of their veto power—if for no other reason. There was another very important reason, however, and that was the realization that the use of force against a major power would likely lead to a third world war. The impotence of the United Nations to deal with big power aggressions had been anticipated, but the readiness of these powers to resort to force as a solution for problems had not been expected. There was no way the founders could have foreseen that not one or two but every one of the five permanent members of the Security Council would send their military forces into another country in violation of the charter that they were pledged to uphold.

The U.N. peace-keeping efforts were also hampered by the fact that both the Soviet Union and France, as well as a dozen small countries, refused to pay their General Assembly assessments for peace-keeping or to make voluntary contributions toward the costs of such operations. The major operations would not have been possible at all if a sizable number of countries had not volunteered to contribute military contingents at minimal cost to the organization.

There was widespread public disappointment over the failure of the United Nations to intervene in the Vietnam War—the largest conflict since World War II. Secretary-general U Thant was deeply concerned by the public reaction and its damage to the U.N. image. He went to great pains to explain the lack of a U.N. role in the conflict. Thant's most comprehensive statement on this subject was made before the Annual Conference of Non-Governmental Organizations in New York on May 12, 1966. One reason, the secretary-general said, was the fact that only one of the participants in the war—the United States—was a member of the United Nations. The other participants were South Vietnam, North Vietnam, the Vietcong, and the People's Republic of China—all of which refused to have anything to do with the organization. "Another reason, which in my view is more basic," Thant declared, "is the disagreement among the big powers regarding the projected United Nations intervention in Vietnam in the field of peace-keeping. Everybody knows that the Soviet Union and France are against United Nations involvement in peace-keeping of any type, of any character, in Vietnam. . . . I have come to the conclusion that the vast majority of the members, large and small, agree that at least for the moment the United Nations cannot be usefully involved in the settlement of the very tragic and very disastrous developments in Vietnam."[3]

Even though the United Nations did not become officially involved in Vietnam, U Thant himself did work privately to bring about a settlement; and, by doing so, he demonstrated once more that the role of the secretary-general can be a significant one in preserving and restoring peace. The author believes and hopes that the recounting in the following pages of the major crises and conflicts since 1946 will contribute to a better understanding of the United Nations' capabilities and limitations, and will help in assessing the blame for its failures and the credit for its successes in peace-keeping.

1

The United Nations' First Year Chilled by Cold War

Regardless of whether or not the United Nations survives, January 10, 1946, will be recorded as a date of some historical significance, for on that day the U.N. General Assembly met for the first time. Until then, the new organization had existed only on paper. The meeting took place in London after weeks of intensive preparations and diplomatic horse-trading on such questions as who would be chosen as secretary-general and which six countries would be selected as nonpermanent members of the Security Council. On the eve of the meeting, King George VI set the solemn tone of the session at a glittering state dinner in St. James's Palace. Gathered around the candle-lit tables in the ancient banquet hall were many of the world's top diplomats, including several prime ministers and some 20 foreign ministers. "It is in your hands," the king said, "to make or mar the happiness of millions yet unborn. It is for you to lay the foundations of a new world where such a conflict as that which lately brought our world to the verge of annihilation must never be repeated."[1]

The next morning the delegates began arriving at the Central Hall of Church House—the main congregation place of England's Methodists—well in advance of the 11 A.M. meeting time. Quietly they took their places at rows of natural-finish oak tables arranged in concentric semicircles before the raised speaker's platform. The galleries were already jammed with aides, wives, and friends of the delegates and with news correspondents from all parts of the world. A huge golden map of the world—a north polar projection—hung behind the rostrum as an unofficial emblem of the United Nations. A hush fell over the assembly as the temporary president—gray-haired, short, bespectacled Dr. Eduardo

ZuletaAngel of Colombia—strode to his seat on the platform. It was 11:03 A.M. when he rapped the gavel on the gold-covered table to call the meeting to order.

His opening remarks were brief and solemn. Perhaps remembering that the day was the twenty-sixth anniversary of another historic event—the birth of the League of Nations at Versailles—he warned the delegates that "We cannot with impunity fail mankind again." He then presented Britain's prime minister, Clement Attlee. In a speech reminiscent of Lincoln's Gettysburg address, Attlee also emphasized the magnitude of the responsibility that must be borne by the assembly. "We who are gathered here today in this ancient home of liberty and order," he said, "are able to meet together because thousands of brave men and women have suffered and died that we may live. It is for us today, bearing in mind the great sacrifices that have been made, to prove ourselves no less courageous in approaching our great task, no less patient, no less self-sacrificing. We must and will succeed."

The delegates immediately plunged into the organizational problems that constituted the first order of business. Paul-Henri Spaak of Belgium was elected president of the assembly; Trygve Lie of Norway was chosen as the first secretary-general; six nonpermanent members of the Security Council were elected; 18 members of the Economic and Social Council were chosen; and the 15 members of the International Court of Justice were elected. With the exception of some minor skirmishes, the elections proceeded smoothly.

The newly elected Security Council members together with the five permanent members—the United States, Britain, France, Nationalist China, and the Soviet Union—gathered on January 17 for a brief ceremonial meeting. It had been assumed that the council would not get down to serious business until the United Nations began operating at its temporary quarters in the United States. But even before the delegates had had time to consider rules of procedure, they found themselves in the midst of an East–West battle. Two days after the opening session, Iran filed a formal complaint charging the Soviet Union with encouraging a separatist movement in its northern province of Azerbaijan, which was still occupied by Soviet troops under a wartime agreement with the United States and Britain. Unwittingly, Iran had dragged the council into what was later to become known as the Cold War. The Soviet Union—convinced that Britain and possibly the United States had inspired the Iranian complaint—decided that the best defense was to attack. The Soviets not only denied the Iranian charges, but filed a complaint of their own alleging the interference of British troops in the internal affairs of Greece. This meant that the fledgling council was faced with two complaints within its first days. To make matters worse, the Soviet Ukraine lodged a separate, unrelated complaint accusing Britain of trying to suppress the nationalist movement in the newly liberated Dutch East Indies, which later became the Republic of Indonesia.[2]

The Greek case proved to be the most serious one. The Iranian question was quickly disposed of after the council agreed on a resolution noting and approving the expressed willingness of both sides to settle the controversy by direct negotiations. The Ukrainian complaint was shelved after brief debate; the council rejected a Ukrainian proposal for the establishment of a commission of inquiry. Debate on the Greek question, however, produced a controversy of major proportions between the Soviet Union and the Western powers. At the center of the storm were two of the least restrained personalities ever to have appeared then or since at the council table—Andrei Y. Vyshinsky, the old Bolshevik prosecutor, and Ernest Bevin, a British labor leader accustomed to shouting down shipowners.

Vyshinsky called the Greek government "fascist scum" and asserted that Britain was endangering international peace by its support. Bevin took the charges as a personal attack and an insult to his government. Shaking a finger at Vyshinsky, he shouted that the charges were lies. Bevin declared that, if he and his government were in fact endangering international peace, the council "ought to tell us to leave this table." "The danger to the peace of the world," he said, "has been the incessant propaganda from Moscow against the British Commonwealth." The Greek question was disposed of when the council adopted a suggestion of the president that it take note of the statements and consider the matter closed. Commenting on this debate, the secretary-general later wrote, "It was a bad omen, and a chill descended upon my optimism. . . . If the atmosphere of this very first debate of the Security Council at which I was present was a sign of future events, I feared that the prospects for further agreements on all the great issues to come might be much poorer than I had thought." Lie had witnessed the first major blast of the Cold War, and it was indeed a preview of the chilling diatribes ahead. More would be heard on the Greek, Iranian, and Indonesian questions in the months and years to come—along with a stream of new issues that contributed to the deepening rift between the former allies. Even in these first weeks, however, the council had begun to set a pattern: In one case, it had sent the problem back to the parties concerned for direct negotiations. In another case, it had simply taken note of a complaint and dropped it. The third case was the first of many Soviet moves that received no support outside the communist bloc.

Even more ominous than the use of the council for propaganda purposes was the outcome of a fourth case that arose in London. It involved the withdrawal of French and British troops from Syria and Lebanon—countries that had been administered by France since World War I under a League of Nations mandate, but had recently become independent. On the surface this appeared to be a noncontroversial issue. Britain and France had stated their readiness to pull the troops out. Syria and Lebanon were satisfied with these assurances, and it seemed to be a simple matter of the council taking note of the statements. However, the Soviets were not satisfied with this. Vyshinsky thought that the language should be tougher. To the surprise of everybody, he voted against the resolution. It was a historic vote—the first veto cast under Article 27 of the U.N. charter, which requires unanimity of the five permanent members of the Security Council on questions of substance.

The president of the council, Norman J. O. Makin of Australia, at first ignored the negative vote of the Soviet Union and declared the resolution approved by a vote of seven to two with Britain and France abstaining. Vyshinsky quickly waved his hand. "I think a mistake has been made," he said, noting the provisions of Article 27. "I did not vote in favor. I voted against." No one questioned the right of the Soviets to veto the resolution, even though everybody wondered why the veto was being used on such a routine question. French Foreign Minister Georges Bidault commented that Vyshinsky's action was "entirely in conformity with the letter and spirit of the charter." The British foreign secretary said, "I agree." The council president then declared that, in view of the opinions expressed, he must conclude that the resolution had been rejected. The veto had no effect on the situation anyway, because both Britain and France stated that it was their intention to accept the majority vote as the sentiment of the council. Commenting later in his memoirs, Trygve Lie called the veto "another chill forewarning of the Cold War to come." Before he left office in 1953, he was to see more than 50 Soviet vetoes.[3]

Two months after those first confrontations in London, some 2,000 newsmen and newswomen gathered at Hunter College in New York City to cover the beginning of the United Nations' operations in the United States. Most of these correspondents—including the writer—had followed the London developments, and were aware of the negative turn they had taken. Because of the publicity that the London clashes had received, there was intense public interest in the United Nations' debut in New York. As preparations were completed for the first Security Council meeting on March 20, 1946, crowds of the curious swarmed around Hunter College—hoping to catch a glimpse of the diplomats that they had read about. The college gymnasium had been converted into a temporary council chamber. The gym walls were concealed by rose-hued drapes suspended from the ceiling. One of the balconies had become the press gallery. The swimming pool was covered to create a huge room for the working press. A council table in the shape of a horseshoe was ready only hours before the opening meeting. Reporters had been on hand for days, to give detailed accounts of the preparations. The Associated Press had assigned a staff of 11 to cover the scheduled council meetings and related events. Like many of the other assembled journalists, the AP staff were or had been foreign correspondents. This was considered a prime assignment.[4]

The March 20 meeting had been called to consider a renewal of the Iranian complaint against the Soviet Union—which had originally been lodged in London. In the new complaint, Iran informed the council that the armed forces of the Soviet Union were still interfering in its internal affairs, that negotiations had failed to resolve the problem, and that the resulting situation might lead to international friction. The issue had been resurrected in New York after Premier Ahmed Qavam had made a fruitless trip to Moscow to urge the withdrawal of Soviet troops in keeping with an agreement that U.S., British, and Soviet troops would be withdrawn by March 2. The Soviets insisted that negotiations on the troop evacuation were in progress and that there was no need for U.N. action. On these grounds they objected to inscription of the Iranian question on the council's agenda. They were represented at the council meetings by a pocker-faced young diplomat, who later was to become a familiar figure both at the United Nations and at other international meeting as Soviet foreign minister. He was Andrei A. Gromyko, then 37 years old and recently named to be the Soviet Union's permanent U.N. representative.

The United States attached sufficient importance to the case to send Secretary of State James F. Byrnes to participate in the discussions. Gromyko's strategy was to try to keep the complaint off the agenda. Failing in this, he pressed for a delay and warned that he would not be able to attend any meetings of the council for the two weeks during which the Iranian question was being discussed. The other delegates were shocked by this; the Netherlands representative, Ellco N. Van Kleffens, described it as a Soviet attempt to "pressure" the council. The Soviet move backfired. When the vote on postponement came the next day—March 27—only Poland voted with the Soviet Union. The council decided to invite the Iranian ambassador, Hussein Ala, to present his case.

First, however, Gromyko asked for and received permission to address the council. Speaking in Russian, as usual, he said; "For reasons which I explained clearly enough in our meeting of yesterday and in today's meeting, Mr. Chairman, I, as representative of the Soviet Union, am not able to participate further in the discussion of the Security Council because my proposal has not been accepted by the council, nor am I able to be present at the meeting of the council and I, therefore, leave the meeting." Few persons at the council table or in the audience were immediately aware of what was happening. In the jammed press gallery, a reporter who understood Russian blurted out, "He's going to walk out." Gromyko did not move until the 67-word statement had been translated first into French and then into English. As the English interpreter—Daniel Hogg—concluded, Gromyko gathered up his papers, removed his shell-rimmed glasses, and stalked briskly from the chamber. He was followed by his advisors. As if nothing had happened, the council proceeded to hear the Iranian ambassador.

The question dominant in everyone's mind was whether the Soviet Union had bolted the United Nations for good—dooming the organization before it had ever gotten under way. No elaboration was immediately forthcoming. Two days later Soviet newspapers published a story on the walkout. According to the official news agency, Tass, Gromyko was unable to take part in the discussions "due to reasons placed upon him by higher ups." Other delegates made no move to get Gromyko back to the table. Several days passed before Moscow newspapers began stressing that the Soviet Union was not pulling out of the United Nations. On April 4—with Gromyko still absent—the council voted to defer action until May 6 and asked the Soviet Union and Iran, meanwhile, to report on troop withdrawals. After missing three meetings, Gromyko resumed his seat without comment. The troops were in fact withdrawn, but the council rejected a request by Gromyko that the issue be dropped from its agenda. Gromyko was not ready to give up, however. He declared the decision to be contrary to the charter and said that "the Soviet delegation is, therefore, not able to participate in the discussions of the Iranian question in the Security Council." But this time, there was no walkout. The Soviets simply ignored the council's request for a report on the troop evacuation. The walkout had been noteworthy primarily because it was a "first," but it served as a grim reminder that the Kremlin would play the game only by its own rules.

After being twice postponed because of the Paris Peace Conference, the second half of the 1946 session of the General Assembly opened in New York on October 23—slightly more than eight months after the London meeting ended. For the first time, the assembly was ready to tackle substantive problems; and now that the time had come, the delegates approached the task with unconcealed pessimism. Much had happened to dampen their initial enthusiasm since they left London. Doubts had already arisen as to whether the new organization could survive the impact of the expanding Cold War. Overshadowing everything else was the fact that the Soviet Union had used the veto power nine times—mostly on seemingly unimportant questions—and seemed to be bent on preventing the Security Council from performing its peace-preserving functions.[5]

Paul-Henri Spaak did not try to minimize the changed atmosphere. Speaking at a City Hall reception, the assembly president took note of the sober restraint with which New York crowds had greeted the delegates this time; and he remarked that perhaps the people were justified in not being "wholly enthusiastic" about the United Nations. Later, at the opening meeting in Flushing Meadows, he again referred to the gloomy outlook. "It is possible," Spaak said, "that one day in the future the pessimists may be right. I do not know. But I do know that today they are wrong." President Truman, in his welcoming address, sought to dispel fears of a third world war with the declaration that "these fears are unwarranted and unjustified." "The American people," he said, "look upon the United Nations not as a temporary expedient but as a permanent partnership—a partnership among the peoples of the world for their common peace and well-being. It must be the determined purpose of all of us to see that the United Nations lives and grows in the minds and hearts of the people."

The first weeks of the session did nothing to dispel the prevailing pessimism, however. The opening general debate consisted largely of an attack on the Soviet use of the veto, and of countercharges from the small but vocal communist bloc that the Soviet Union's critics were attempting to promote another war. Although it was not until the 1947 session that Vyshinsky first used the term "warmongers," the Soviets were already using the warmonger theme in 1946. This phase of the Cold War reached its peak at the 1947 assembly when Vyshinsky asserted that a war plot existed in the United States. He demanded the "enchainment" of John Foster Dulles and Warren Austin (permanent U. S.

representative at the United Nations), Britain's chief delegate Hector McNeil, and other prominent Western leaders. He said that they should be put in the same class with those who disseminate pornography and traffic in women and children.

The historic first session of the assembly came to an end in the early morning hours of December 16, after five weeks of meetings in London and eight weeks in New York. To deal with urgent postwar problems, it had established an International Refugee Organization (IRO) and created special economic commissions for Europe and Asia to aid in the reconstruction of war-devastated areas. There were a number of notable failures. Efforts to restrict the use of the veto got nowhere. The assembly even refused to censure the Soviet Union for abuse of this big power privilege. In the end it adopted a watered-down resolution urging the big powers to refrain from using the veto except in cases of major importance and to try to work out procedures and practices for voluntary restrictions. The antiveto advocates had hoped at least to mobilize public opinion against the abuses. They did do that, but the Soviets—as always—paid little attention to public opinion. They would use the veto 12 times in 1947, as against 9 times in 1946. One effect of the debate, nevertheless, was to advertise this weakness of the United Nations.

Another failure experienced by the 1946 assembly involved its efforts to get rid of the Franco regime in Spain. Under Generalissimo Francisco Franco, Spain had been an Axis partner during World War II and had been barred from U.N. membership by the delegates to the San Francisco Conference. The assembly decided to go one step further and impose a diplomatic quarantine on Spain. It recommended that all member nations recall their ministers and ambassadors from Madrid and that the Franco government be barred from membership in all international agencies created by the United Nations or affiliated with it. These recommendations failed to have the desired effect of ousting Franco— partly because many countries gave them only lukewarm support, partly because some governments openly ignored the assembly's proposed sanctions, and partly because the action was a halfway compromise in the first place.

Even worse than the failure to get rid of Franco was the damage done to the image of the United Nations itself by the large-scale noncompliance of member states. The United States and Britain had opposed the recommendations, along with a number of other influential members; but once the resolution was adopted, they complied. On the other hand, the Argentine's President Juan Perón openly defied the organization. Argentina had no ambassador in Madrid at the time, but Perón promptly sent one. It was not long before other countries decided to ignore the assembly resolution. By 1950 sixteen member states had either reestablished full diplomatic representation in Madrid or announced that they would do so. The list included Argentina, Bolivia, Brazil, Columbia, Costa Rica, the Dominican Republic, Egypt, El Salvador, Haiti, Iceland, Iraq, Lebanon, Nicaragua, Paraguay, Peru, and Syria. In view of the widespread revolt against the U.N. majority, the United States announced that it was prepared to support a resolution to rescind the 1946 resolution, if such a proposal were submitted. The assembly ended this sad experience by wiping the resolution from its books on November 4, 1950. The circle was completed when Spain was admitted as a member to the United Nations five years later.

2

Headquarters in New York: Good, Bad, or Maybe

Trygve Lie once remarked that the decision to locate U.N. headquarters in the United States was part of the strategy of peace. What he meant was that the decision was motivated primarily by the desire of the sponsors to ensure the fullest possible participation of the United States in the world organization. In his memoirs, Lie said: "A repetition of the tragedy of the League of Nations, stemming not the least from the United States' refusal to join, could not be permitted." Some diplomats, including Lie, believed that the U.S. public would be more likely to remain enthusiastic if it could see and hear the discussions and accept the organization as a reality.[1]

Not everybody agreed on the desirability of locating the United Nations in the United States. There was indeed a strong sentiment for establishing its headquarters in Europe. And, after the choice had been made to locate in the United States, there was an even wider disagreement as to the specific part of the country to be selected. The world leaders were aware that the choice of a headquarters site was much more than a procedural matter. Basically, they had to answer these questions: If the United Nations were to select a European site, would it be haunted by the ghost of the League of Nations? If it were located in the United States, would it be better off in an urban setting or a more isolated area? And would the East Coast be preferable to the West Coast?

Strange as it may now seem, no government invited the organization to be its permanent guest. This included the United States. Although 22 U.S. communities were actively lobbying in London to get the U.N. headquarters, the U.S. government initially followed a hands-off policy not only on these bids but even on the question as to whether the United Nations should locate in

Europe or the United States. Adlai Stevenson, the U.S. representative in the Preparatory Commission's Committee Eight, said that, although the United States was strictly neutral on the subject, the United Nations would be welcomed if it decided to make its home in the United States. As the debate progressed, it became clear that the committee was divided almost evenly between those who favored a European site and those who wanted to locate in the United States. The Soviet Union led the pro-U.S. group, while two of the United States's leading allies—Britain and France—were pushing for Europe. The key vote in London was 23 in favor of Europe, 25 against, and 2 abstaining. The decision quite likely would have gone the other way if any country in Europe had shown an interest in playing host.

France proposed that the headquarters be located in Vienna or Copenhagen—but did not invite it to Paris. Britain's representative, Philip Noel-Baker, pressed for Geneva—but said nothing about a British site. Switzerland, which was not then and still is not a member of the United Nations, was reluctant to have the Security Council take enforcement action on Swiss soil, for fear her neutrality might be compromised. London, Paris, and Brussels were mentioned as possible sites, but none found much support. The initial decision in London was simply a choice of the United States over Europe, with the exact location in the United States left for later determination.

This turned out to be as controversial as the selection of the United States. The debate eventually reached such intensity that some delegations began a move to reconsider the original decision and take the United Nations to Europe, after all. The trouble started in December 1945 when an interim site committee, headed by Dr. Stoyan Gavrilovic of Yugoslavia, recommended that the headquarters be located in the Greenwich-Stamford area of Connecticut, just across the line from Westchester County in New York State. This was a suburban community largely the domain of rich and near-rich commuters. While a growing number of communities were campaigning for the headquarters, this one definitely was not. Publication of the Gavrilovic committee's report touched off a wave of protest meetings. The concept of the headquarters site at that time was of an international enclave covering some 40 square miles, complete with shops, hotels, restaurants, and everything needed to make it self-contained. This would necessarily have involved a large-scale relocation of the residents. The prospect of losing their homes angered and alarmed the Connecticut property owners. And those adjacent to the proposed enclave felt that the influx of thousands of delegates and staff members of all nationalities, races, and religions would be felt for miles around. In a referendum on the question, residents of the area voted two to one against the recommendation. These developments were reflected in the debate that took place in London and New York. The General Assembly's Permanent Headquarters Committee kept the controversy alive by refusing to exclude the Greenwich-Stamford area. It did, however, make the recommendation more flexible by declaring that the headquarters should be located near New York City, either in Westchester County, New York, or in

Fairfield County, Connecticut. The committee proposed that alternative plans be prepared for sites of 2, 5, 10, 20 or 40 square miles. Meanwhile, it was decided that temporary headquarters would be located in New York City.[2]

At this stage it seemed virtually certain that the headquarters would be on the East Coast and most likely in the general vicinity of New York City, but it soon became clear that the question was by no means settled. By the time the discussions were resumed in the fall of 1946 in New York, more than 50 communities had extended invitations to the United Nations. They came from the East, West, North, and South—from large cities and remote rural areas. The United Nations was assured a welcome in such varied locales as Jekyll Island, Georgia: Sunrise Mountain, North Carolina; the Black Hills of South Dakota; the Smokey Mountains of Tennessee; Cape Cod, Massachusetts; the Delaware Valley in Pennsylvania; the Bronx, New York; the San Francisco Bay area of California; Boston; and Philadelphia. Most of the invitations were eliminated without much difficulty, but it soon became apparent that many countries were interested in areas other than New York City and that the search should be widened.

It must be remembered that the discussions were taking place during the early days of the Cold War. Although East–West differences dominated most U.N. debates in those days, they played only a minimal role in the consideration of the headquarters question. When it came to a choice between East Coast and West Coast, for example, the governments were motivated mainly by what would be most convenient for them. As might be expected, China, Australia, the Philippines, and other countries of Asia and the Far East preferred San Francisco, while the European countries generally favored the East Coast. However, the European countries were not all sold on the location recommended by the Headquarters Committee in London. As a result, this committee voted on November 14 to broaden the search to include Boston, Philadelphia, and San Francisco, in addition to New York.

Through it all, the United States tried to avoid taking sides, although it was accused of doing so when President Truman finally offered to make available the Presidio—a San Francisco military installation—if the United Nations should want it. The biggest crisis came when the Soviet representative, Georgi Saksin, told the Headquarters Committee: "Under no circumstances shall the delegation of the Soviet Union go to San Francisco and I take it no other self-respecting delegation will accept a decision in so flagrant a contradiction to the resolution of the General Assembly." Saksin further declared that "If the United Nations goes to San Francisco, it will degenerate into a second rate organization with second rate officials because not one self-respecting country will permit its delegates to cross three or four continents—to take this terrible journey—and as a consequence the United Nations will follow the path of the League of Nations."

The Soviet declaration forced the United States to break its silence. After a cabinet meeting in Washington, the U.S. ambassador to the United Nations,

Warren Austin, announced that the Truman administration favored an East Coast site. While not specifying whether the United States preferred New York, Philadelphia, or Boston, Austin said: "The United States is not for establishing headquarters on the West coast. The United States is for headquarters on the Atlantic coast." Apparently referring to the strong support given the East Coast by Britain and the Soviet Union, he said that "we must have regard for the countries who will always be the main support for the United Nations." He denied that the United States had at any time attempted to influence other delegations in the choice of a site.

The issue was finally decided by the Rockefeller family. On December 11, 1946, John D. Rockefeller, Jr., offered the United Nations a gift of $8,500,000 to be used for the purchase of a 17-acre tract of land alongside the East River in midtown Manhattan. Advocates of San Francisco staged a last-ditch fight led by Australia's Norman J. O. Makin. He was joined by India, Saudi Arabia, Iraq, Egypt, Lebanon, and Syria in opposing acceptance of the Rockefeller gift, but 33 countries voted for it. Only at the last minute did China abandon the ranks of those advocating San Francisco and vote with the majority. France abstained. Thus, the decision was made. One cannot help but wonder what the effect would have been if the United Nations had established its base of operations in Europe or in another U.S. location, say San Francisco or the Black Hills. There can be no clear-cut answer; but, in retrospect, many observers have had second thoughts as to the wisdom of that early 1947 decision.

In one important respect, the decision to locate on the East Coast later proved to have been correct. It was to mean thousands of miles less travel for representatives of the new African countries, for U.N. Secretariat members flying to and from meetings in Africa, and for U.N. technical experts sent on African missions. Gromyko had objected to the West Coast largely because of the 6,000 miles of additional travel for European delegates. With the admission of two-score member states in Africa during the 1960s, the validity of his argument was reinforced. True, the same savings would have been accomplished if the headquarters had been located in Europe, but then the travel costs of the Western hemisphere delegates would have been more.

Both the U.S. government and the people of the United States were immensely pleased to have the permanent U.N. headquarters in their country. The Truman administration showed its appreciation by providing an interest-free loan of $65 million to finance the new buildings, and the City of New York—equally pleased—put up more millions to acquire additional land for the site and to improve its approaches. As Lie told the assembly on November 20, 1947, the United States as host country was giving "tangible evidence of its faith in the United Nations and of its determination to see it firmly established for all time to come." Although it was the policy of the Truman administration— and those that followed it—to support the United Nations without reservation, there were many in the State Department who had their doubts, nevertheless. One of these was Dean Acheson, who—as under secretary of state—was assigned the task of getting the Senate to ratify the charter. "I did my duty faithfully and successfully," Acheson wrote in his memoirs, "but always believed that the charter was impractical."[3]

Beginning with the first Security Council meetings at Hunter College, the United Nations was to lead a nomadic existence for the next five years while the permanent headquarters was being planned and completed. For a few weeks the organization had its administrative offices in Rockefeller Center. After Hunter College, the Security Council and some subsidiary organs, including the Atomic Energy Commission, met at a former nightclub in the Henry Hudson Hotel. The plenary meetings of the General Assembly were held in one of the 1939 World's Fair buildings in Flushing Meadows. In 1948 and 1951 the assembly met in the Palais de Chaillot in Paris.

Except for the assembly meetings, the United Nations had moved all its operations to a temporary headquarters at Lake Success on Long Island by August 1946. Lake Success is a residential suburb about 25 miles from the center of New York City; before its U.N. days the town was noted primarily as the home of the Sperry Gyroscope Company, which had built a huge complex there during World War II. Only part of the 30-acre plant was needed to fill postwar needs. Therefore, the Sperry Company leased its four-story administration building and one-third of its factory over to the United Nations, which then spent $2.5 million converting the factory into offices, council chambers, committee rooms, and a luxurious delegates' lounge—one of the showplaces of the temporary headquarters. The annual rent was approximately $200,000.

The Lake Success dateline disappeared from the world press in June 1951, after being almost synonymous with the United Nations for just under five years. The final meetings there were held on May 18 when two bodies—the Commission on the Status of Women, and the Statistical Commission—wound up their spring sessions. The flags of the United Nations were hauled down for the last time at the temporary headquarters after these meetings were adjourned.

The surrender of the temporary headquarters marked the end of a dramatic epoch in diplomatic history. The Security Council had held more than 500 meetings in the improvised chamber, and had seen more than 40 Soviet vetoes. The big (then 60-nation) General Assembly committees—often meeting simultaneously in the four spacious committee rooms—transacted most of the assembly's business at Lake Success. Hundreds of thousands of visitors had come by bus, automobile, and the Long Island Rail Road to attend meetings and to tour the building. Singer Paul Robeson had even led a protest sitdown strike in the lobby. And in another incident, a peace advocate had dropped a small homemade bomb from a rented single-engine plane while flying over the administration building.

During those five years, miracles had occurred on Manhattan's East Side— where a shabby, down-at-the-heels neighborhood had been transformed into the world's greatest international center. Not only had the plush U.N. headquarters itself—with its slender glass-and-marble tower—become one of New York's best known landmarks, but building after building had gone up in the surrounding area to house organizations and activities attracted by the organization. Nowhere else in the world is there such a concentration of agencies, individuals, and facilities devoted to global affairs. U.N. Plaza, the broad avenue that separates these glittering new buildings from the 17-acre U.N. enclave, has become one of the most popular places in the world for demonstrations and picketing on international issues. Depending on the issue of the moment, you may find anyone from magenta-robed Tibetan monks to bearded supporters of Fidel Castro, each group pleading its cause on the picket line.

It has been said that, while the Soviet Union gained an empire from World War II, the United States gained an international organization. Undoubtedly, the United States would have played a leading role in the United Nations no matter where it had been headquartered, but being its host did make a difference. There have been disadvantages as well as advantages. The people of the United States have been exposed to large doses of the United Nations on television and in the press. Often the Americans are impressed, but sometimes their faith has been shaken by what they see. The same goes for the delegates and the U.N. staff. Much of what they encounter in New York City has been to their liking, but occasionally they are upset by rude or thoughtless behavior, racial discrimination, and customs that they do not understand. Unlike Washington, D.C., New York was not accustomed to the ways of diplomacy. At times there has been evidence of hostility on the part of the public toward this new group of "privileged characters" whose automobiles bear the "DPL" registration plates. The situation wasn't helped any by those diplomats who abused their privileges by double-parking and otherwise flouting the law. One New York newspaper—exasperated with the parking abuses—suggested to its readers that they might correct the problem by deflating the tires of any "DPL" vehicle illegally parked.

Another problem stemmed from the fact that U.N. delegates and staff members are of so many different races. Even in the early days—before the heavy influx of Africans—some delegates were plagued with discrimination in housing and restaurants; there were cases in which they received scurrilous letters threatening their safety. In one incident—for example—the Indian ambassador, en route to a U.N. meeting in San Francisco, was refused service in a restaurant at the Dallas airport. Even U Thant was involved in a case of rent gouging in regard to a furnished apartment that he rented when he was Burma's permanent U.N. representative. The case received wide publicity when New York State Rent Administrator Robert E. Herman filed suit against William S. Whaley, who had sublet the apartment to Thant. Whaley was accused of charging Thant $1,200 instead of the legal maximum of $402.50. Whaley contended that part of the $1,200-a-month was deferred payment of $6,447 in alleged damage to the furnishings during Thant's tenure. There was no mention in court as to how the damage had occurred, but Whaley later blamed it on Thant's cat. "He tore the damask curtains, ripped up the carpets and upholstery," Whaley said. "We had to throw out a lot of stuff." But then he hastened to add that "Mr. Thant is a fine gentleman. As soon as he realized what happened to the furniture, he had the cat's claws cut." A spokesman for Thant admitted that the diplomat did have a cat, but said he doubted that one cat could do so much damage.

The problem of playing host could be time consuming, as well. Consider the case of Gregory Stadnik, a member of the Ukrainian delegation, who was shot in a New York delicatessen during the early morning hours of November 21, 1946. This was one of the first major incidents involving a U.N. diplomat. Therefore, the matter was handled personally by Secretary of State James F. Byrnes and the Ukrainian foreign minister, Dmitri Manuilsky. It would have been just another police case had not Manuilsky charged that the attack on Stadnik and a colleague, Alexis Voina, was "a premeditated attempt on the lives of two delegates to the General Assembly of the United Nations." Stadnik received a serious wound in the thigh, during what the police called an attempted robbery. Manuilsky rejected the police theory. "The delegation of the Ukrainian Soviet Socialist Republic," he said in a protest to Byrnes, "draws your attention to the fact that acts directed against the lives and security of the members of the delegation to the United Nations are taking place in the locality of the organization of the United Nations and, what is more, the criminals have not been apprehended up to now." In his reply, Byrnes denied Manuilsky's charge and said that everything possible was being done to apprehend the assailants. In his words: "While we deeply regret that a delegate to the General Assembly should have been the victim of this crime, I know you will be glad to learn that in the opinion of the police commissioner, based upon the evidence of witnesses, it was not as you feared, a premeditated attempt to kill two members of your delegation. . . . The fact that the primary purpose of the criminals was robbery and not to kill the two delegates does not lessen their crime and certainly it does not lessen my regret that one of your representatives should have been the victim of such a criminal act."

There seemed little doubt that this incident was indeed a holdup, and the fact that U.N. delegates were involved was no more than coincidental. The difficulty arose mainly because it occurred during the Cold War. There probably would have been no protest had U.N. headquarters not been located in the United States. As it turned out, however, the location of the United Nations was at least partially responsible for a substantial amount of U.S.–Soviet friction. One illustration was the controversy over the tax-free status of the Soviet estate at Glen Cove on Long Island; the matter lasted for several years, causing ill feelings on the part of both the Soviets and the Glen Cove community. The dispute began when village authorities refused to recognize the tax exemption granted to the Soviets under terms of the Headquarters Agreement. The Soviet mission, backed by the State Department, fought the matter in court and finally won.

The Soviets themselves did much to poison the atmosphere. One serious problem was their use of the Soviet mission and the Soviet members of the U.N. Secretariat for espionage purposes. This started even when the United Nations was still at its temporary headquarters in Lake Success. The first known case involved a Soviet member of the Secretariat, Valentin Gubichev, who was arrested in 1949 with a U.S. woman, Judith Coplon, on espionage charges. The Soviet Embassy in Washington demanded Gubichev's immediate release; it claimed diplomatic immunity for him. U.N. legal experts held, however, that immunity did not apply in Gubichev's case. He was tried, convicted, and deported to the Soviet Union. Like other similar cases later, the espionage here was directed not against the United Nations, but against the United States. As Trygve Lie commented: "There was nothing to spy on in the United Nations. Governments did not give it secret information they wished to withhold. Its meetings and documents were public property. . . . The United Nations was about as barren a field for spies as could be imagined." The Gubichev and subsequent communist espionage incidents hurt the United Nations' image in the United States; such incidents were relished by U.N. critics, who labeled the organization "a nest of spies." Although this was patently an exaggeration, the willingness of the Soviets to abuse their privileges as guests of the United States had a souring effect on the public. Over the years, there continued to be repeated charges of espionage lodged against communist members of the U.N. secretariat and members of Soviet bloc delegations. In almost all cases, the outcome was the same: expulsion.

As to domestic events in the United States itself, few commanded such wide attention in the United Nations as the developing crisis over racial integration in the public schools. The impact of the violent and dramatic conflicts at Little Rock, Oxford (Mississippi), Birmingham, Selma, Savannah, Philadelphia, New York City, and later Boston was tremendous. U.S. policymakers were frankly concerned. They disagreed only on the extent of the damage to U.S. relations with Asian and African countries.

The new countries were sensitive to U.S. racial incidents for at least three reasons: (1) personal experiences with racial discrimination in the United States; (2) the preoccupation of Asian and African countries with the apartheid policies of South Africa; and (3) communist efforts to exploit the U.S. racial problem with the aim of discrediting the United States. In 1964 Secretary of State Dean Rusk told a congressional committee that the communists regarded racial discrimination in the United States "as one of their most valuable assets." He warned that, unless Congress acted to remove discriminatory practices, "hostile propaganda might be expected to hurt us more than it has hurt us until now." Adlai Stevenson said that he found U.N. diplomats to be generally tolerant and understanding, but that even they were "shocked by what they had seen and heard." Ralph Bunche, the U.S. Negro who was U.N. under secretary for political affairs in 1958, said that the "repressions" of blacks had hurt the image of the United States because it had always been thought of as "a democratic nation leading the cause of world freedom." A Soviet delegate, Platon D.

Morozov, told a U.N. committee that the "unbridled racism" in the United States had proved there was no moral basis for the claim that Americans were the defenders of human rights in the world. No African sought publicly to place the United States in the same category as South Africa, but the prime minister of Uganda, Milton Obote, told a meeting of African leaders in Addis Ababa that "the key to the successful projection of the United States image in Africa lies more in the solution of the Negro problem than in foreign aid." Commenting on discrimination against blacks in housing and restaurants in New York, Ambassador Gershon B. O. Collier of Sierra Leone said: "Your American Negroes understand this kind of prejudice and are used to it. We are not."

Another sore spot in the U.S. culture—perhaps even more serious than racial discrimination, in terms of this country's role as host to the United Nations—was the hostility of New Yorkers toward Arab and communist delegates. These manifestations began during the early days and have continued right down to the present—one of the most notable in recent years being the demonstrations against Yashir Arafat, leader of the Palestine Liberation Organization. One of the worst periods was in 1971 when Arab and communist delegates interrupted a debate on Chinese representation to protest against a series of such incidents, including the firing of four rifle shots into the Soviet Mission—allegedly by members of the Jewish Defense League, headed by Rabbi Meyer Kahane. The ensuing discussions took up three entire meetings of the General Assembly. When George Bush was U.S. permanent representative, he regarded harassment of delegates as one of the most trying problems. "It could have a very serious effect on the movement to take the U.N. to another country," Bush said. "The diplomats are sick and tired of some of the abuse and some of the violence they are subjected to. Some of this is due to the fact that political pressure groups and political extremists, in an effort to embarrass the United States, provoke attacks upon certain countries here. I think if these outrageous attacks continue there will be more talk about moving the United Nations abroad. It is a disgrace that all Americans resent deeply."

There were problems from two other sources, also. One of these had an especially significant impact on U.S. public opinion. This was the element in Congress most notably represented by Senator Joseph McCarthy of Wisconsin and Senator Patrick McCarran of Nevada—who was chairman of the Senate Subcommittee on Internal Security—which placed the United Nations under a cloud of suspicion by charging that the organization was packed with communists. A number of U.S. members of the Secretariat were dismissed from duty by their government for taking the Fifth Amendment during the so-called loyalty investigations in the 1950s. Trygve Lie called the inquiries a "witch hunt," which he said distorted the facts and smeared the entire Secretariat. Lie compared the McCarthy–McCarran attacks to Soviet charges that the Secretariat was dominated by Americans. "It was indeed ironic," he wrote, "that the secretariat should have been subjected at the time to attacks in the United States for exactly the opposite reasons." The net effect was a serious slump in the morale of the staff and a loss of confidence in the organization by many persons who believed the accusations. Referring to this, Dean Acheson later said, "If I needed confirmation of my opposition to having the U.N. headquarters in New York—which I did not—we had plenty of it during the autumn of 1952."

The other groups involved in attacking the United Nations were of the "America First" type—such as the John Birch Society—which kept up a continuous barrage of fabricated charges that found a substantial following in some parts of the country, notably in the Midwest, the South, and the West Coast. These groups reported authoritatively from time to time that the United Nations was secretly organizing a huge army of Chinese communists with the object of wiping out 200 million or 300 million people, that it was planning a one-world police state, and that the organization was totally under the control of: (1) communists, (2) Zionists, (3) spies and narcotics smugglers, (4) international bankers, and/or (5) atheists. Diplomats and other U.N. speakers were heckled in some parts of the country by individuals armed with this type of material in the form of loaded questions. In addition to the John Birch Society, other groups distributing similar "information" included the American Mercury, the Committee to Restore the Constitution, and the Smoot Report. They attacked every phase of the United Nations—including UNICEF, which they alleged was communist dominated. In every case, the avowed goal was generally the same: To get the United States out of the United Nations and the United Nations out of the United States.

Fortunately, neither the U.S. public nor the U.N. members took such groups too seriously. There has never been significant movement either by the people of the United States or by the government to get rid of the United Nations. Furthermore, none of the other countries has expressed any more desire to play host to the organization than they did in 1945 and 1946.

3

The United States Responds to Soviet Balkan Vetoes with the Truman Doctrine

On June 26, 1945, President Harry S. Truman addressed the San Francisco Conference following the signing of the U.N. Charter, with these words:

> You have created a great instrument for peace and security and for human progress in the world. The world must now use it. If we fail to use it, we shall betray those who have died in order that we might meet here in freedom and safety to create it. If we seek to use it selfishly—for the advantage of any one nation or any group of nations— we shall be equally guilty of betrayal.

Before the end of 1946 it had become obvious that the Soviet bloc was trying to use the United Nations to cover up their aid to Greek guerrillas who were operating in the northern section of that country. The Greek problem had been raised at the London meetings of the Security Council, but had been shelved after a brief debate. It came up again in New York in the form of a Soviet verbal attack on the Greek government. While the Soviets were accusing the Greeks of border violations against their northern neighbors, these neighbors were actually sending military supplies to the Greek rebel forces. Recognizing the fabricated claims, the Security Council rejected four Soviet-sponsored resolutions that declared Greece guilty of border violations. Then Greece filed its own complaint charging the communist bloc with aiding the guerrillas.

On December 19, some 11 months after the issue first came before the council, that body voted to establish a Commission of Investigation to make an on-the-spot inquiry and make recommendations to the council. Surprisingly, the Soviet Union and Poland supported the establishment of the commission and took part in its investigation, along with representatives of nine other countries serving on the council in 1947.

That was the end of their cooperation, however. They were incensed when it became apparent that the commission would find Albania, Bulgaria, and Yugoslavia guilty of sending supplies to the Greek rebels. Their first reaction was to oppose the creation of a subcommission that would keep an eye on Greece's northern border after the commission left. The Soviet Union had already used the veto four times during consideration of the Balkan question, but this time they abstained. The subcommission was established, but the communist countries refused to cooperate with it. The Soviet Union used the veto two more times in August 1947 to kill two resolutions based on the findings of the full commission. With this failure, the council decided to drop the question from its agenda, in order to clear the way for consideration by the veto-free General Assembly.

By January and February 1947, the situation in Greece had deteriorated badly. Diplomatic reports reaching Washington indicated a possible collapse of the Greek government, with a subsequent communist takeover. On top of these alarming reports, the U.S. State Department was notified that British aid to Greece would end in six weeks. The British wanted the United States to assume the burden of both the tottering Greek government and the Turkish government as well. The Turks needed large-scale financial help to maintain their military forces and carry on economic recovery.[1]

Despite President Truman's declaration on the need to use the United Nations, he had already realized by 1947 that there were limits to what the organization could do. Greece and Turkey were deemed to be pivotal in U.S. foreign policy. Therefore, their existing governments had to be preserved—by action outside the United Nations, if this could not be achieved within the organization. This was the reasoning behind the launching of the so-called Truman Doctrine, which was unveiled to the world in the form of a presidential message to Congress on March 12, 1947, in the midst of the Security Council debate on the Balkan problem.[2]

The heart of Truman's message was a proposal for a $400 million grant to Greece and Turkey for economic and military assistance. The communists were furious with this, as was to be expected. But also, the way in which the plan was presented came as a shock to the U.S. public and to friendly nations. As Lie said in his memoirs, "The Truman Doctrine burst like a bombshell upon the world with no advance notice whatever." Neither the secretary-general nor the permanent U.S. representative, Warren Austin, had been informed in advance. There resulted an outburst of protests declaring that the United Nations had been bypassed and that its authority had been undermined.

One of those angered by the action was Arthur Vandenberg, the Republican leader of the U.S. Senate. Another was Mrs. Eleanor Roosevelt, a member of the U.S. delegation at the United Nations. Vandenberg said, "The administration has made a colossal blunder in ignoring the U.N." He immediately drafted a series of amendments to the proposed legislation, in an attempt to rectify the apparent snub of the world organization. Mrs. Roosevelt was indignant over the failure of the administration to inform the United Nations and the U.S. delegation beforehand. In her newspaper column, "My Day," she wrote, "I hope never again this type of action will be taken without at least consulting with the secretary-general and with our permanent member of the Security Council." She asked what would happen if the Soviets were to follow the U.S. precedent and say "Since you acted without consulting the United Nations, we are free to do the same." She added further: "Feeling as I do that our hope for peace lies in the United Nations, I naturally grieve to see this country do anything which harms the strength of the United Nations."

Quite apart from the final verdict on the wisdom of the Truman Doctrine, it does seem clear that the announcement was handled ineptly. Trygve Lie was one of those who eventually became convinced that Truman's decision had indeed curbed communist expansion. But in his memoirs, Lie says that the State Department "served him ill in one important respect. . . . It would seem to be obvious that a government so strongly committed to the principle that the United Nations was the 'cornerstone of its foreign policy' should first announce to the Security Council its intention of undertaking this program of aid, and the reasons for it."[3]

In his message to Congress, Truman more or less wrote off the possibility of any effective U.N. action to help Greece. "We have considered how the United Nations might assist in this crisis," he asserted, "but the situation is an urgent one requiring immediate action, and the United Nations and its related organizations are not in a position to extend help of the kind that is required." In another reference to the world organization, the president said, "In helping free and independent nations to maintain their freedom, the United States will be giving effect to the principles of the charter of the United Nations."

Truman had expected criticism from the communists, but he was completely surprised by the vehemence of the reaction in the U.S. press and among such influential congressional leaders as Senator Vandenberg. Ambassador Austin—angered at being kept in the dark—rushed off to Washington to see what could be done to blunt the charge that the United States had bypassed the United Nations. Meanwhile, in cooperation with the pro-U.N. senators, the State Department began working on amendments to the authorizing legislation in an effort to bring the world organization into the picture. Dean Acheson later admitted the fault was his that a gesture had not been made in the direction of the United Nations.[4]

Commenting in the New York *Times* on the congressional debate regarding the Truman proposal, James Reston wrote, "Everybody in the debate so far agrees on the one point that, in helping Greece and Turkey, the United States should not hurt the United Nations, one group arguing that the world organization will be hurt if it is not asked to deal with the Greek and Turkish cases and the other that it will be hurt immeasurably more if it is compelled to deal with it." The problem was this: Could the United States show its confidence in the United Nations without forcing the organization to deal with a question it could not possibly handle? Among the proposals advanced in Congress was one by Senator Claude Pepper of Florida under which Truman would turn over to the United Nations $100 million immediately and $150 million later, for Greece alone. The plan called for a special session of the General Assembly to handle the fund.

The Senate, however, preferred to go along with the Vandenberg amendments. Although they were obviously an afterthought, they served the purpose of taking some of the edge off the criticism by linking the Truman Doctrine loosely to the United Nations—without going so far as to place the funds under U.N. control. One of the amendments directed the president to withdraw the aid allocated for Greece and Turkey if requested to do so by the government of either country "representing a majority of the people" or if the president found that the purpose of the aid had been accomplished by any intergovernmental body or if the Security Council or the General Assembly found that U.N. action had made the aid unnecessary or undesirable. The key phrase was that U.N. action had to be a determining factor in any request to halt U.S. aid. Acheson felt that the amendments left the Truman Doctrine intact. In his memoirs, he said that the changes were "window dressing and must have sounded silly or cynical or both in London, Paris or Moscow."

The amendments were welcomed by Austin, but they did not avert a long debate in the Security Council, where Gromyko did his best to use the issue as a means of diverting attention from the charges against Albania, Bulgaria, and Yugoslavia. In a speech before the council on April 7, 1947, Gromyko accused the United States of unilateral action that contradicted the principles of the United Nations and dealt "a serious blow to its authority." Stressing the fact that the U.S. grant to Greece and Turkey included military as well as economic aid, the Soviet delegate said, "The actual material aid which the Greek people are in need of, can and must be real aid, and must not serve as a screen for purposes which have nothing in common with aid at all. Aid must be rendered through the United Nations, in which case it will exclude all possibilities of any foreign influence on this country." In a later speech on April 14, Gromyko formally proposed that the council establish a special commission to see that the U.S. aid to Greece was used only "in the best interests of the Greek people."[5]

Although initially some U.S. allies had been unhappy with the way the Truman Doctrine was launched, they quickly lined up behind the United States in this confrontation with the Soviet Union. Sir Alexander Cadogan told the Security Council that the U.S. action was "in full accord with the purposes and principles of the United Nations." He said it had been clear that Greece was in immediate need of relief and that the United Nations was in no position to provide it. Colonel W. R. Hodgson of Australia was even more positive:

In the view of my government, the action proposed by the United States is not only justified and correct in principle but should be welcomed with gratitude by all the United

Nations. As the United States representative has pointed out, the present emergency and temporary program will not conflict with the long-term responsibility of the United Nations for the reconstruction of Greece. The United States has also taken two steps of great significance for the future of the United Nations. The United States, far from ignoring or by-passing the United Nations, has done exactly the opposite. First we have an assurance that any agreement entered into with Greece in connection with the execution of this program will immediately be registered for publication by the secretary-general. In the second place, we have the action of the United States in coming before this council to explain its proposals and the reasons for them. The Australian delegation feels that these steps show an admirable recognition of the role of the United Nations and a clear desire to do nothing which would impair its strength or prestige.

The delegate of China, Dr. Quo Tai-Chi, said that the "Security Council naturally would have welcomed a communication from the United States representative on or before March 12 when President Truman proposed the program of assistance to Greece." He added, however, that the United States had later made a comprehensive statement on the subject—"which in itself shows clearly that the United States did not and does not intend to by-pass the United Nations."

The Soviet proposal for the establishment of a special commission was put to the vote on April 18. In a final statement Gromyko said, "You gentlemen must decide for yourselves what is absurd: the Soviet proposal, which calls for the external help to be used in the interests of the Greek people, or statements which distort the situation and make believe the Soviet proposal is directed against the interests of the Greek people. Decide for yourselves, gentlemen where there is absurdity and where there is truth." The council gave the United States a vote of confidence—in effect—by rejecting the Soviet proposal. Only Poland joined the Soviet Union in supporting the resolution, while Australia, Belgium, Brazil, and Britain voted against it. China, Colombia, France, Syria, and the United States abstained.

The Balkan question was taken up by the General Assembly in the fall of 1946. On October 21, the assembly called on Greece's three northern neighbors to stop aiding the Greek guerrillas and to cooperate in settling their differences with Greece through peaceful negotiations. The assembly also established an 11-nation Special Committee on the Balkans (UNSCOB) to replace the Security Council's Commission of Investigation. As members of the Security Council, the Soviet Union and Poland were entitled to places on the new committee; but, by this time, communist cooperation on the Balkan inquiry had ceased. The two countries announced that they would boycott UNSCOB because, in their view, its creation violated the sovereignty of Albania, Bulgaria, and Yugoslavia. In 1948, 1949, 1950, and 1951 UNSCOB reported that communist countries were continuing their support of the guerrillas and, as a result, they were a threat to Greece's independence and territorial integrity. By 1949 Yugoslav aid had been discontinued, but the 1951 report said that aid was going to the guerrillas from Czechoslovakia, Hungary, Poland, and Rumania in addition to Albania and Bulgaria. One could only conclude that U.N. efforts had produced absolutely no effect on the flow of communist aid to the Greek guerrillas. Actually, the communist aid had increased during the five years from 1947 through 1951. In 1951 UNSCOB was replaced by a Balkan Subcommission of the Peace Observation Commission, but this body was able to operate only on the Greek side of the border. This subcommission continued to function until 1954 when it was finally discontinued at the request of Greece.

So far as the United Nations was concerned, this was the end of the Balkan problem, except for its unsuccessful efforts to repatriate 25,000 Greek children who had been removed from their homeland and transferred to communist countries. Year after year, the assembly urged the return of the children. The International Committee of the Red Cross joined in the effort. Most of the children who were being held in Yugoslavia were returned after Marshal Tito's break with Moscow, but thousands remained in other countries—despite the pleas of the United Nations.

Although the Marshall Plan was intended to operate outside the United Nations, its launching—a few months after the announcement of the Truman Doctrine—was handled more skillfully. In his Harvard speech of June 5, 1947, Secretary of State George C. Marshall studiously avoided the likelihood that critics might link the new initiative with the Truman Doctrine as another unilateral U.S. program. He stressed that this was a program to be designed by the Europeans themselves and that it should be a joint program for any European countries wishing to participate. British Foreign Secretary Ernest Bevin and French Foreign Minister Georges Bidault did meet initially with Soviet Foreign Minister Vyacheslav Molotov to discuss the plan, but Molotov quickly withdrew after receipt of a telegram from Moscow. Bevin and Bidault immediately issued a joint statement inviting 22 other European governments to send representatives to Paris to draft a blueprint for what later became known as the European Recovery Program. The meeting was boycotted by all the Soviet bloc countries. The Soviet rejection of the Marshall Plan no doubt was an important factor in winning congressional support for the huge appropriations needed to finance the program. Although the Marshall Plan had bypassed the United Nations, pro-U.N. groups were muted somewhat by the fact that the program received the full support of the U.N. secretary-general.

The emergence of the Cold War was responsible for another shift in the U.S. postwar international contributions. The United States had been the leading supporter of the United Nations Relief and Rehabilitation Administration (UNRRA), which had been created to take care of the millions left homeless and destitute at the end of the war. This was operated by the Allied nations and predated the founding of the United Nations, even though it used that name. By 1946 UNRRA was being liquidated, and its functions transferred to newly created U.N. agencies. One of these was the controversial International Refugee Organization (IRO), which was to take over the rehabilitation and repatriation of the hordes of displaced persons. The Soviet Union had fought the draft constitution of the IRO through two sessions of the Economic and Social Council and the General Assembly, but had failed to gain its objective—the required return of all refugees to their country of origin, whether they wanted to go back or not. Other delegates objected on other grounds. The assembly finally voted to establish the IRO, but six months later only 19 of the 55 member nations had ratified its constitution. The Soviet bloc refused to accept it.

The late Fiorello H. La Guardia, director-general of UNRRA, was infuriated by the United Nations' handling of the refugee problem. He had begged for speed so that there might be no interim gap between the expiration of UNRRA and the effective operation of the new refugee agency; he had stressed the difficulties he faced in keeping his organization intact, in view of its impending liquidation; and he had warned that chaotic conditions might result unless the United Nations acted quickly. The only thing that saved the situation was a six-month extension of UNRRA's mandate.

In the summer of 1946 La Guardia went before the Economic and Social Council with a warning that the expiration of UNRRA's emergency food relief program would leave an equally serious situation in Europe. In a fighting speech, he pounded the table and shouted that thousands would face starvation unless the United Nations provided additional food relief. "And they can't eat resolutions," he added with a growl. He promised to present a plan of action. When this plan—providing for a $400,000,000 emergency food fund to be administered by an international committee—was forthwith submitted to the assembly, La Guardia was there in person to fight for it. The United States, which had contributed 72 percent of UNRRA's funds, was asked to provide 49 percent of the proposed emergency fund—or approximately $200,000,000. The success of the plan naturally depended on its acceptance by the United States and Britain, the second-largest prospective contributor. Both turned it down. They decided that they were tired of Yugoslavia, Albania, Poland, and other Soviet satellites biting the hand that fed them. Britain and the United States would continue to give assistance to needy countries—they announced—but not through an international agency.[6]

La Guardia, who was supported by a majority of the assembly, put up a dramatic fight for the $400,000,000 fund, but he recognized that he was beaten. He accused the United States of attempting to use food as a political weapon, and said, "There is a tendency to revert back to the nation—the national system, the old system of mighty and rich, weak and poor. It's morally wrong, It's wicked." Pushing his glasses back on his forehead and chewing a stubby cigar, he pounded the table and shouted; "They have the dollars. They'll have their way. We want an international agency, but if the United States and the United Kingdom won't come along there is no use. Gentlemen, I ask you if that is a veto. I'm discouraged. May God have mercy on the hungry people of the world."

La Guardia was angered still more when British Delegate Percy Wells referred to him as one who talked with "carefree and confident irresponsibility." In his answer to Wells, La Guardia repeatedly referred to him sarcastically as "Sir Percy." When Wells was finally provoked into saying that he was just "plain Mr. Wells," LaGuardia retorted, "Make a couple more speeches like yesterday and the accolade of knighthood may be bestowed upon you. And brother, a few more and you may become first lord of the king's navy." La Guardia lost his fight. The General Assembly adopted a compromise plan, which called for a technical committee to make estimates of the needs of various countries but left the actual supplying of relief in the hands of individual nations.

4

The United Nations Gets a Tough One: Palestine

When the United Nations was born, the British had been administering Palestine for a quarter century under a League of Nations mandate. It had not been a happy experience. From the beginning, the administration had been caught in the middle of a bitter and often violent struggle between Arab and Jewish groups over the future of the Holy Land. By 1947 the British had had a bellyful and wanted out. It was apparent by then that the Palestine problem was about to be dumped in the lap of the United Nations, even though the organization was barely a year old. Some 18 separate groups had investigated the situation without finding a formula acceptable to both Jews and Arabs. Politicians in the United States were making capital of Britain's restrictions on immigration, while Jewish terrorist groups were turning the British administrative machinery into a shambles. The Labor government of Clement Attlee was under attack for failure to solve the problem; and, at the same time, it was assailing the United States for meddling without being willing to share the responsibilities.

Unfortunately, the United Nations was still feeling its way along. No one knew just what it could have done, but many—including President Truman—regarded it as a "slightly mythical entity" able to solve problems that had baffled its individual member nations. The British frankly acknowledged their failure to solve the problem. In cooperation with the United States, they had already tried to work out a solution through the Morrison–Grady inquiry and later through the Anglo–American Committee of Inquiry. In the end, they concluded that agreement between the Jews and Arabs was unattainable and that the only recourse left was to terminate their League of Nations mandate and let the United Nations try its hand.

The British had no plan to lay before the United Nations. It soon became clear that not only were they surrendering their responsibility for Palestine, but they were withdrawing from any active role in the U.N. deliberations, as well. The United States began to realize that it would have to take over the leadership, since no one else—with the exception of the Soviet Union—was willing to do so. Dean Acheson, as under secretary of state, brought this question up in a conversation with Chief of Near Eastern Division Loy Henderson in February 1947. In his book *Present at the Creation*, Acheson recalls telling Henderson that there was no way the United States could safely avoid assuming some leadership. "Whatever the United Nations might propose, we would be asked to finance it," Acheson said. "It is to our interest, therefore, that the United Nations proposal should be as sensible as possible." At this stage, the United States had not given serious consideration to the direction its Palestine role should take.[1]

There were several alternatives. One was simple termination of the mandate by Britain. This was what the Arabs wanted. It would have permitted the establishment of an independent Palestinian state, ruled by the Arab majority. Such a step would have spelled the end of Zionist hopes for a Jewish homeland. Another possibility was to surrender the mandate to the U.S. trusteeship system—thus shifting the responsibility from Britain to the United Nations, but leaving the internal strife and the whole problem of Jewish immigration unresolved. A third alternative was the so-called Morrison–Grady plan, which called for a federation of Jewish and Arab cantons. A fourth possibility was the partition of Palestine into separate Jewish and Arab states.

The Truman administration approached this long-range problem with caution—limiting its pronouncements mainly to the need for increased immigration into Palestine. Although Britain had sought to bring the United States into the picture through such joint endeavors as the Morrison-Grady committee and the Anglo–American Committee of Inquiry, the U.S. government had avoided endorsing any plan. The nearest approach to endorsement had come in the Yom Kippur statement of October 4, 1946, when Truman stated that some plan based on partition "would command the support of public opinion in the United States." A month later the British ambassador, Lord Inverchapel, tried to pin the State Department down as to whether the United States would support partition. The best he could get was a statement that partition would be the easiest plan for the United States to support, because of domestic opinion and because—in Washington's view—opposition in Palestine was likely to be more vocal than physical.

This was the situation when Britain proposed on April 2, 1947, that a special session of the General Assembly be summoned as soon as possible to launch an inquiry into possible courses of action. The special session was convened on April 28. The United States and many other countries believed that the only question to be decided would be a routine one of establishing a committee of inquiry, and that this would be disposed of quickly. The five Arab states, however, seized the opportunity to press for a full debate on Palestine independence. This was one thing the United States did not want at this stage. Its position was that the proposed committee should be composed of neutral countries and that no pressure should be exerted to influence its decision. The United States soon found itself not only opposing the Arab demands, but engaged in battles on two other issues: (1) whether the committee of inquiry should include the big powers, as the Soviet Union demanded; and (2) whether the General Assembly should hear the views of the Jewish Agency and the Arab Higher Committee.

In all three cases, the United States' views prevailed. The assembly rejected the Arab proposal for a full debate on the substance of the Palestine problem; it decided that the committee of inquiry should be composed of small countries; and it voted to hear the views of Jewish and Arab representatives in the assembly's political committee, rather than in plenary sessions. These were "mechanical" victories, which had no lasting impact on the long-range situation. It may be worth noting, however, that the Soviet Union favored hearing the Jewish Agency in the General Assembly—just as it favored hearing Yasir Arafat, leader of the Palestine Liberation Organization, more than 25 years later. The United States, on the other hand, was consistent in claiming that—in both cases—such a procedure was a violation of the U.N. charter and that only representatives of member nations should address the assembly. The difference between 1947 and 1974 was that the Soviet Union was on the losing side in the first test and on the winning side in the second.

On May 15, 1947, the assembly voted 46 to 7 to create a small-nation committee of 11 members to make an unrestricted investigation into the Palestine problem and make recommendations to the regular fall session of the assembly. In the closing hours of the special session, the Soviet Union gave up its fight to include the Big Five powers on the committee. After abstaining on the paragraph naming Australia, Canada, Czechoslovakia, Guatemala, India, Iran, the Netherlands, Peru, Sweden, Uruguay, and Yugoslavia to committee membership, the Soviets voted for the resolution as a whole. Only Turkey and Afghanistan joined the Arab states—Saudi Arabia, Syria, Lebanon, Iraq, and Egypt—in voting against establishment of the committee. During the discussions, which lasted from April 28 through May 15, the United States scrupulously refrained from making any declaration that might prejudice the outcome of the committee's investigation. On the next-to-the-last day of the special session, however, Andrei Gromyko stated that the Kremlin favored the creation of a joint Jewish–Arab nation in Palestine, but would accept partition as its second choice. It ruled out the possibility of a single state—whether Jewish or Arab. In effect, Gromyko's statement was a major boost for partition, since most delegates considered a federated state to be only remotely possible. In voting against the creation of the U.N. Special Committee on Palestine (UNSCOP), the Arab countries had declared in advance that they would accept neither federation nor partition.

U.S. Secretary of State George Marshall was pleased with the outcome of the special session, but within a few weeks he was beginning to have second thoughts. The U.S. government—from the White House down—had been indulging in wishful thinking that somehow the Jews and Arabs would eventually accept a U.N. decision and try to make the best of it. It was becoming increasingly clear that this was not going to happen. In June 1947, Marshall wrote to Warren Austin that "An agreed settlement no longer appears possible. A certain degree of force may be required [for] any solution." He added that there must be a comprehensive review of the situation, to make certain that any solution could "be defended before the world both now and in the future."

Between May 26 and August 31, the U.N. Special Committee on Palestine held 16 public and 36 private meetings at Lake Success, Jerusalem, Beirut, and Geneva. As expected, the committee found it impossible to make a unanimous recommendation. Seven of the eleven members recommended the partition of the Holy Land. These were Canada, Czechoslovakia, Guatemala, the Netherlands, Peru, Sweden, and Uruguay. India, Iran, and Yugoslavia proposed a single federated state, while the eleventh member—Australia—supported neither recommendation.

With the publication of the committee's report, the stage was set for the historic debate that was to dominate the 1947 General Assembly session. Almost nobody was completely satisfied with the majority proposal for partition, but this appeared to be the only plan with the slightest chance for approval. The Arabs had repeatedly declared that they would not accept partition. The Jews were far from happy with it. The United States was still uncommitted, and an influential group in the State Department was working behind the scenes to forestall U.S. support. Zionist leaders in the United States, on the other hand, were exerting tremendous pressure on the White House and on the governments of friendly countries to back the majority recommendation. The British government stated at the outset that it had no intention of implementing any plan unless both Jews and Arabs accepted it.[2]

It was not until November 22 that the United States made an unequivocal declaration that it would support the partition plan as "the most practicable and most just present solution of the Palestine problem." Without such support, the plan certainly would not have won approval. Although the Soviet Union had already endorsed it, the most vocal backers were the representatives of two small Latin American countries—Garcia Granados of Guatemala, and Rodriguez Fabregat of Uruguay—who scarcely carried enough weight to put the plan across. It was generally acknowledged that the influence of the United States helped determine the votes of enough wavering countries to make the difference between victory and defeat. Another thing that undoubtedly helped was a declaration by the Jewish Agency on October 2 that it was prepared "most reluctantly" to accept partition. Rabbi Abba Hillel Silver, chairman of the American Section of the Jewish Agency, told the assembly's Palestine committee that enforcement measures would be essential to implementation of the plan.

He was highly critical of Britain's decision to pull out of Palestine and to refuse cooperation in any plan not acceptable to both Jews and Arabs. "One questions whether in taking such a position," he said, "the United Kingdom is helping to solve this difficult problem and whether its course will enhance the authority and prestige of the United Nations which has assumed responsibility over the Palestine question."

The outcome of the vote remained in doubt down to the last minute. When the assembly adjourned on November 27, there were 28 members who had definitely declared for partition, but this was not expected to be enough in view of the substantial number of abstainers and the known opponents. By this time the United States had thrown its full weight into the fight for the majority plan. Ambassador Herschel V. Johnson appealed especially to those who had abstained in the preliminary voting. "How by abstaining can any delegation think they are furthering a solution?" he asked. "The time now is for decision." Declaring that the United States was ready to support the implementation of the partition plan without reservation, Johnson said, "The plan makes the Security Council responsible for security elements. Certainly if a situation arises under chapters VI and VII of the charter, my government will perform its duty under the charter in carrying out Security Council decisions." The reference to Chapter VII was interpreted as a commitment to support the use of armed forces, if necessary, to implement partition.

Curiously enough, in the concluding speeches, there were many references to pressure. It is true that a number of delegations did switch their positions, without explanation—but nobody specified the source of the pressure. Among those who changed at the last minute were the Philippines, Haiti, and Liberia. Muhammad Zafrullah Khan of Pakistan—one of the most eloquent spokesmen against partition—spoke of intense lobbying, and declared that he was certain the vote had been influenced. As he said, "The United Nations today is on trial. The world is watching. It will see if any room is to be left for honest judgements in important questions." Colombian Ambassador Alfonso Lopez asserted that the partition plan never would have reached the assembly without the "powerful backing" of the United States and the Soviet Union. "It is a minority proposal," he said. "No wonder the plan has had to come across the Atlantic to find the supporters it failed to find in the Near East and the Mediterranean." The vote finally came on November 29 after an unsuccessful attempt to postpone action until the spring of 1948. The partition plan was adopted by a vote of 33 to 13, with 10 abstaining. This was not the kind of victory that could justify either unrestrained satisfaction or complacency on the part of the victors. It should have been clear to all that the decision had by no means solved the Palestine problem.

It was certainly significant that 23 member states refused to follow the leadership of the two big powers. Equally significant was the large number of Asian and Latin American countries abstaining or voting against the partition plan. The Third World had not yet been born, but there was a message in the

November 29 vote for anyone looking for it. One delegate who did read the signs correctly was Zafrullah Khan, who advised the supporters of partition that "you may need friends tomorrow, you may need allies in the Middle East. I beg of you not to ruin and blast your credit in those lands." One of the big mysteries was the attitude of the Soviet Union. Why—in the midst of the Cold War— did the Kremlin line up with the United States? It was definitely within the power of the Soviet Union to have blocked the partition plan by joining its Arab, Asian, and Latin American opponents. But for some reason the Soviets preferred to see the plan approved. The United States—among others—was suspicious of their motives. There was a feeling in the State Department that the Soviet move was a cynical political gambit to keep the pot boiling in the Middle East. As Margaret Truman wrote in the biography of her father: "Stalin himself was anti-Semitic and anti-Zionist, but Russia was looking for any opportunity to establish a foothold on the shores of the Mediterranean." A similar view was expressed by Alfred Lilienthal, an ardent anti-Zionist, in his book *What Price Israel?* "Why did no one in America pay attention to the transparent objectives of the pro-Zionist Soviet gambit?" he asked. "Because no portion of the globe has been concealed from American view by a thicker veil of ignorance and misinformation than the Middle East."[3]

Within a few weeks after the adoption of the partition plan, it became obvious that the worst fears were being realized. The Arabs showed no sign of retreating from their pledge to ignore the assembly's action. They had walked out as a group after the November 29 vote. Syrian Delegate Emir Adel Arslan had shouted, "The charter is dead—not of a natural death—it was murdered. All the consequences will fall on your heads, not on ours." On February 6, 1948, a representative of the Arab Higher Committee wrote to Secretary-general Lie: "The Arabs of Palestine . . . will never submit or yield to any power going to Palestine to enforce partition. The only way to establish partition is first to wipe them out—man, woman and child." No one should have been surprised. In recommending the plan, the Special Committee on Palestine had warned that "enforcement measures on an extensive scale may be necessary for some time." Noting the mounting strife in the Holy Land and the Arab resistance, the United Nations' newly created Palestine Commission—which came to be known as the "Five Lonely Pilgrims"—began sending up distress signals almost immediately. Britain objected to the commission's entry into Palestine earlier than two weeks before termination of the mandate—which had been set for May 15. London would not permit formation of a Palestine militia as recommended by the assembly. It refused to facilitate delimitation of the frontier between the proposed Jewish and Arab states. It further refused to evacuate by February 1 a seaport and hinterland territory to provide for the authorized immigration into the new Jewish state. In Lie's opinion, "The British approach proved to be not in accord with either the letter or the spirit of the partition plan." Despite all this, the United States kept hoping that, in some way, the Jews and Arabs would work the problem out.[4]

As a member of the U.S. delegation, Eleanor Roosevelt was deeply concerned about Washington's reluctance to back up the assembly's decision. She joined Sumner Welles, Herbert Lehman, and Senator Elbert D. Thomas in supporting a four-point plan proposed by the American Association for the United Nations to enforce partition. The signatories declared that the Arab resistance "poses the question of the authority of the United Nations." If its authority could be challenged successfully "by these weak states in the Middle East, what confidence can be placed in the ability of the U.N. to meet and master future crises to which, perhaps, major powers may be a party?" Despite this public pressure and the pleadings of Secretary-general Lie, the antipartition faction in the State Department stood firm. Less than four months after the approval of partition, the United States reversed itself with a request that the Security Council instruct the Palestine Commission to "suspend its efforts to implement the proposed partition plan." It proposed instead that Palestine be placed under a temporary U.N. trusteeship. In his statement to the council, Warren Austin maintained that the United Nations did not have the authority to enforce the November 29 decision and that, therefore, the plan must be abandoned, at least for the moment.

Having laid down a blueprint for a Palestine solution, the United Nations now found itself facing a number of questions: Could the Arabs be forced to cooperate? Could Britain be required to adhere to the timetable laid down by the United Nations? Would the backers of the partition plan be willing to take the necessary enforcement measures? The Five Lonely Pilgrims said frankly that they could not discharge their responsibilities—on termination of the British mandate—without armed forces. "In the view of the commission," they asserted, "a basic issue of international order is involved. A dangerous and tragic precedent will have been established, if force or the threat of force is to prove an effective deterrent to the will of the United Nations." Lie began making private soundings as to the possibility of a U.N. force being established to implement partition. He found the United States backing away from the partition plan. It was ready neither to send troops nor to have the Soviet Union do so. Lie was convinced that the United Nations was obligated to implement its decision, even if this should require force, and that it had the legal competence to use force. Any other response, he felt, would discredit the organization in the eyes of the public. In a memorandum to the Palestine Commission, Lie asserted that

the Security Council has the power required to carry out the responsibilities assigned to it by the General Assembly. It is submitted that if the Security Council deemed that it was within its competence to accept responsibilities for the carrying out of certain provisions of a treaty [the Trieste treaty] negotiated and concluded outside the United Nations, it is still more appropriate that it should accept responsibilities for the implementation of a plan adopted by the General Assembly.

Few U.S. decisions have inspired such a barrage of criticism as the switch on the partition of Palestine. On March 21, 1948, the New York *Times* assailed the change of heart as "a plain and unmistakable surrender to the threat of force." It said that the switch came as a climax "to a series of moves which has seldom been matched for ineptness in the handling of any international issue by an American administration." The New York *Herald Tribune* declared that the trusteeship proposal would have no better chance of acceptance than partition and that "the day of reckoning is only postponed." One of the critics was Eleanor Roosevelt who, as usual, felt that the United States should do everything possible to strengthen the United Nations. In a letter to Adlai Stevenson, Mrs. Roosevelt said, "I am very unhappy about going back on the assembly decision on Palestine and I feel the handling of it up to this time has brought about much of the Arab arrogance and violence."[5]

As she predicted, the United States did have difficulty getting other nations to dance to the new tune. At a special session of the General Assembly—opening on April 16, 1948—the trusteeship proposal was debated for a month; but, in the end, the United States was able to win little support. In his memoirs, Lie wrote, "The American turnabout on partition has never been explained. . . . In any case, the American reversal was a blow to the United Nations and showed a profoundly disheartening disregard for its effectiveness and standing. I could not help asking myself what the future of the United Nations would be if this was the measure of support it could expect from the United States."[6]

Truman himself tried to salvage something by emphasizing that the trusteeship was a temporary measure only, and that there had been no reversal. But Lie said that Austin's statement had taken the "heart of any support which the Security Council might have mobilized to enforce peace and maintain the decision on partition." In the biography of her father, Margaret Truman offers a somewhat belated explanation that throws some additional light on the U.S. performance in these events. According to a memorandum scribbled by President Truman on his calendar, the State Department had simply "pulled the rug from under" him. He had approved a speech to be given at the United Nations, but it was not the speech delivered by Austin. "This morning," Truman wrote, "I find the State Department has reversed the Palestine policy. The first I know about it is what I see in the papers. Isn't that hell?" Margaret described this as one of the worst messes of her father's career. He never disclosed the details, she said, because he believed it would have made him and the whole government look ridiculous. In his memo, Truman blamed the reversal on "third and fourth level" people in the State Department.[7]

Two months later Truman turned the tables on the State Department in a surprise action of his own. This was the de facto recognition of the State of Israel on May 14—the date on which the mandate was surrendered by the British, and Israel became independent. What made his action so unusual was that it came during the General Assembly debate on the establishment of a temporary international regime for Jerusalem. At the time the announcement was made by the White House, the U.S. delegation—in all innocence—was urging other countries to maintain the status quo in Palestine. Trygve Lie described the announcement as another "reversal of policy." Warren Austin angrily talked of resigning, but was persuaded by his colleagues to stay on. Writing about the announcement, Margaret Truman later said, "This was a decision made by Dad alone, in spite of the State Department conspirators who for a time even had the Secretary of State convinced that recognition should be withheld." Eleanor Roosevelt was just as upset as Austin. She wrote to Secretary of State Marshall that the president's announcement had created complete consternation in the United Nations. She herself wanted to see Israel recognized, Mrs. Roosevelt declared, but the way this had been handled once more weakened the influence of the United States and weakened the United Nations. Several delegates from other countries had stated quite frankly, she said, that they did not see how they could every follow the United States' lead because the United States changed so often without any consultation.

The U.S. action was all but forgotten in the next few hours, however. On May 15, the Arab states began their armed invasion of Palestine in an attempt to overturn the November 29 decision. Lie immediately called on the Security Council to take "a decisive stand in support of the authority of the charter and of the United Nations." He added that "A failure of the Security Council to act under these circumstances can only result in the most serious injury to its prestige and the hopes for its future effectiveness. . . . Moreover, it may undermine the progress already made by the Council in other security problems with which it is now dealing." The Council did little, however, beyond appointing Count Folke Bernadotte as mediator and adopting a series of resolutions calling for cease-fires or truces. Some of these were effective temporarily, but it was not until July 1949 that the last of four armistice agreements ended the fighting on the Egyptian, Jordanian, Lebanese, and Syrian borders of Palestine. The State of Israel had survived the war, but there was no Arab Palestinian state, no economic union, no internationalized city of Jerusalem, and no permanent peace.

Two of Trygve Lie's close associates, Andrew W. Cordier and Wilder Foote— writing years later—blamed "American vacillation" for the failure of the United Nations to implement partition. "Though the Arab leadership bitterly opposed the partition plan and the creation of Israel," they said, "one may wonder if the timely dispatch of an effective United Nations force in 1948 and establishment of a strong and permanent international presence in Jerusalem might not have led to a better answer than the bloodshed of three wars and countless border incidents, the tragedy and shame of more than a million Arab refugees, and the undiminished hostility we have witnessed in the twenty years since that time."[8]

5

Korea: The United Nations Goes to War

The Korean problem was another one that should have been settled by negotiations. Instead, between June 25, 1950, and July 27, 1953, some three million men were killed or wounded in a war that nobody wanted and few understood. Some critics claim that the Truman administration laid the foundation for the war, by its haste in withdrawing U.S. wartime military forces from South Korea and by suggesting that Korea was outside the U.S. defense perimeter. Others contend that the Soviets misjudged the will of the free world to resist communist aggression. As World War II neared its end, the United States had hoped to take over the entire Korean peninsula as a condition of the Japanese surrender. A last-minute change was necessitated, however, when the Soviet Union entered the war against Japan on August 8, 1945, and sent their military forces into the northern part of Korea four days later. To prevent the occupation of the whole of the peninsula by the Soviet Union's forces, which had advanced as far as Seoul, the United States proposed that Soviet authorities accept the Japanese surrender of territory north of the 38th parallel and that the U.S. authorities take over the territory south of this line. The Soviets agreed. Soviet units that had crossed the 38th parallel withdrew when U.S. forces arrived. This arrangement was not a "sellout" plotted at Yalta—as has sometimes been alleged—but a matter of expediency to prevent the loss of Korea in its entirety to the Soviet Union. The result was a divided country, with the north under the administration of a Soviet military government and the south under U.S. military rule. This did not appear to present any serious problem, since the United States and the Soviet Union had agreed to abide by the Cairo Declaration of 1943 calling for an ultimately free and independent Korea. Things did go smoothly for a while. Washington and Moscow agreed to set up a provisional democratic government for Korea and established a joint U.S.–Soviet commission to implement the agreement. However, the discussions in the joint commission ran into one difficulty after another, until they collapsed completely on August 11, 1946—a victim of the Cold War.

The shooting war was still four years in the future. U.S. officials were primarily disturbed by the prospect of an indefinite military occupation of South Korea—which would not only tie down two divisions of U.S. troops, but would lead to a progressive acceleration of political problems both in Korea and in the United States. Economic conditions in Korea were chaotic; the government was badly in need of huge sums of money, which the U.S. Congress was reluctant to provide. Korean political groups were impatient for independence. This all added up to the conclusion that the disadvantages of continuing the military government in South Korea far outweighed whatever advantages there might be. In the words of Leland M. Goodrich "The problem which the United States government faced in the summer and fall of 1947 was how to extricate itself from an embarrassing situation in Korea while salvaging the substance of what it had hoped to achieve, namely, an independent Korea organized in accordance with American conceptions of democracy, friendly to the United States, and prepared to cooperate with the West in resisting the expanding pressure of Communism.' " It was this objective that led the United States to approach the United Nations in an effort to break the stalemate.[1]

Up to this point, the United States had taken no major initiative in the United Nations on any problem. Therefore, it was something of an occasion when the U.S. delegation requested on September 17, 1947, that the "problem of the independence of Korea" be placed on the agenda of the second session of the General Assembly. U.S. Secretary of State George Marshall acknowledged the failure of the two powers to reach agreement and declared that further attempts to settle the problem through bilateral negotiations "will only serve to delay the establishment of an independent, united Korea." It turned out that the United States had no proposal to present to the assembly except the one that had already been rejected by the Soviet Union. This called for early elections to choose a provisional legislature for all Korea. The United States was anxious to get the moral endorsement of the world community for its position, even though the odds were against a reversal of policy by the Soviets.

There was no doubt in anyone's mind that the United States was in full command of the U.N. majority at the time, and could count on approval of any U.S. initiative. This was demonstrated from the very first in the General Committee by the inscription of the U.S. item on the agenda. Soviet Ambassador Andrei Gromyko objected vigorously to discussion of the Korean problem in the assembly, on the ground that it should be dealt with according to the Moscow Agreement—in the joint commission. The General Committee supported the United States by a vote of 12 to 2 and its decision was later upheld by the assembly. Despite this rebuff, the Soviets did take part in the ensuing discussions. They made several proposals, including one that representatives of North and South Korea be invited to participate. The United States countered with a proposal for the establishment of a temporary commission, whose functions would be to supervise the election of Korean representatives to take part in future U.N. debate. On November 14, 1947, the General Assembly adopted a resolution calling for elections to be held before March 31, 1948, to choose members of a national assembly. The resolution also established a temporary commission of nine members to arrange and supervise the elections. The Soviet Ukraine—one of the nine—announced immediately that it would not take part. And, more importantly, the Soviet military government in North Korea refused to have anything to do with the commission. This doomed any hope of holding national elections for a unified government.

Members of the commission found themselves facing a dilemma. If they were unable to arrange for national elections—as they had been instructed to do—should they go ahead with elections in South Korea alone? This was possible—but some members of the commission, including Canada and Australia, feared that such a decision might result in freezing the division of Korea. They believed that the elections should be delayed until all possible efforts had been made to win the cooperation of the North Korean authorities and the Soviet Union. The commission finally decided that it needed new instructions from the Interim Committee of the General Assembly, which had been established in November 1947 to act between regular sessions of the assembly. This added another twist to an already complicated situation, since the Soviet Union and other communist countries were boycotting the Interim Committee on the ground that it was illegally constituted. In the Interim Committee, U.S. Ambassador Philip C. Jessup proposed that the elections be held in South Korea, and the elected representatives recognized as the Korean National Assembly—even though one-third of the country would not have participated. Jessup suggested that negotiations could be conducted later regarding the participation of North Koreans in the National Assembly. Although the United States was clearly in a position to call the signals, the Jessup proposals were not accepted without opposition. Canada questioned both their wisdom and legality. Australia also saw dangers ahead. The Australian delegation warned that, in the event of threats from North Korea, "the United Nations might be placed in the difficult position of having either actively to support, or else to renounce all responsibility for, the government it had established." The United States pushed ahead, nevertheless, and won approval of its proposal by a vote of 31 to 2 with 11 abstentions.

From the beginning, the Korean question had been tied to the Cold War. It was now involving the United Nations more and more deeply in the dispute between the two superpowers. As Leland Goodrich wrote, "The United States could, with some justification, be accused of giving the United Nations a hot potato, of passing to the international organization a responsibility which the latter was far too weak to assume, and which the United States was unwilling to continue to carry." With the Soviet Union contesting the legality of the entire proceedings, the United States continued to have its way. The elections were held in South Korea, and a government was established in Seoul on August 15, 1948. In December, the General Assembly recognized the South Korean government as the only lawful government of Korea and called for the withdrawal of occupying military forces from both zones. A new commission was established to bring about the reunification of the country. The situation continued to deteriorate, however. Despite warnings from Syngman Rhee, president of the newly created Republic of Korea, the United States proceeded to withdraw its armed forces.

The decision to pull the U.S. forces out had been made before the question was brought to the General Assembly, and the actual withdrawal began before the Republic of Korea had time to organize its own defense force. Thus, the Republic of Korea was left vulnerable. This was undoubtedly discussed by Stalin and Mao during the latter's Moscow visit early in 1949. At any rate, it later became known that, soon after the Soviet Union announced the withdrawal of its forces, a North Korean army was organized around a nucleus of the battle-trained Korean refugees and exiles who had served in the Soviet army. They were equipped with the latest Soviet assault equipment.

While this was taking place, U.S. Secretary of State Dean Acheson made his ill-timed National Press Club statement of January 12, 1949, in which he asserted that the U.S. defense perimeter against Asian aggression started from the Philippines, continued through the Ryukyu Archipelago, then bent backward through Japan and the Aleutian Islands. As for attacks outside this perimeter, he said, "The initial reliance must be on the people attacked to resist it and then upon the commitments of the entire civilized world under the charter of the United Nations, which so far has not proved a weak reed to lean on by any people who are determined to protect their independence against outside aggression." The significance of the declaration in relation to the Korean problem was that the entire Korean peninsula was outside the defense perimeter drawn by Acheson. His speech touched off congressional demands for his resignation and led to the defeat of a Truman-administration appropriations bill to provide economic aid to South Korea. In recounting these events, Acheson noted that he had been accused of giving "the green light" to the attack on South Korea, but—he declared—"this was specious, for Australia and New Zealand were not included either, and the first of all our mutual defense agreements was made with Korea." Be that as it may, six months later the North Korean forces attacked the South Koreans across the 38th parallel—beginning the long and costly war.[2]

The June 25 attack posed the most important policy questions to Moscow and Washington. The United States was fully aware that South Korea had only 100,000 men under arms, as against some 175,000 for North Korea. It was also known that the South Koreans had no air force, no tanks, and only small infantry weapons—while North Korea had planes, tanks, and heavy artillery.

For once, there was no doubt in Washington as to what the response should be. The attack across the 38th parallel was the first communist incursion across a frontier or demarcation line since the end of World War II. Nobody in the Truman administration accepted the attack as some foolhardy North Korean adventure. It was recognized as a communist challenge, organized and initiated by the Soviet Union and the Chinese communists. In the words of President Truman, "whatever has to be done to meet this aggression has to be done." There was no suggestion from anyone—either in the U.S. government or the United Nations—that the challenge be ignored.

By 1950 the United States was committed without reservation to halting the spread of communism. Even though it had failed to save Mainland China from Mao, it had been successful in Europe—largely through the Truman Doctrine and the Marshall Plan. Having failed to back up U.N. decisions on Palestine and having been accused of bypassing the organization with the Truman Doctrine, the United States recognized that it must either be prepared to resist the communist invasion of South Korea or be a party to the undermining of U.N. prestige and authority. Failure of the Kremlin to understand this, writes Charles W. Yost, "was at least as gross a miscalculation as any which the Americans had previously made." Yost attributed the Soviet miscalculation to their "psychological isolation" and "the total breakdown of rational communication between the two blocs."[3]

Regardless of the culpability of the parties before the outbreak of hostilities, the United States was the unchallenged defender of the United Nations in 1950, and the Soviet Union was the enemy. Boycotts and vetoes were one thing, but a military attack on the United Nations itself was more than the members could accept. Right from the beginning, Secretary-general Lie spoke out in condemnation of the communist attack; and, as the war progressed, he dropped all pretense of impartiality. His break with the Soviet Union became irreversible on June 25, 1950, when he took the floor in the Security Council to denounce the Communist attack as a violation of the U.N. charter and "a threat to international peace." When the United States decided to respond to the attack with force, Lie was quick to throw his support behind the U.S. action. From that day until the day he left office, the Soviet Union refused to recognize Lie as secretary-general. On June 26 he told a radio news conference that he welcomed the prompt and vigorous action taken by the Security Council. Lie asserted that "every incident, every conflict must, in my opinion, be met squarely by the United Nations." In a speech in Chicago on September 8, 1950, he said, "It would have been disastrous for the United Nations and for the cause of peace if an act of armed aggression had succeeded in these circumstances. It did not succeed because of the immediate action by the Security Council and the equally prompt intervention of the armed forces of the United States, later backed by other members of the United Nations. The world owes a great debt of gratitude to the president and people of the United States for the courageous decision they made between June 25 and June 27 and for the leadership they were able to give to the United Nations as a result of these decisions." Looking back on this period, Lie commented that the Soviets had to make up their minds whether they would resume their place in the United Nations or withdraw permanently and form their own rival organization composed of communist nations.[4]

Until the beginning of the Korean War, Trygve Lie had been contemplating retirement at the end of his five-year term on February 1, 1951. However, during the spring and summer—before the Korean crisis—a movement had been begun to persuade him to accept a second term. He had been told during talks in Moscow and Washington that he would have the support of both the Soviet Union and the United States if he would agree to continue. After June 25, the situation changed. He was attacked in the Soviet press as "an accessory to the American aggressors" and "a direct and active accomplice of the United States armed aggression in Korea." It was apparent that Lie would no longer have the support of the Soviets for a second term. He also faced a likely veto by Nationalist China because of his position on China's representation. As a result of the Soviet attacks, Lie began to have second thoughts. He decided that, if he quit under attack, he would appear to be leaving as a man defeated and pushed out by the Soviet Union. He definitely did not want another five-year term as secretary-general, but he was inclined to accept an extension of his term for one or two years as a means of blocking a Soviet triumph. The Soviet Union was determined to prevent his reelection or any extension of his term. The United States had never used the veto up to this time, but it threatened to do so to prevent the election of any other nominee. At a Security Council meeting on October 11, Soviet Delegate Jacov Malik reaffirmed Lie's unacceptability and proposed the nomination of the Polish foreign minister, Zygmunt Modzelewski. Only the Soviet Union voted for Modzelewski. Four members voted against the nomination, and six abstained. The council then voted for a Yugoslav motion to reappoint Lie. Nine members voted in the affirmative, but a negative vote by Malik blocked the proposal. Nationalist China abstained.

The Western bloc—led by the United States—took the position that the General Assembly had the authority to extend Lie's term without a recommendation of the Security Council. The argument was that the Security Council had recommended Lie's appointment in 1946 and that no further recommendation was needed. The Soviet Union took the position that this procedure was illegal. Malik declared that "if the appointment of Mr. Lie is imposed, the USSR will not take Mr. Lie into account and will not consider him as secretary-general of the United Nations." When the decision was made on October 31, 1950, the General Assembly voted overwhelmingly to extend Lie's term for three years. Only the five Soviet bloc countries voted against the proposal. True to its threat, the Soviet Union never dealt directly with Lie again, but addressed official communications to "The Office of the Secretary-General" and not to Lie by name.

Lie was not happy with the situation. In the summer of 1952—some 18 months before the terminal date of his extended term—he decided to resign. His decision was announced in the General Assembly on November 10, with a provision that he would stay on until a successor was chosen. Lie did not refer specifically to his difficulties with the Soviets, but concluded his statement by saying: "I am stepping aside now because I hope that this may help the United Nations to save the peace and serve better the cause of freedom and progress for all mankind." It was not until the following March 31 that the Security Council agreed on the nomination of Dag Hammarskjöld to take over the job.[5]

In a final statement before the General Assembly on April 7, 1953, Lie said that "It is my duty to leave no door unopened" for strengthening the prospects for peace, and then added, "It was to provide an opportunity to you to open one door that—not because of me—had been closed since 1950 that I submitted my resignation four months ago. By your election today of a secretary-general recognized as such by all five permanent members of the Security Council, you have opened the door to the office of the secretary-general."

The United Nations became a party to the Korean War through the adoption of a series of resolutions by the Security Council on June 25, June 27, and July 7, 1950. The first was general in nature—simply calling for a cease-fire, the withdrawal of the North Korean forces to the 38th parallel, and assistance to the United Nations by member states in the execution of the resolution. The June 27 resolution, which noted that the communist authorities had ignored the first resolution, recommended that member nations furnish such assistance to the Republic of Korea as might be necessary to repel the armed attack and restore peace to the area. The U.N. umbrella was fully raised with the action of July 7. This resolution welcomed the support that states had given to the previous appeals for assistance, recommended that countries providing military forces make them available to a unified command under the United States, requested the United States to name a commander, and authorized the use of the U.N. flag by the unified command. In effect—with the exception of the latter provision—the action was an endorsement of the military response already made by the United States to the communist attack.[6]

No one except the Soviet Union, however, appeared to be greatly concerned by the fact that Washington's initiative during these early stages was running a few steps ahead of the U.N. actions. The Soviets protested every inch of the way. They had blundered by their boycott of the Security Council over the Chinese representation issue at the time of the North Korean attack. This had not only eliminated the threat of a Soviet veto, but also the possibility of parliamentary maneuvers that could have tied the hands of the council members and caused costly—if not fatal—delays. It is often said that history might have been different had the Soviet Union not been boycotting the council at that time. Perhaps this is an overstatement. The fact is that the Security Council's actions were recommendations, rather than binding directives. They might have been made by a special session of the General Assembly, as well—although not so quickly.

Having realized their mistake, the Soviets sought to make up for it by charges that the council's actions were illegal and that the secretary-general and members of the council had acted "as tools utilized by the ruling circles of the United States for the unleashing of the war." Gromyko accused the United States and the Republic of Korea of aggression against North Korea. Jacov Malik, who was the Soviet U.N. representative at the time, ended his boycott and returned to the Security Council in August 1950, when it became his turn—under the alphabetical rotation system—to take over the presidency. Malik transformed the council into a propaganda forum, and tied it in such a knot through procedural wrangling and with the aid of the veto that it was not able to adopt a single resolution during the month. Malik's performance—most of it carried by television to the U.S. public—earned him the nickname of the "Great Stone Face" and did tremendous damage to the image of the United Nations. Ecuadorean Ambassador Antonio J. Quevado declared in the council that "the world would not accept the version that the invaded Republic of Korea was the aggressor, or that the United Nations Commission on Korea, composed of representatives of sovereign states, could be a mere tool of the United States." Jean Chauvel of France accused the Soviets of failing in their obligations by being absent from the Security Council during the Korean decisions. Statements such as these did not halt the Soviet campaign. On August 22, Malik said, "The whole world knew that armed intervention in the internal affairs of the Korean people, armed aggression in Korea, was being carried out by the United States on the personal orders of President Truman and under the command of a United States general. No illegal resolutions could veil or justify that aggression."

Malik convinced nobody. It was U.S. Ambassador Austin who dominated the U.N. scene and who emerged as the real champion of the United Nations. In one of the most dramatic speeches heard in the Security Council up to that time, Austin answered the Soviet charges—in language that the man on the street understood:

Whose troops are attacking deep in somebody else's territory? Those of the North Koreans. Whose territory is overrun by an invading army? That of the Republic of Korea. Who is assisting the Republic of Korea to defend itself? The United States with the support of 53 of the 59 members. Who has the influence and the power to call off the invading North Korean army? The Soviet Union. Who is responsible for the bombing and bloodshed that inevitably ensued from the act of aggression? The North Koreans and those who support them. Who, then, can stop the bombing and bloodshed? The North Koreans and those who support them. What member of the Security Council is supporting the North Korean regime in the Security Council? The Soviet Union. What kind of "peaceful settlement" has the Soviet Union proposed? The kind of settlement that would send the United Nations police away and leave the bandits to plunder Korea at will. Who, then, is supporting the United Nations charter and really working for peace? The fifty-three members of the United Nations which are supporting the Republic of Korea. Is the USSR one of the fifty-three? No.

Austin's mention of 53 nations is somewhat misleading. This was the number that actually declared their approval of the collective action—not the number that contributed military forces or other assistance. By early 1951 there were 16 U.N. members who had forces either in Korea or on their way. Many others furnished supplies or provided token services in one way or another. The United States contributed slightly more than half the ground forces, 85 percent of the naval forces, and 93 percent of the air forces. This means that the total contribution of the other participants was less than sensational. This was a U.S. show all the way. The United States provided the manpower, the weapons, the money, and the strategy.

In the United Nations no one spoke of a war to halt communist aggression. Instead, it was called a "police action." U.S. politicians and generals liked to say that, because of its link with the United Nations, the Korean War was a "no win" war—the only one in history that the United States had ever fought without the objective of defeating the enemy. Those who were less chauvinistic described the conflict with a new phrase: "limited war." One U.S. officer was quoted as saying: "We need not only combat troops but a corps of lawyers to fight this damned thing." The main difficulty was the confusion as to who was running the war—the United States or the United Nations. One important party who was mixed up over this was Gen. Douglas MacArthur, head of the Unified Command, who had to be fired by President Truman as a result. MacArthur was simply unable to distinguish between his role as commander of a U.N. operation and his lifelong position as a soldier of the United States.

For the most part, the conduct of the war was left in the hands of the United States. Since the Americans had taken charge in the beginning and were bearing the heaviest burden, there was no alternative. Trygve Lie was anxious to keep the United Nations in the picture as much as possible, but the United Nations had no machinery capable of commanding large-scale military operations. The secretary-general suggested the creation of a Committee on Coordination of Assistance for Korea, to work with the Unified Command; but the United States turned the idea down. Lie also proposed that a joint command be established, including officers from other participating countries; but this was not acceptable to Washington. The United States also rejected a suggestion by the secretary-general that the operating headquarters of the ground forces be designated as the "First U.N. Army." Eventually the countries with military units in Korea did establish a liaison committee in Washington. However, this was not an advisory group, but one to which the United States passed along information. The Unified Command's only obligation to the United Nations was to report periodically; but these reports were transmitted months after the events they dealt with, and usually after their contents had been made public in Washington. For many years, critics of the United Nations made allegations that U.S. soldiers had been killed because Soviet members of the U.N. Secretariat were transmitting military secrets to Moscow. There was absolutely no foundation for such allegations.

The United States soon found that it was not easy to carry on under the U.N. banner, even with U.S. authority unlimited. There were bound to arise questions that would be answered one way if the United States were waging war on its own, and another way if it were acting in the name of the United Nations. Such a question did arise in September 1950 after the Inchon landing and the successful breakout of the Pusan perimeter. The question was whether the Unified Command should push on across the 38th parallel or consider that its mission had been accomplished with the expulsion of the invading forces. Despite the clamor of the hawks in the United States for a total victory, President Truman decided to seek U.N. approval before going ahead with a decision to unify Korea by force. Meanwhile, Secretary-general Lie had privately circulated a memorandum called "Suggested Terms of Settlement of the Korean Question"; but he withdrew it when he learned that Washington had already decided to take the war to the north. Because of the deadlock in the Security Council, the United States took the question before the General Assembly in a resolution recommending that "all necessary steps be taken to ensure conditions of peace through the whole of Korea" and that elections be held under U.N. auspices to set up a unified, independent government for all Korea. The resolution was adopted substantially in this form on October 7—thus giving the United Nations' blessing to the Truman decision. It looked like a brilliant stroke, as MacArthur's forces swept northward toward the Chinese border at the Yalu River.

But on November 29 "disaster struck"—in the words of Lie—in the form of Chinese communist intervention, just as victory appeared at hand. The confused U.N. forces retreated in the face of a massive counterattack. The entry of the Chinese into the war once more altered the situation and raised new issues that concerned the United Nations as well as the United States. It became a new war, in which the United Nations found itself opposed by a major power. The Chinese entry touched off a new wave of second-guessing as to whether or not the United States and the United Nations would have been better off had the Unified Command stopped at the 38th parallel, instead of now having to settle for that as the demarcation line in the armistice agreement of 1953. As it was, the fighting continued during the months of negotiations at Panmunjom, and both sides suffered heavy losses.[7]

When it was all over, it seemed relevant to ask what lessons had been learned. For example, what advantages—if any—did the United States gain by pursuing its objectives through the United Nations? In view of the Truman administration's policy of halting the spread of communism, it would have been ruinous if the United States had not been prepared to meet the attack on South Korea. The choice to be made was whether this would be best done unilaterally or through the United Nations. There had never been a collective response to aggression since the founding of the United Nations; and there was no machinery for it, although the charter did provide for both collective self-defense and military sanctions. Without hesitation, President Truman chose to act through the United Nations. Since the organization was deeply involved in the Korean problem, its prestige was on the line. The president and the State Department feared that the United Nations would not only look ridiculous if the North Korean attack went unanswered, but that it would suffer the fate that had befallen the League of Nations when it failed to meet fascist aggression. There-fore, the United States had double motives—neither of which offered much in the way of advantages to the United States, except indirectly. As a matter of fact, the war was unpopular from the beginning in the United States and was almost as much a political liability as the Vietnam War was to become later on. Use of the United Nations, however, put the United States on the side of right. The move was morally correct, in the view of a majority of the U.N. members.

Finally, when the war ended in something less that a sweeping victory, doubts were expressed as to whether the United Nations had contributed enough support to balance the frustrations of fighting a limited war. Although Lie cited the U.N. police action as a victory for collective security, it was a "one-of-a-kind" operation that no one had any desire to repeat. One advantage that has been underemphasized was the inhibiting effect that the Korean War had on the Soviet Union. It would have been much easier for the Soviets to have intervened openly—instead of merely supplying materials of war—had the war not been waged under the U.N. banner. Communist China, as a nonmember, did not have the same reluctance. Ruth B. Russell has written that the consequences of the Korean War for the United States were: "widespread disillusionment with collective security possibilities through the United Nations; an even greater concentration on 'international communism' as the sole threat to world peace; and the eventual development of further regional and special security arrange-ments that have since formed the chief bases of United States strategic policy."[8]

Writing about the war from another angle, Inis L. Claude, Jr., said that the participants finally emerged from the war "with a sense of relief, not a sense of triumph. They felt fortunate at being able to muddle out of a messy and po-tentially disastrous situation, not heroic at having performed admirably in a noble cause. When the Korean war was finished, the general reaction was more nearly 'Whew, Never again!' than 'Now, let's arrange things so that we can repeat this whenever necessary!' "[9]

6

Quiet Diplomacy Ends the Berlin Blockade

The Berlin crisis was part of a broader East–West cleavage manifested by the Truman Doctrine, the Communist coup in Czechoslovakia, and the drawing together of the free nations of Europe in what later became the North Atlantic Treaty Organization (NATO). All these developments took place mainly outside the United Nations, but the organization was either drawn into each of them at one stage or another, or else adversely affected by being excluded. If any one event can be blamed for the beginning of the Berlin crisis, it was the announcement on February 9, 1948, of the Anglo–American Bi-zonal Charter for the rehabilitation of West Germany. The Soviets reacted by walking out of the Allied Control Council in Berlin—declaring that this council no longer served any purpose, since the West had abandoned the four-power government arrangement in Germany. The situation deteriorated further when the Soviet Union imposed a series of minor restrictions on communications between the Western-occupied sectors of Berlin and the rest of West Germany. The most obvious result—and perhaps the most important—was the termination of France's differences with the United States and Britain, which thereby opened the way for a coordinated policy for West Germany as set forth in the London Agreement of June 7, 1948. But this was the period when the superpowers were impelled to rush full speed ahead toward a Cold War showdown. The Soviet Union predictably responded with another walkout—this time from the four-power Kommandatura of Berlin.

The whole thing seems to have snowballed unnecessarily from one petty decision to another. A question of currency reform became the key issue. The West made the first move by introducing a new currency in the Western sectors of Berlin. Then the Soviets—fearing that the economy of Germany's Eastern zone would be adversely affected—took similar steps in the Soviet sector of Berlin. Currency from the Eastern zone began circulating throughout the whole city. The Western powers responded by employing specially marked currency from West Germany in their sectors. The crucial act came with the announcement by the Soviet Union that all land communications between the Western sectors of Berlin and the Western Zones of Germany were cut off because of "technical difficulties." This was a clear-cut case of reprisals; the pretense of technical difficulties was never seriously argued.

This was undoubtedly the most threatening confrontation yet between the superpowers of East and West. Some 2.5 million Germans in Berlin's Western sectors suddenly found themselves subjected to a piecemeal strangulation. The question was whether the Western powers would accept the Soviet challenge and use force to break the blockade. There were some who believed that the Western powers should immediately send an armored column on the autobahn with instructions to blast its way through to Berlin. General Lucius D. Clay, the U.S. commander in Germany, and his political advisor, Robert Murphy, recommended the dispatch of an armed convoy "equipped with engineering material to overcome the 'technical difficulties' " mentioned by the Soviets. Clay believed that the chances of such a convoy being met by force were small. "I was confident," Clay said, "that it would get through to Berlin and that the highway blockade would be ended." The recommendations were turned down by the U.S. Joint Chiefs of Staff and Secretary of State Marshall as well as by the governments of Britain and France. They were all afraid that—just possibly—the Soviet Union might not be bluffing.[1]

Instead of a direct challenge on land, the Western powers launched a massive airlift to break the Soviet stranglehold on the West Berliners. For 11 months—from June 28, 1948 to May 12, 1949—U.S. and British aircraft flew vital supplies into West Berlin—using three airfields and the waters of the Havel River to land 130 flights a day. During this period they flew in a total of 1,583,686 tons of essential cargo and brought out many thousands of tons of exports to help maintain the city's economy. The airlift cost a total of $170 million; but it was generally accepted as a major psychological victory as well as a political triumph for the West. Dean Acheson—for one—was firmly convinced that the Soviet decision to lift the blockade was influenced primarily by the success of the airlift.

The United Nations was fully preoccupied with the Balkan problem, the Kashmir conflict, and the Palestine partition controversy; it watched the development of the Berlin crisis with concern. During the first months of 1948, however, the situation was almost universally regarded as a problem for the Big Four—and there was no inclination on their part to ask for U.N. intervention. In fact, the first call for U.N. action came from the Senate of Greater Berlin on June 29, 1948, five days after the beginning of the total land blockade. Since the appeal did not come from a member state—or even from a national government—it was not recognized by U.N. officials as a formal request. At the time, Trygve Lie was already making private soundings among the Big Four representatives on a possible move by the secretary-general to bring the issue before the Security Council. He dropped the idea when he received no support from any of the big powers. Lie was upset when word of his private feelers was leaked to the press. To offset the rumors, he issued a statement on June 29 saying that he was watching the situation closely but that "at this time I do not plan any action under Article 99." In the introduction to his 1948 annual report—issued on July 5—Lie declared that nothing would contribute more to the effectiveness of the United Nations than settlement of the German problem. "It is difficult," he said, "for me to judge whether any of the machinery for mediation and conciliation possessed by the Security Council and the General Assembly would be helpful or not in the settlement of these differences. If consideration is given to bringing the whole problem of Germany before the United Nations, I can only urge in the strongest terms that it be done in the spirit of a genuine attempt to reach a settlement."

Meanwhile, the blockade continued, the airlift continued, and discussions among the four powers dragged on through the summer months without results. By the end of August, the Soviet commandant—Marshal Vasili Sokolovsky—was talking about tightening the blockade by restricting access to Berlin by air. It was then that the Western powers first began to give serious consideration to bringing the Berlin problem to the United Nations. This they did in separate notes on September 29, 1948, appealing to the Security Council to act against what they called a Soviet threat to international peace. By this time, few were prepared to argue that peace was not in jeopardy.

The question finally came before the council on October 4—some eight months after the crisis began. The meeting was held in Paris since the General Assembly was in session there and most of the foreign ministers were attending. It was obvious from the beginning that the only chance for positive results would be through mediation. In view of the Soviet objections to any U.N. intervention, it certainly was unlikely that the council could take any enforcement action against the Soviet Union without running up against a veto. The situation was especially difficult because the Soviets challenged the United Nations' legal competence to deal with the question. They insisted that, under Article 107 of the charter, all matters relating to enemies of the Allies in World War II must be handled exclusively by the Big Four. The Western powers, on the other hand, argued that the Berlin question was "not the problem of Germany but the threat to international peace and security caused by measures taken by the USSR in relation to France, the United Kingdom and the United States." The Berlin item was inscribed on the agenda over the objections of the Soviet Union and the Soviet Ukraine. On grounds that the action was illegal, the two objectors refused to take part in the discussions during any of the eight meetings devoted to the subject. On October 25 the Soviet Union suspended its boycott long enough to veto a six-nation resolution urging the Big Four to resume negotiations in the Council of Foreign Ministers.[2]

Having made their gesture toward the United Nations and aired their charges of Soviet intransigence, the Western powers were neither surprised nor particularly displeased with the outcome. In fact, they were in a somewhat awkward position to enter into negotiations on a major problem. Because of French fears of a united Germany, the West had no plan for German unification and was glad to have an excuse for delaying negotiations with the Soviets. There were other factors, including the impending U.S. presidential election and the interregnum period between the election and the January inauguration of a new administration. At the time, political experts favored Thomas E. Dewey to defeat Truman, and John Foster Dulles was standing by to become secretary of state. In France also, national politics were in a state of confusion; four successive ministries had resigned within three weeks. The Soviet veto had provided a welcome breather.

Following the October 25 vote, U.N. diplomats tried new approaches. Under the leadership of Argentine Foreign Minister Juan A. Bramuglia, who was president of the Security Council at the time, the six neutral council members launched a series of private talks in an effort to work out a solution behind the scenes. Bramuglia set up a Technical Committee on Currency and Trade composed of these six countries—Argentina, Belgium, Canada, China, Colombia, and Syria—to draft proposals for the reintroduction of a uniform currency in Berlin, but the group found no acceptable formula. In a separate effort, Lie appointed experts from the U.N. Secretariat—a special group headed by Gunnar Myrdal—to work on the Berlin currency problem. This effort also failed to win agreement of the two sides. Meanwhile, Mexico had introduced a General Assembly resolution appealing to the Big Four to renew their negotiations. The Mexican resolution was adopted unanimously on November 3, with the concurring votes of the big powers; but this was really nothing more than a hope. In the same category—and no more successful—was a joint appeal sent to the heads of the Big Four governments by Secretary-general Lie and Herbert V. Evatt of Australia, president of the assembly. They offered to use their good offices in helping resolve the controversy, which they described as a "danger to peace"; but their offer was politely ignored. "Every day that the deadlock over Berlin continues," the Lie–Evatt appeal said, "the danger to the peace and security of all nations continued undiminished. Fear of another war is crippling the efforts of all nations to repair the damage of the last war and return once more to the ways of peace. The work of the General Assembly and of the United Nations as a whole in every field of its endeavor is being delayed and undermined."[3]

The Soviet Union said that it was ready for an immediate resumption of negotiations, but said nothing about lifting the blockade. The Western powers restated their position that no talks could take place until after the blockade had been ended. After receiving these replies, Lie and Evatt issued a joint statement saying that the parties to the dispute had in effect expressed a willingness to accept mediation by the Security Council. The statement created a minor diplomatic furor in the Western capitals. The British suggested that Lie and Evatt should have directed their original appeal to the Soviets alone, since there was no doubt as to who was at fault. "They were right up to a point," Lie said in his memoirs, "but I for one had genuine doubts in signing it that the Foreign Office and all elements in the State Department at that time cared for a compromise solution from which no party would emerge wholly "victorious."

The first new element was injected into the situation in January 1949 when Stalin replied to four questions submitted to him by Kingsbury Smith, the European general manager for the International News Service. The key question was this: Would the U.S.S.R. be willing to remove its restrictions on traffic to Berlin if the United States, Britain, and France agreed not to establish a separate West German state, pending a meeting of the Council of Foreign Ministers to discuss the German problem as a whole? Stalin replied that it would—if the Western powers accepted the conditions stated in the question and removed their counterrestrictions against traffic in the Soviet zone.

The United States read the reply as a signal that the Soviet Union was ready to lift the blockade for a price. Dean Acheson, who was now the U.S. secretary of state—Truman having won a second term—felt that the price would be too high if it required abandonment of the three-power plans for West Germany. The Soviet signal obviously called for some acknowledgment, and for a return signal that the United States was at least interested in exploring the question further. Acheson decided that the best way to do this would be at a regularly scheduled press conference. One of the significant aspects of the Stalin interview had been the failure of the Soviet leader to mention the currency issue. Realizing this but not wishing to dramatize it, Acheson sidestepped a direct answer when asked what significance he attached to the omission. With the approval of President Truman, he decided to have a discreet inquiry made through the U.S. delegation at the United Nations as to whether the omission meant what it appeared to mean—that Stalin might be ready to lift the blockade without a prior settlement of the currency controversy. Ambassador Philip C. Jessup was instructed to approach the Soviet delegate, Jacov A. Malik, privately and informally in New York.[4]

No better illustration of quiet diplomacy can be found than what happened during the ensuing weeks. Upon his return from Washington, Jessup began watching for an opportunity to raise the question casually. The opportunity soon arrived. He ran into Malik in the Delegates' Lounge a few minutes before a Security Council meeting; and, after the usual exchange of diplomatic small talk, Jessup mentioned Stalin's omission of the currency problem and asked whether the omission had any particular significance. Malik said that he would find out. He consulted the Foreign Ministry in Moscow and a month later informed Jessup that the failure to mention the currency issue was "not accidental." On instructions from the State Department, Jessup arranged a secret meeting with Malik—and out of this came more meetings. Malik told Jessup that the currency question was important but that it could be discussed by the Council of Foreign Ministers, once such a meeting had been arranged. Jessup then inquired whether this meant after the lifting of the blockade. Malik replied that he had no instructions on that question. "Why don't you ask?" Jessup said. On March 21, the answer came back that, if a definite date could be set for the foreign ministers' meeting, the blockade could be lifted before the meeting took place. Malik, in his turn, asked whether the Western powers would suspend preparations for a West German government until after the Council of Foreign Ministers met. Jessup answered that the Western powers expected to continue preparations for a West German government, but that this would take time and that nothing was likely to happen before the proposed meeting.

Up to this point, Britain and France had been told nothing about the U.S.– Soviet talks. In view of the progress being made, Jessup was authorized to inform Sir Alexander Cadogan and the French U.N. representative, Jean Chauvel, about what was taking place and to keep them informed on future developments. While the discussions were in progress in New York, British Foreign Secretary Ernest Bevin and French Foreign Minister Robert Schuman met with Acheson in Washington, D.C., to be sure of a unified Western approach. Acheson saw little risk in agreeing to a meeting of the Council of Foreign Ministers so long as the West continued tripartite preparations for a West German government. He wrote later that, in his view, the blockade would not be reimposed if the council meeting failed to reach agreement on the broader German problem. "Stalin was lifting it," Acheson said, "because as a means to his end—allied withdrawal from Berlin—it had failed and was hurting him. He would not walk back into the trap."

Unconditional agreement was announced in a Big Four communiqué on May 5, 1949. The main point was the lifting of the blockade on May 12, nearly 11 months after the severing of all land communications between the Western sectors of Berlin and the remainder of West Germany. The four powers also agreed to convene the Council of Foreign Ministers in Paris on May 23 to consider questions relating to Germany, including the Berlin currency dispute.[5]

Acheson felt that the agreement—while terminating the blockade—left the German problem as a whole just about where it had been a year earlier. Looking back, he said in his memoirs: "I did not expect the Council of Foreign Ministers to accomplish much more than an uneasy *modus vivendi* with the Russians."

Except for the fact that the negotiations took place between the U.N. representatives of the United States and the Soviet Union, the role of the United Nations was limited and unimpressive. The Security Council had been unable to act positively—first, because of Soviet nonparticipation; and finally, because of a Soviet veto. The appeal of the General Assembly—although unopposed by the big powers—had been unproductive. So was the appeal by the secretary-general and the assembly president. Nor were efforts by the neutral members of the Security Council any more successful. Despite these setbacks, Trygve Lie was convinced that the U.N. efforts had been helpful. In an address to the

General Assembly on May 18, Lie summarized the various U.N. actions and concluded with these words:

It was by United Nations delegates in United Nations delegation offices that these conversations were brought to their successful conclusion, which resulted in the lifting of the blockade and the calling into session once again of the Council of Foreign Ministers. What does the record show? It shows that the United Nations has generated persistent and powerful influence for the peaceful settlement of the most dangerous dispute that has arisen since the end of the war. These influences for peace have persisted and re-asserted themselves in one form or another despite all setbacks, until eventually they have prevailed.

7

India and Pakistan Battle over Kashmir

In the midst of the controversies over the partition of Palestine, the Berlin blockade, and the Balkan dispute, the United Nations was confronted with an armed conflict between India and Pakistan. The Indian subcontinent—with its 400 million inhabitants—had long been in turmoil. The problem became more acute when the Indian Independence Act became effective on August 15, 1947. It was apparent soon afterward that the United Nations would have to become involved in some way, but no one could foresee that this was the beginning of a 40-year headache for the organization.

The keystone of the Independence Act was partition of the subcontinent to pull the Muslim minority out of India and create a new dominion within the British Commonwealth as Pakistan. The act also provided that the princely states previously under British rule would have the option of acceding to either India or Pakistan. One of these—the state of Jammu and Kashmir—had already become a problem before the British rule ended. This state posed special problems since it was governed by a Hindu maharaja, while 85 percent of its four million inhabitants were Muslim.

The final decision as to whether Kashmir was affiliated with India or Pakistan was of no great concern to the world in general. There has been a serious concern, however, over the behavior of the parties to the dispute and the effect that their actions have had on the United Nations and its prestige. Three times the United Nations has stopped large-scale fighting in Kashmir. In all probability the United Nations has prevented a full-scale war on the subcontinent. It still keeps a lid on the smouldering conflict by maintaining U.N. military observers in Kashmir, but the controversy over this remote princedom remains.

The resort to force by India and Pakistan in the early years of the United Nations demonstrated that the organization would face challenges from many directions in addition to those already produced by the Cold War and the Israeli–Arab conflict. U.N. diplomats were shocked, particularly, by India's readiness to use force in settling disputes. The Mahatma Gandhi's legend of nonviolence had somehow led the world to believe that India would follow his path. Muslim Pakistan was involved in this conflict, however. There being a built-in enmity between Hindus and Muslims, it was very difficult for the two countries to exist side by side in peace.

Despite pressure from Lord Louis Mountbatten, the British viceroy, the maharaja of Jammu and Kashmir found one excuse after another to delay a decision on accession. First he concluded a standstill agreement with the government of Pakistan, and then he launched a series of repressive measures against the advocates of accession to Pakistan. The militant Muslims resisted, and the resistance quickly developed into open revolt. Faced with the threat of defeat, the maharaja requested accession to India. Prime Minister Jawaharlal Nehru agreed, but declared that "the fate of Kashmir is ultimately to be decided by the people; that pledge we have given not only to the people of Kashmir, but to the world and cannot back out of it."

The question of taking the controversy before the United Nations was first raised by the Pakistani prime minister in a press statement in mid-November 1947 in which he said:

The fundamental principle of the charter of the United Nations is to prevent might prevailing over right. This whole dispute should, therefore, he brought before the bar of international opinion. We are ready to request the United Nations Organization immediately to appoint a representative in the Jammu and Kashmir state in order to put a stop to fighting and the repression of Muslims in the state, to arrange the program of withdrawal of outside forces, set up an impartial administration in the state until a plebiscite is held, and conduct the plebiscite under its direction and control for the purpose of ascertaining the free and unfettered will of the people of the state on the question of accession.

Nevertheless, Pakistan made no formal request for U.N. action. When the situation was finally brought officially to the notice of the United Nations, it was India who complained. In a note dated January 1, 1948, India charged Pakistan with aggression and asked the Security Council to halt Pakistani assistance to the rebel tribesmen in Kashmir. Pakistan responded with a counter complaint accusing India of "widespread genocide against the Muslim population," nonfulfillment of agreements reached immediately after partition, and illegal acceptance of the accession of Kashmir. With these complaints, the long U.N. involvement began. It was only after a full year of debate in the Security Council and intensive on-the-scene mediation efforts that a cease-fire ended the fighting. An additional seven months were required to reach agreement on the demarcation of the cease-fire line.[1]

On the surface, the Kashmir question appeared to be a simple one, since both India and Pakistan had agreed from the beginning to abide by the outcome of a plebiscite. By the time the United Nations entered the controversy, however, it had become complicated by the intervention of both Indian and Pakistani military forces. In both countries, the situation was now a political issue so highly charged with emotion as to be difficult to discuss rationally. For example, Dean Acheson found it impossible to hold a frank talk with Nehru on the Kashmir problem when the Indian leader visited Washington in 1949. All he could get, Acheson recalled, was "a curious combination of a public speech and flashes of anger and deep dislike for his opponents." Nehru insisted that Pakistan had no legitimate claim on Kashmir and that no settlement could be made until Pakistan's alleged aggression had been purged by the complete withdrawal of Pakistani troops and pro-Pakistani tribesmen from the territory.[2]

Time after time India repeated that it was willing to have the question decided by plebiscite, but there was always a condition attached: Pakistan's alleged aggression must be purged. During all the years that the question was before the United Nations, India found little support for her position. The Security Council never found Pakistan guilty of aggression, nor did it accept India's contention that this was a legitimate condition for conducting the proposed plebiscite. One of the first U.N. moves was to send a five-nation commission to the subcontinent, to seek initially a cease-fire and then a settlement of the dispute. The chairman of the commission, Josef Korbel of Czechoslovakia, asked Nehru to agree to an unconditional cease-fire. The Indian leader rejected the proposal angrily. "How can you ask for something like that?" he asked. "It means you are putting us on the same platform as the other side. It is your duty as a commission to condemn Pakistan for having an army on our soil. You should compel them to withdraw. Otherwise it would be as though a thief had broken into my house and you would then tell him to stay and not move out until some further measure had been taken. You treat the thief and the owner of the house as equals. First, the thief must get out, and then we can discuss further steps."

In early 1949, there was a brief period when the commission believed the situation was improving. In fact, India and Pakistan did agree informally on a plebiscite, and the commission asked Secretary-general Lie to nominate a plebiscite administrator. Lie promptly named U.S. Fleet Admiral Chester W. Nimitz, who was to be appointed by the government by Jammu and Kashmir when details of the plebiscite were settled. Then, when the commission presented its plans to the two parties and asked for acceptance without reservation, the plan fell through. The commission proposed arbitration of the points at issue, but India refused.[3]

Except for a personal mediation effort by General A. G. L. McNaughton of Canada, who had succeeded Korbel to the chairmanship, the commission had completed its work. Without success, McNaughton submitted to the two parties a set of proposals for the demilitarization of Jammu and Kashmir prior to the proposed plebiscite. The effort was dropped when the parties suggested amendments that were mutually unacceptable. The commission was abolished by the Security Council in March 1950. It would not be fair to say that it had achieved nothing. It was largely through the commission's endeavors that the cease-fire of January 1, 1949, had been brought about and that the agreement on a demarcation line separating the military forces of India and Pakistan had been reached on July 27. By this time, the cease-fire line was under the surveillance of the U.N. Military Observer Group in India and Pakistan (UNMOGIP), made up of officers from various member states; and quiet had been restored. The cease-fire left between one-third and one-half of the territory of Jammu and Kashmir in the hands of Pakistan and the remainder under Indian control.

Meanwhile, the United Nations continued its efforts to end the dispute. There is no need to repeat here the various charges and countercharges, the proposals for settlement rejected by one side or the other, the record-breaking lengths of the speeches made by representatives of the two sides, or the numerous breaches of the cease-fire. When the Security Council voted the commission out of existence, it transferred its responsibilities to a U.N. representative, Sir Owen Dixon of Australia. After six months of talks with officials of India and Pakistan, Dixon concluded that his efforts were being wasted. He asked to be relieved of his responsibilities. In April 1951 the council named Frank P. Graham of the United States as his successor. Graham did remarkably well in view of Nehru's feelings against having a big-power national in such a key role. In connection with the nomination of Nimitz as plebiscite administrator, the Indian leader had expressed doubts as to the wisdom of the choice. However admirable the individual might be, Nehru said, the appointment of citizen of a big power would needlessly create suspicion "not in my mind necessarily, but in some other big power's mind." Nehru offered no objection to the appointment of Graham who continued to make recommendations to the two parties until 1958. Like the mediators before him, however, he got nowhere.

On January 16, 1957, nine years after it was first raised, the Kashmir question came before the United Nations in another crucial test. This time Pakistan suggested that the Security Council follow the pattern used in the Suez crisis—the establishment of a U.N. police force for Jammu and Kashmir. Under the Pakistani proposal, this force would move in as Indian and Pakistani troops withdrew and would maintain order until a U.N.-supervised plebiscite could be held. When this suggestion was embodied in a resolution, it was vetoed by the Soviet Union, which had been a staunch supporter of India throughout the dispute. A few weeks later, the council asked its president, Gunnar Jarring of Sweden, to undertake a personal peace mission to the subcontinent. Jarring soon concluded that there was even less chance for a settlement than before.[4]

The new factor was a much more rigid political situation, Jarring noted. The most important development was the meeting of the so-called constituent assembly at Srinagar—the capital of Kashmir—late in 1956. The assembly had drafted a constitution integrating the state into India. India had referred to the changed situation at the January meeting of the Security Council, and had declared that India could not forever consider past proposals as applicable or binding. It was clear that the Indians were in effect contending that the decision of the constituent assembly had eliminated the need for a plebiscite. This was in direct contradiction to the position taken by the Security Council. The council had stated in a resolution on March 30, 1951, that any action a constituent assembly might take to determine the future of Jammu and Kashmir "would not constitute a disposition of the state."[5]

Pakistan was not itself without blame in the controversy, but it now had good reason to feel let down by the United Nations. Pakistani leaders could not fail to see that India was presenting the world with a fait accompli and that the integration of the Indian-occupied parts of Jammu and Kashmir had eliminated all chances for a plebiscite. What other interpretation could be given to India's statement that it could not forever consider past proposals as applicable or binding?

The world press was almost unanimous in its condemnation of Nehru. There was also a substantial amount of criticism directed at the United Nations for its failure to meet the Indian challenge to its authority. And there was concern in many responsible newspapers for the possible adverse effect that the situation might have on the prestige and effectiveness of the organization. In an editorial on January 30, 1957, the London *Daily Express* said:

Nehru, as leader of the anticolonial nations, may feel himself strong enough to defy the U.N. Let the U.N. prove itself stronger. Sanctions are the test. Failure to put them into operation against India will finally expose the U.N.'s double standard—high principles for one nation, expediency for another.

The St. Louis *Post-Dispatch* said:

Can the United Nations ignore what India has done? An agency which does not enforce its authority is liable to lose it. That is why India has struck a hard blow against the United Nations whose jurisdiction it acknowledged in accepting the 1949 truce.

The New York *Times* commented:

This unilateral action on the part of India does not, in our judgment, relieve the United Nations of its responsibility. The Kashmir issue is still before the United Nations and the international body had committed itself not merely to a cease-fire in the hostilities that have taken place but to the larger framework of a free, popular ballot under external supervision.

This was not the last that the United Nations was to hear of the Kashmir question.

By 1961 the United Nations had become accustomed to seeing its members resort to force to settle disputes. A glaring example occurred on December 18 when Indian troops seized the territories of Goa, Daman, and Diu—which had been ruled by Portugal since 1505. The three enclaves, with a population of just under a million, were located near Bombay and had been claimed by India since that country attained its independence in 1947. The situation reached an unexpected crisis six weeks after U Thant took office as acting secretary-general.[6]

The question was brought to the attention of the Security Council in a series of letters from Portugal between December 6 and 16. Portugal charged that India was massing forces to carry out its declared intention of annexing the territories. India, in turn, accused the Portuguese of attacking Indian villages. On December 14 Thant intervened personally in an attempt to head off the threatened military conflict. In an appeal to the two governments, the secretary-general said, "I respectfully appeal to your excellency and your government to ensure that the situation does not deteriorate to the extent that it might constitute a threat to peace and security. I would urge immediate negotiations with a view to achieving an early solution of the problem." The appeal was ignored. The issue was settled four days later when Indian troops took over the disputed territories. Recognizing the fait accompli, the Security Council never took up the question.

There was no substantial change in the Kashmir situation until August 5, 1965, when cease-fire violations began accelerating at an unprecedented rate. There was heavy and prolonged artillery fire from the Pakistani side on August 15–16. Between then and September 1, Indian troops crossed the cease-fire line at several points, and occupied Pakistani positions. Australia Major General Robert H. Nimmo, chief of the U.N. military observer group, warned U Thant that the situation was deteriorating rapidly. The secretary-general offered to send Under Secretary Ralph Bunche as his personal representative to seek an end to the violence. Both sides laid down such intransigent conditions, however, that he was forced to consider the mission not feasible. Instead, he summoned Nimmo to headquarters for consultations.[7]

On September 1 Thant sent urgent appeals to Mohammad Ayub Khan, president of Pakistan, and Sri Bahadur Shastri, prime minister of India, for a restoration of the cease-fire. "I must point out," he said, "that resort to force for the settlement of a dispute of this kind is contrary to both the spirit and letter of the charter of the United Nations and the obligations undertaken by your country as a member of the organization." By the time they received his appeals, the cease-fire had collapsed completely, and heavy fighting was in progress. In an urgent meeting on Saturday, September 4, the Security Council adopted a resolution calling for restoration of the cease-fire.[8]

The fighting continued, however, and the council met again two days later. After listening to statements by India and Pakistan—both of whom defended their refusal to agree to a cease-fire—the council again called on them to end the fighting and withdraw their forces to the positions held before August 5. The resolution further requested the secretary-general "to exert every possible effort to give effect to this resolution." After private consultations, Thant concluded that the council intended he should undertake a personal peace mission to the Indian subcontinent. He left the next day for a nine-day visit to Rawalpindi and New Delhi. After conferring with the leaders of the two countries, the secretary-general formally called upon them to halt the fighting by September 14; but again, both laid down conditions that he could not accept. He left on September 15 to report urgently to the Security Council.[9]

In his final communication to the two leaders, Thant proposed a face-to-face meeting and offered his assistance in any role desired by the parties. Nothing came of his proposal immediately; but the two leaders did meet four months later at Tashkent in the Soviet Union—at the invitation of Soviet Premier Alexei Kosygin—and agreed to withdraw their forces not later than February 25, 1966, to the August 5 positions. Meanwhile, they had already accepted a Security Council cease-fire deadline of September 22; and the fighting did end on that date, some six weeks after the outbreak of hostilities.

The dispute itself did not end, however, even after the Tashkent meeting. Shastri had expressed concern that he might not be able to sell the Tashkent Declaration to the Indian people. His concern was justified. Soon there were riots both in India and Pakistan. Within three months Pakistan was again pressing its claims to Kashmir. Meanwhile, Shastri had been succeeded by Indira Gandhi, who endorsed the declaration but added: "If we have to fight, it is inevitable we will fight and fight successfully, too."

There was an uneasy peace between India and Pakistan until 1971 when they once more became engaged in a major military conflict. The new crisis began as an internal struggle in Pakistan, grew into a rebellion of the predominantly Bengali population of East Pakistan, and eventually involved India. No one was surprised when the internal political structure of Pakistan broke down. It had been foreordained by the improbable marriage between two culturally incompatible peoples at the time Pakistan became independent in 1947. This country with separate eastern and western regions was unique among the nations of the world. East Pakistan and West Pakistan were divided not only by divergent cultures and history, but by a corridor 1,100 miles wide running through Indian territory. From the beginning, the East Pakistanis had felt themselves oppressed by the Punjabis in West Pakistan. Talk of separation was common. Support for the Aswami League, which advocated autonomy for Bengal, was widespread. The league had a popular and able leader in Sheik Mujibur Rahman, known by his followers affectionately as "Mujib."[10]

The trouble came to a head when the blunt and intensely nationalistic General Agha Mohammed Yahya Khan took over the Pakistan government in 1969. He immediately imposed martial law and declared, "I'll be damned if I'll see Pakistan divided." Surprisingly, Yahya ordered national elections—the first in the 23-year history of the country. These were held on December 7, 1970, just three weeks after a devastating cyclone left hundreds of thousands dead in East Pakistan. For Yahya the time was unfortunate since it came when the East Pakistanis were bitterly complaining about what they believed to be the national government's indifference to their suffering. When the Bengalis went to the polls, they voted in such numbers that Mujib's Aswami League won 167 of the 169 seats allotted to the East in the 313-member national assembly. That gave the league a majority, and should have assured Mujib the post of prime minister of Pakistan. However, West Pakistan's popular leader, Zulficar Ali Bhutto, refused to participate in the assembly; and President Yahya abruptly postponed its opening indefinitely. Within hours, Mujib called a general strike in East Pakistan. He demanded limited autonomy under which East Pakistan would control its own taxation, trade, and foreign aid. Yahya met with him; but, even while they were talking, the government began flying in military reinforcements for a huge troop buildup in East Pakistan. Yahya suddenly broke off the talks, flew back to Islamabad, and outlawed the Aswami League.

The carnage began on March 25, 1971. Tanks crashed through the street of Dacca, the capital of East Pakistan. Flamethrowers torched sections of the city. Machine guns mowed down fleeing citizens. The campus of Dacca University—a beehive of separatist activity—was reduced to shambles. In cities throughout Bengal, the carnage was repeated. In rural areas, crops were burned. By mid-April the campaign had been completed. Estimates of the number of dead ranged from 200,000 to half a million. Meanwhile, Bengalis by the hundreds of thousands trudged across their borders into India and scattered into some 1,500 refugee camps.

Up to this time the United Nations had not intervened in the political conflict because it was regarded as an internal affair outside the competence of the organization. Thant had limited his initiative to the humanitarian field. On April 1, during the height of the fighting, a U.N. spokesman said, "If the government of Pakistan were to request the secretary-general to assist in humanitarian efforts, he would be happy to do everything in his power in this regard." Pakistan, however, was reluctant to ask for U.N. intervention, even to this extent. It was not until some six weeks later that Yahya gave the go-ahead enabling the secretary-general to appeal for contributions and to designate Sadruddin Khan, U.N. high commissioner of refugees, to coordinate the international assistance program.

It should be noted that—up to this time—the Pakistani bloodshed was still a domestic affair, except for the massive influx of refugees into India. By mid-summer, however, Thant was convinced that the situation had become a threat to international peace, and was therefore a matter for possible U.N. action. He hesitated to take any initiative on his own under Article 99 of the charter because, upon consulting members of the Security Council, he found them sharply divided as to whether U.N. intervention would do any good. Instead, on July 20, he took the unusual step of sending to all members of the council a secret aide memoire urging the council to intervene. "The time is past," Thant said, "when the international community can continue to stand by, watching the situation deteriorate and hoping that relief programs, humanitarian efforts and good intentions will be enough to turn the tide of human misery and political disaster."

The Security Council continued to avoid facing up to the seriousness of the situation. Thant finally made his aide memoire public on August 2—after distorted versions had appeared in print—but the council still did not act. On October 20, Thant sent messages to the governments of India and Pakistan; he declared the situation to be so serious that it "could all too easily give rise to open hostilities which would not only be disastrous to the two countries principally concerned but might also constitute a major threat to a wider peace."

At that time India still had not openly intervened in the Pakistani civil conflict, but Thant was disturbed by increasing border incidents and the massing of troops along both sides of the border. "In this potentially dangerous situation," he said, "I feel that it is my duty as secretary-general to do all I can to assist the governments immediately concerned in avoiding any development which might lead to disaster." He proceeded to offer his good offices to the two countries, but they were not accepted. By then, India and Pakistan were already on the brink of war. Full-scale war began on December 3 when Indian troops attacked across the border into East Pakistan and along the cease-fire line in Jammu and Kashmir. Despite the fact that India had invaded Pakistani territory, no one sought to press charges of aggression. It was generally conceded that the Pakistani excesses against the Bengalis largely justified the intervention on the part of India. The Indian initiative definitely had the approval of the Indian public, which had never accepted the geographic oddity that left a segment of Pakistan deep inside Indian territory. Some hawks in New Delhi were unhappy that the Indians had not pushed their advantage to destroy Pakistan, once and for all.

Finally, the Security Council did meet, after the fighting started; but efforts to appeal for a cease-fire were stymied by Soviet vetoes—as expected. Henry Cabot Lodge was critical of the United Nations' failure to act during the massacre in East Pakistan. In his book, *The Storm Has Many Eyes*, Lodge wrote,

In 1971 the United Nations did not make a determined effort to persuade the government of Pakistan to cease its brutal behavior toward the East Pakistanis. It is true that the United Nations charter forbids interference in a state's "internal affairs"—and the conduct of Pakistani officials in Pakistan, in one sense was very "internal." But the U.N. can, without using force, intervene in a nation's internal affairs when it fears that developments there constitute a threat to peace. This was not done with regard to Pakistan. Nor did the U.N. prevent—or try to prevent—India from invading Pakistan.[11]

Unfortunately, Lodge was not the U.S. representative in 1971 (but he had been, from 1953 to 1960). The United States was one of the Security Council members who did not take the initiative—despite Secretary-general Thant's request—to bring the Pakistani situation up for consideration before the fighting started.

On December 7 the secretary-general went before the General Assembly in a personal appeal that all parties to the conflict "take every possible measure to spare the lives of the innocent civilian population which is afflicted and threatened by the present hostilities." The fighting ended ten days later, after some 30,000 soldiers and civilians had died. In the east, the Pakistani troops had fallen back rapidly to Dacca without giving any serious resistance. They were ordered to hold Dacca at any cost, but local commanders surrendered when it became clear that their forces had no hope for reinforcements or escape. A short time later a cease-fire was arranged on the Jammu and Kashmir cease-fire line and further south. Pakistan had lost East Pakistan for good.

Jubilation swept East Pakistan in the following days when General Yahya and other high officers were purged from the government and the military, for their part in the disaster. Some politicians claimed that the east could have been saved except for the "bloody-mindedness" of these leaders. Another cause for jubilation was the release of Mujib, who had been imprisoned by Yahya. The surrender of the Pakistani forces in Dacca had cleared the way for the emergence of East Pakistan as the independent country of Bangladesh. The new provisional government arrived in Dacca behind Indian tanks and paratroops. Some Western diplomats thought that the Pakistani national government was better off without the former East Pakistan and its 75 million people—who lived 1,300 people to the square mile, in crushing poverty. The United States and the People's Republic of China had watched in helpless frustration as their ally Pakistan went down in defeat. On the other hand, the Soviet Union had backed India all the way, and thereby greatly increased its prestige in New Delhi.[12]

8

The Suez War

During its first ten years, the United Nations had been battered by various kinds of abuses, including the use of military force to thwart its decisions. But for sheer callousness in flouting the obligations of U.N. membership, nothing came close to the invasion of Egypt by Israel, Britain, and France in October and November 1956. U.S. Secretary of State John Foster Dulles called the invasion "a grave error, inconsistent with the principles and purposes of the charter, and one which if persisted in would gravely undermine our charter and undermine this organization." The world was not only shocked by the use of force, but even more so by the aggressors' deception and collusion, their improper use of the United Nations, and their attempts to belittle the U.N. organization in the eyes of the public. This was the first time that permanent members of the Security Council had taken part in a clear-cut act of aggression against another member nation. The involvement of Britain was a particularly heavy blow, because from the beginning the British had been considered among the staunchest supporters of the United Nations. France's relations with the United Nations had been poor because of the organization's position on Morocco, Tunisia, and Algeria; but even France's closest allies—such as the United States—found it difficult to believe that it would conspire in such a scheme. And Israel had been created by the United Nations!

The story of the collusion has been told many times, but it is essential to review the main steps briefly because of their relevance to the question of U.N. prestige and public confidence. This was much more than an attack on one member nation by three other members. The plan was actually drafted while the participants were engaging in U.N. discussions, presumably in good faith.

The Security Council, in fact, was used to direct attention away from the undercover activities and to lull the member states into a sense of false security.

The first talk of coordinated military action against Egypt took place in June 1955—more than a year before the nationalization of the Suez Canal Company on July 26, 1956. Nothing came of this first discussion except an agreement for the secret delivery of French arms to Israel. Ostensibly, the first reaction to the nationalization of the canal was a meeting of 18 interested countries in London on August 16, 1956, to consider the problem. A more significant meeting, however, took place secretly in Paris on August 7, between French and Israeli officials. It was here that France advanced the concept of a joint French–Israeli attack—a proposal that Israel quickly accepted. Britain was not involved in the initial agreement, although Anthony Eden—at that time prime minister—had been considering the idea of a possible Anglo–French military action against Egypt as early as March 1956.[1]

Up to mid-September, British Foreign Office officials had cautioned against collaboration with Israel because of potential damage to Britain's traditional ties with the Arab countries. The first British discussions with Israel on the subject took place about the same time that Britain and France brought the Suez crisis to the attention of the Security Council. The council held a preliminary meeting on September 26 at which they agreed to consider the British–French complaint and also a complaint by Egypt. The substantive discussion began on October 5. This was a key date. It was on October 5, 1956, that Israel completed plans for the invasion of Egypt and gave it the code name KADESH. It was also on this date that Egyptian President Gamal Abdel Nasser sent a message to his foreign minister, Mahmoud Fawzi, at U.N. headquarters, authorizing him to agree to the creation of an international Suez advisory board—if he saw fit—during the New York discussions. By this time—although it was a closely guarded secret—Britain had committed itself to take part in the attack on Egypt, along with France and Israel. At an October 24 meeting in Sèvres, France, a plan that spelled out the role of each participant was put into writing.[2]

The United States had no inkling of this developing collusion, but President Eisenhower was disturbed by Britain's increasingly tough attitude. On October 5—just before the Security Council debate began—Secretary of State Dulles met with Selwyn Lloyd and Christian Pineau, the British and French foreign ministers, to prepare for the council meeting. Dulles found that his two colleagues were practically writing off any possibility of a peaceful settlement. He disagreed as emphatically as he could. The Soviet Union sensed that Britain and France did not expect any useful action from the council. The Soviet foreign minister, Dmitri Shepilov, proved to be prophetic when he pictured the two Western powers as saying: "You have urged us to appeal to the United Nations. We have done so. We have appealed to the Security Council. But, as you see, it is powerless, it can do nothing. Negotiations with Egypt are useless. Other steps must be taken."

It seemed for a while that something might come of the discussions at the United Nations, after all. During private talks under Secretary-general Dag Hammarskjöld's aegis, Lloyd had listed six principles for a Suez settlement, and the Egyptians—much to Lloyd's surprise—had accepted them. The British and French were not looking for protracted negotiations at this stage, however. With military plans already in motion, they submitted last-minute conditions (in the form of a rider to the six principles) that they were sure Nasser would not accept. The Soviet Union—backing up Nasser—vetoed the Anglo–French rider.[3]

As it was finally worked out, the attack plan called for Israel to attack across the Sinai Peninsula and for Britain and France to launch a "police action" to halt the fighting in the absence of any effective international machinery to deal with the situation. The strategy was a two-track approach—with efforts on the one hand to discredit the United Nations, and on the other to picture the proposed intervention as a disinterested peace move. There was even an effort by Britain to equate the Suez invasion with the U.S. intervention in Korea. There were obvious differences, however—the main one being that the U.S. action had been a response to aggression against a government established under U.N. auspices, while the Anglo–French attack was inspired by a desire to destroy Nasser and was launched under a phoney pretext manufactured in advance by the parties. In addition to its violation of major U.N. principles, the Suez invasion was a betrayal of the NATO allies—particularly the United States, which was the closest friend of all three participants. They had not only gone against the advice of the United States, but had done their best to keep the United States in the dark about their plans. The Israeli military commander, Moshe Dayan—writing in his diary just before the attack—said that he was struck by the "hollowness" of the warnings given by Eisenhower against military action. They show, he said, that Eisenhower "thinks the imminent conflict is likely to erupt between Israel and Jordan and that Britain and France will cooperate with him in preventing this. How uninformed he is of the situation! In all its aspects, the reality is the reverse of his assumptions."

Eisenhower's assumptions were not surprising, in view of the elaborate effort made by Israel to create the impression that the mobilization of its forces was inspired by raids from Jordan and by the reported movement of Iraqi troops into Jordan. The fake crisis between Jordan and Israel was so realistic, in fact, that only quick action by Prime Minister Eden prevented the British military from going to the aid of Jordan under terms of their Anglo–Jordanian alliance. This would have seriously complicated the Anglo–French plans for war against Nasser. The reports about the entry of Iraqi troops into Jordan were being spread by the Israeli intelligence branch. Dayan said that this was part "of the deception plan to produce the impression that our activity is aimed at Jordan and Iraq." The Jordanian red herring—carried out with the knowledge of Britain and France—even included bloody retaliatory raids, Israel's withdrawal from the Israeli–Jordanian Mixed Armistice Commission, and the prohibition of U.N.

military observers from investigating incidents on Israeli territory. Almost everybody fell for the ruse, including Israeli troops and Canadian General E. L. M.
Burns, chief of the U.N. Truce Supervision Organization.

A key part of the attack plan was an ultimatum to be issued after the Israeli
attack, giving Israel and Egypt 12 hours to agree on a cease-fire and to withdraw
their forces to a distance of ten miles from the canal. If either of the parties
refused to agree, the ultimatum said, "United Kingdom and French forces will
intervene in whatever strength may be necessary to secure compliance." This
was to be the pretext for the intervention of British and French forces. The
text was agreed on by Britain, France, and Israel on October 24—five days
before the Israeli attack. The three parties also agreed that Israel would withhold
its reply until Egypt's answer was known. Although they expected Egypt to reject
the ultimatum, they wanted to make sure that the pretext would not be destroyed
by a surprise Egyptian acceptance. In that case, Israel would reject the ultimatum.

On October 29—according to plan—the attack was launched by Israel. Paratroops were dropped at a number of points. Within hours Israeli troops had
penetrated deep into the Sinai. Then came step number two—the Anglo–French
ultimatum—which was sent to Israel and Egypt on October 30 as a communication purported to have been drafted during British–French consultations in
London on that date. The Security Council had been alerted during the night;
it met on the morning of October 30 at the request of the United States. The
council was not aware at the time that it faced anything more than an Israeli
attack, but all kinds of rumors had been circulating to the effect that much
more was involved. Soviet Ambassador Arkady Sobolev—for example—said,
"It is plain from everything that is happening that Israel could not have made
this attack without encouragement and help from these aggressive circles which
are not interested in the preservation of peace in the Middle East and are trying
to find some pretext for moving their troops into this area."[4]

The British and French representatives took the position that, on the basis
of past experience, the Security Council did not have the ability to deal with
the problem and that they themselves must step in to fill the vacuum. Sir Pierson
Dixon, the British representative, asked, "How can we have confidence, much
as we would like to, that some future injunction by the Security Council would
in fact prove to be effective to deal, in time—and time is of the essence—with
a situation which is rapidly getting out of control?" He concluded that "there
is no action that the Security Council can constructively take which would
contribute to the twin objectives of stopping the fighting and safeguarding free
passage through the Suez canal." The United States—in an open break with
its major European allies—introduced a resolution calling on Israel to withdraw
to the established armistice lines and urging all members "to refrain from the
use of force or threat of force in the area in any manner inconsistent with the
purposes of the United Nations." It also called on U.N. members to "refrain
from giving any military, economic or financial assistance to Israel as long as it
has not complied with this resolution."

For once, the United States and the Soviet Union were aligned against Britain and France. Despite their repeated attacks on the Soviet Union for using the veto to thwart the will of the majority, Britain and France invoked the veto to kill the U.S. resolution. It was Britain's first veto, and France's third. The Soviet Union then introduced a resolution of its own—similar to that of the United States, except that it eliminated the appeal for members to refrain from the use of force and from aiding Israel. In other words, it simply urged Israel to withdraw its forces. But this also was vetoed by Britain and France. That was the situation when the ultimatum expired at midnight (New York time) on October 30. The vetoes set the stage for transfer of the debate to an emergency session of the General Assembly, under the Uniting for Peace Resolution.

Ironically, it was communist Yugoslavia that invoked the Uniting for Peace procedure and called the first emergency session since the resolution was adopted six years earlier. John Foster Dulles, who had helped push the resolution through the assembly in 1950, now watched it being used to get around the vetoes not of the Soviet Union, but of the United States' main NATO allies—and with the support of the Soviets, who had always denounced the resolution as a violation of the charter. In fact, it was the Soviet Union that cast the seventh and deciding vote.

With the publication of the ultimatum and the reception of news dispatches telling of massive British naval movements through the eastern Mediterranean toward Egypt, it soon became apparent that there was substance to what Sobolev had said. James Reston reported in the New York *Times* that, when Eisenhower learned of the ultimatum, "the White House crackled with barrack-room language the like of which had not been heard since the days of General Grant." The president sent messages to British Prime Minister Eden and French Premier Guy Mollet, saying: "I must urgently express to you my deep concern at the prospect of this drastic action at the very time when the matter is under consideration, as it is today, by the United Nations Security Council. It is my sincere belief that peaceful processes can and should prevail." The Anglo–French action had been taken without the knowledge of the British Commonwealth governments or the U.N. secretary-general, who had been engaged right up to the time of the attack in trying to arrange further negotiations to resolve the Suez problem. Brian Urquhart—one of Hammarskjöld's closest associates in the Secretariat—said in his biography of the late secretary-general: "The Anglo–French ultimatum shocked and outraged Hammarskjöld. In spite of rumors, hints and disturbing pieces of evidence, he found it hard to believe that two permanent members of the Security Council, the two Western European countries which he most admired and which he believed to represent the best traditions of European civilization, could be guilty of so shoddy a deception or of so disastrous a course of action." In fact, shortly before the attack, Hammarskjöld had told the Egyptian foreign minister, Mahmoud Fawzi, that there was nothing to fear. "I cannot conceive that Britain would resort to force," he said. "As for the French, they have their internal troubles [Algeria] and these are enough."[5]

Eisenhower was in the midst of a presidential campaign at the time, and the three aggressor countries had counted on this to prevent any strong anti-Israel reaction on his part—which might have alienated Jewish voters. Realizing the danger of this kind of thinking, Eisenhower had already sent word to Prime Minister David Ben-Gurion through Israeli Ambassador Abba Eban that "I don't give a damn whether I'm re-elected" and that he intended to keep the peace in the Middle East. His anger was still apparent in a speech he made on October 31. Eisenhower said:

The United States, was not consulted in any way about any phase of these actions. Nor were we informed of them in advance. As it is the manifest right of any nations to take such decisions and actions, it is likewise our right—if our judgment so dictates—to dissent. We believe these actions have been taken in error. For we do not accept the use of force as a wise or proper instrument for the settlement of international disputes.[6]

Hammarskjöld was so upset by the collusion that he felt he must take a public stand. While not condemning the three attacking countries by name, he declared that a

secretary-general cannot serve on any other assumption than that—within the necessary limits of human frailty and honest differences of opinion—all member nations honor their pledges to observe all articles of the charter. . . . The bearing of what I have just said must be obvious to all without any elaboration from my side. Were the members to consider that another view of the duties of the secretary-general than the one here stated would better serve the interests of the organization, it is their obvious right to act accordingly.

He clearly intended to confront the members with a question of confidence, and his statement was so understood by those present in the Security Council. All of them, including the representatives of Britain and France, expressed their full confidence in him.

The emergency session of the General Assembly began on November 1. By that time Britain and France had already launched large-scale air attacks on Cairo and other Egyptian cities. Paratroops were poised at bases on the island of Cyprus, while troop transports steamed across the eastern Mediterranean toward Port Said. At the United Nations, Secretary of State Dulles personally led the U.S. effort to halt the fighting. The abhorrence of the world community was reflected in the one-sided vote by which the assembly adopted the U.S. resolution on November 2: It was 65 to 5, with only Australia and New Zealand standing by the three aggressors. The resolution called for: (1) an immediate cease-fire and a halt to the movement of armed forces into the area, and (2) prompt withdrawal behind the armistice lines of 1949. Britain, France, and Israel ignored the resolution. On November 5—while the assembly continued to discuss the situation—the invasion of British and French airborne and sea-borne forces began. In all, about 20,000 troops poured in from Cyprus and Malta before the two big powers agreed to abide by a U.N. cease-fire on November 6. The British government claimed that there were only 100 Egyptians killed and 540 wounded in the 24 hours of fighting by British and French forces and by Anglo–French air attacks. British correspondents on the scene, however, hotly disputed these figures. The correspondent for the London *Daily Express* said that he had seen many more casualties; he estimated 1,000 killed, 5,000 wounded, and 25,000 homeless. In any event, it was clear that London and Paris had blundered in assuming that Egypt would not resist and that their venture would result in little or no bloodshed.[7]

Although the British and French had sought to justify their use of force by arguing that the United Nations was incapable of dealing with the problem, it was the United Nations that provided the machinery—and the excuse—for bringing the war to an end. As soon as the two powers realized that they could achieve their objective only with large-scale fighting, they knew that they had miscalculated. They were not prepared to continue the war in the face of strong public reaction both at home and abroad. The way out was provided when Canada's minister for external affairs, Lester B. Pearson, proposed to the General Assembly in the predawn hours of November 2 that Dag Hammarskjöld be authorized to organize an international police force that would step in until a political settlement could be reached. Pearson had been talking privately about such a move for some days. Originally, he was thinking in terms of combining U.N. troops with those of the British and French to form a buffer between the Egyptians and the Israelis. His main objective was to halt the fighting, but he was also anxious to get the two Western allies off the hook before any permanent damage had been done to NATO and the British Commonwealth. The United States was opposed to the original Pearson concept. Instead, Washington favored an international force made up of small countries, with the details of planning and organizing left in the hands of the secretary-general. This was the form in which Pearson presented it on November 2. The British and French quickly endorsed the Pearson proposal. British Delegate Dixon told the assembly that "if the United Nations were willing to take over the physical task of maintaining peace in the area, no one would be better pleased than we." On November 3 Eden told the British people in a radio broadcast: "We have stepped in because the United Nations could not do so in time. If the United Nations will take over this police action we shall welcome it." The first step toward the establishment of the U.N. Emergency Force (UNEF) was formalized in the early hours of November 4, when the General Assembly adopted a resolution requesting the secretary-general to submit plans for the proposed force within 48 hours. On November 7, the assembly accepted Hammarskjöld's blueprint for UNEF. The vote was 64 to 0, with 12 countries abstaining. Among the latter were the nine communist countries, Israel, Egypt, and South Africa.[8]

From there on, the arrangements were in the hands of the secretary-general and the newly appointed chief of UNEF, General Burns. By early February, 6,000 officers and men from seven countries had arrived in Egypt to maintain a peace watch along the cease-fire line. In addition to its role in facilitating the withdrawal of British and French military forces, UNEF had historical significance as the first international police force. Although its establishment had been approved without a dissenting vote, the question of financing the operation was not disposed of so smoothly. Nine communist countries—Albania, Bulgaria, Byelorussia, Czechoslovakia, Hungary, Poland, Rumania, the Soviet Ukraine, and the Soviet Union—voted against a proposal by the secretary-general that the costs be borne by the member states on the basis of apportionment in the General Assembly. These countries declared that they would not participate in financing the force because, in their opinion, the procedure was illegal. Only the Security Council was competent to make such decisions, they argued. This was the beginning of the United Nations' peace-keeping deficits, which were later to be the center of an Article 19 controversy. A number of other countries refused to pay their UNEF assessments, but for different reasons. Egypt, for example, was one of a half-dozen Arab states that were withholding payment on grounds that the aggressors should be made to pay. Israel paid its assessments; but it rebuffed U.N. proposals that UNEF units be stationed on the Israeli side of the cease-fire line, as well as on the Egyptian side. Ben-Gurion—as the only victor in the war—was not happy with U.N. intervention. He told the Israeli Knesset on November 7: "Israel will not consent, under any circumstances, that a foreign force—called whatever it may be—take up positions whether on Israeli soil or in any area held by Israel." Israel had occupied Gaza, most of the Sinai Peninsula, and the Strait of Tiran—which gave Israeli shipping free passage through the Gulf of Aqaba to the Red Sea. The British and French, on the other hand, had to pull out of Egypt with nothing to show for their efforts. They had failed to break Egypt's control of the Suez Canal and had lost their bid to oust Nasser. To make matters worse, the canal had been blocked by the sinking of some 50 ships—some by British bombing, but most by Egyptian scuttling—and was to remain closed until April 1957. One of the tasks assigned to the United Nations was the clearing of the canal—which was accomplished at a cost of $8.2 million.[9]

Much has been said here about the abuse of the United Nations and the violation of the charter perpetrated by the countries involved in this attack on Egypt. The United Nations not only survived the ordeal, but came through it with greatly enhanced prestige. Many member states—the United States, in particular—realized that this was a supreme test for the organization. Observers generally agreed that the U.S. performance at the United Nations—the United States' firm stand against the action of its closest allies, and its leadership throughout the Suez crisis—was one of the high points in U.S. foreign policy. By joining with the Soviet Union and the Afro–Asian countries, it put new life into the United Nations at a time when many were writing the organization off—as the British and French were. Henry Cabot Lodge, who was then U.S. ambassador to the United Nations, said that the U.N. action in the Middle East was "the decisive factor in preventing a war." "If the United Nations had not taken the stand it did," he declared, "it would have ceased to be a respectable organization and the whole world would have slipped into international anarchy." French Foreign Minister Pineau acknowledged that pressure from the United States was one of the factors leading France to agree to a cease-fire. He asserted, however, in a speech before the General Assembly that the U.N. organization had a long record of failures. "If we look back on the principal questions before the United Nations," Pineau said, "we note that actually the United Nations has been unable to solve most of the problems referred to it." British Prime Minister Eden sought to justify his country's action by claiming that the United Nations would never have taken the vigorous action that it did, had it not been prodded by the Anglo–French intervention.[10]

Two U.N. officials who were intimately involved in the Suez discussions— Hammarskjöld's executive assistant, Andrew W. Cordier, and his press spokesman, Wilder Foote—gave the following appraisal, some years later:

The sixty days from November 2 to December 31, 1956, were the most inventive and fruitful two months in the first twenty-five years of the history of the United Nations. This was the time when the attack on Egypt was halted, the United Nations Emergency Force was created and began its deployment, the British and French withdrew their troops, and the Suez Canal clearance operation was organized and launched."[11]

9

The Soviet Union Intervenes in Hungary

It has been said that the Suez invasion was planned to occur at a time when the Soviet Union was preoccupied with unrest in Hungary and the United States was engaged in a presidential election campaign. It has also been alleged that the Soviets felt they could act with impunity in crushing the Hungarian revolt because the Western alliance was split by the Suez adventure. There is undoubtedly some truth in both contentions, although there is no concrete evidence that any of the parties actually foresaw what circumstances would be prevailing at the time their interventions took place. In any event, the timing did work out well for the Soviets and for the British and French. Under other circumstances, either of these flagrant acts of aggression might have touched off a third world war. One writer called it "a heaven-sent coincidence" that the major powers had their hands full with their own problems.

As already mentioned, the Suez attack had been planned in advance. On the other hand, the Hungarian uprising was spontaneous, and so was the Soviet response. It so happened that the growing Hungarian unrest surfaced on the evening of October 23, 1956, just as the British, French, and Israelis were finalizing their attack plans at the Sèvres meeting—and that the use of Soviet force against the Hungarian rebels in the streets of Budapest peaked simultaneously with the Suez fighting. The United Nations thus found itself confronted with two major crises at the same time—each involving the use of massive military force, and each involving permanent members of the Security Council. Beyond this, there was little similarity. The United Nations was credited with one of its most brilliant performances in ending the Suez war. In the eyes of the public, it failed miserably in its handling of the Hungarian crisis. Even some officials—like Hernane Tavares de Sa, former U.N. under secretary for public information—felt that the inability of the United Nations to take effective action against the Soviet Union constituted "one of the least honorable chapters" in the history of the organization.[1]

The key to the United Nations' reaction—or lack of it—was held by the United States. President Eisenhower concluded that nothing short of U.S. intervention would cause the Soviets to reverse their course of action, and that geography made it "out of the question" for such a response to be made either alone or through NATO. He was also convinced that no U.N. mandate could or would be forthcoming, such as had sanctioned the Korean intervention as collective defense. Furthermore, there was a strong feeling in the State Department that Nikita Khrushchev (who became Communist party secretary in the U.S.S.R. after Stalin's death) had faced no other choice but to smack the Hungarian revolt down by force. There had already been trouble in Poland, and the Kremlin saw signs of ferment all through the Soviet bloc as a result of its de-Stalinization policy. Robert Murphy, U.S. deputy under secretary of state, said that the Soviets had acted when it became apparent that their "entire Eastern European security system was at stake," but that they had done so reluctantly. "From the Russian point of view," Murphy wrote in his memoirs, "this was an absolute political and military necessity, and once the offensive was launched, they followed through. Putting ethics and the humanities aside, their judgment was sound." Washington also recognized that the Soviet Union was taking a page from U.S. policy regarding spheres of influence. Only two years earlier, in 1954, the United States had organized and backed an invasion of Guatemala to overthrow a government considered to be procommunist. The difference between the two cases was mainly one of degree.[2]

Nevertheless, it was the United States that took the main initiatives against the Soviet Union in the United Nations, limited as those initiatives turned out to be. One of the problems confronting U.N. diplomats was the confused political situation in Hungary, and the conflicting news coming from Budapest. It was difficult for outsiders to know who was running the country—whether they were Soviet stooges, or whether they represented the rebels. Imre Nagy, who had been expelled from the Hungarian Communist party as a "right deviationist" in 1955, was rehabilitated after Khrushchev's denunciation of Stalin's crimes in February 1956. Both Nagy and János Kádár—because of their popular following—were brought back into the government on October 24 after the first outbreak of fighting. Nagy was named prime minister; but the power remained in the hands of Erno Gero—first secretary of the Central Committee—who had been associated with the repressions during the Stalin era. The United States was highly suspicious of Nagy at first; it regarded him as a figurehead, and linked him with the request for Soviet assistance. Whether the Soviet Union ever actually received such an appeal—and, if so, from whom—was to play an important part in the U.N. debate. After he assumed real authority in the reorganized government on October 27, Nagy denied that he had asked for Soviet help, and said that he did not know who did.

As the disorders in Hungary continued, the United States began consultations with Britain, France, and other members of the Security Council on October 26 with a view to bringing the Hungarian situation before the council. This was still three days before Israel's invasion of Egypt. On October 27, the three Western powers joined in a request for Security Council action to halt the "repression of the rights of the Hungarian people." There was some doubt in the State Department as to what could be done. The opinion in Washington was that Soviet troops had a right to be in Hungary under terms of the Warsaw Pact. There remained the question as to whether these troops could be used legitimately to put down an insurrection. Some U.S. officials acknowledged that U.S. forces abroad probably could be used in the same way if confronted with a communist-led uprising—say, in Italy.

The U.N. debate on the Hungarian situation began on Sunday afternoon, October 28—five days after the initial violence broke out in Budapest. U.S. Ambassador Henry Cabot Lodge told the Security Council that the Hungarian people were "being subjected to violent repressive measures by foreign military forces" and were reported to be suffering heavy casualties. "The members of the United Nations clearly have a deep interest in this situation and cannot remain indifferent to it," he said. "They must assert their serious concern and consider how best they might discharge the obligations which they have assumed under the charter." It quickly became apparent that the Soviet Union would use its veto to block any action by the council. Soviet Ambassador Arkady A. Sobolev contended that the situation in Hungary was an internal matter and was, therefore, not within the competence of the United Nations. The secretary-general received a letter from the Hungarian government before the council meeting; it protested that any U.N. discussion would amount to "a serious violation of the sovereignty of the Hungarian People's Republic." Sobolev proposed that the council postpone debate for three or four days "to watch events and see how they went." The French representative, Bernard Cornut-Gentille, asserted that "there is every reason to believe that the foreign intervention was spontaneous and that it occurred before any appeal was made by the Hungarian government." The council rejected the proposed postponement and decided by a vote of nine to one (the Soviet Union) to place the Hungarian question on its agenda. The eleventh member—Yugoslavia—abstained.[3]

No one pressed for immediate action. And, for a while, it appeared that no action would be necessary. The most significant development was a declaration by the Soviet Union on October 30 in which it expressed regret at the bloodshed and indicated that the Soviet intervention was about to end. The declaration stated specifically that the Soviet government had given instructions to the military command to "withdraw the Soviet army units from Budapest as soon as this is considered necessary by the Hungarian government." It stated further that the Soviets were ready to enter into negotiations with the Hungarians and other parties to the Warsaw Pact on the presence of Soviet troops in other parts of Hungary. Some Soviet units actually were withdrawn from their positions guarding the Danube River bridges—which led to reports that a full Soviet retreat from Budapest was under way. Negotiations were begun between Soviet and Hungarian military leaders on the "technical aspects" of the withdrawal. The immediate reaction at the United Nations and in the capitals of the world was one of relief. But the relief was short-lived. New dispatches soon reported fresh columns of Soviet troops moving across the border into Hungary. On November 1, Nagy sent a note to Secretary-general Hammarskjöld asking for U.N. help. He said that additional Soviet military forces were entering Hungary—while negotiations still were in progress—and that he had protested without success to the Soviet ambassador. Nagy declared that Hungary was repudiating the Warsaw treaty and proclaiming its neutrality. Nagy sent a second appeal to the secretary-general on November 2, urging him "to call upon the great powers to recognize the neutrality of Hungary and ask the Security Council to instruct the Soviet and Hungarian governments to start negotiations immediately" on the withdrawal of Soviet troops.

By this time, it had become clear to the Soviet Union that there could be no reconciliation with the Nagy government. If any hope remained, it was dispelled on November 3 with the formation of a multiparty government in Budapest—including such prominent noncommunists as Social Democrat Anna Kethely and Istvan Szabo of the Smallholders Party, along with former President Zoltán Tildy and Bala Kovacs, who had also served in the cabinet formed on October 27. Among the communists remaining in the government was János Kádár. The main news from Hungary that day—in addition to the government changes—was that Soviet and Hungarian representatives had opened negotiations on the question of Soviet troop withdrawals. A broadcast by Free Radio Kossuth said: "The Soviet delegation has promised that no further trains carrying Soviet troops will cross the Hungarian frontier."

That was the situation when the U.N. Security Council met on the evening of November 3, which was a Saturday. The United States laid before the council a resolution "deploring the use of Soviet military forces to suppress the efforts of the Hungarian people to reassert their rights." Action was postponed until the following Monday, however, after Soviet Ambassador Sobolev and the Hungarian representative, János Szabo, gave assurances that negotiations on the withdrawal of Soviet troops were in progress. Szabo told the council of the Soviet promise that no more troops would cross into Hungary. One of the most incredible performances in the history of the United Nations was the role played by the British and French in condemning the Soviet behavior at this very moment when their own planes were bombing Egyptians and their invasion forces were steaming toward Suez objectives. Louis de Guiringaud of France recalled the Soviet coup in Czechoslovakia in 1948 and asked whether the Soviet Union were not trying to do the same in Budapest. "If the Soviet Union does wish to negotiate with Hungary, then it certainly can withdraw its troops. Why should it need tanks and troops for negotiations? For all these reasons, the representatives of the Soviet Union cannot come here and submit that the situation is a highly confused one and that consequently, the Soviet Union must await clarification of the situation before taking action. It is just because the situation is confused that we must act." Speaking for Britain, Sir Pierson Dixon said it was a matter of history that many nations who had negotiated with the Soviet Union had reaped no results but misfortune.

It was to be a busy night for U.N. delegates. The emergency session of the General Assembly had already scheduled a Saturday night meeting to deal with the worsening Suez situation. As the delegates gathered, Lester Pearson of Canada was putting the final touches on his speech proposing the dispatch of a U.N. force to the Middle East. At almost the same hour in which Pearson addressed the assembly, a dramatic radio announcement was broadcast in Hungary. At 5:19 A.M. (11:19 P.M. New York time), the Hungarian national anthem was heard on Radio Free Kossuth—followed by these words: "This is Imre Nagy speaking, the president of the Council of Ministers of the Hungarian People's Republic. Today at daybreak Soviet forces started an attack against our capital, obviously with the intention to overthrow the legal Hungarian democratic government. Our troops are fighting." Until 7:10 A.M. (Hungarian time), this station remained in the hands of the Nagy government. At 6 A.M., however, a broadcast was heard from a station calling itself Kádár Government Radio, announcing the formation of a new government under János Kádár. "Hungarians, brothers, patriots, soldiers, citizens," the broadcast said. "We must put an end to the excesses of the counter-revolutionary elements. The hour of action has struck. The interest of the people and the nation is to have a strong government. That is why we have formed the Hungarian Revolutionary Worker-Peasant Government."

These events were taking place while the General Assembly was discussing the Canadian resolution that called on the secretary-general to draft a blueprint in 48 hours for a Middle East police force—a resolution that was to win for Pearson a Nobel Peace Prize.[4]

Long before approval of the UNEF resolution at 1:42 A.M., news of the Hungarian events began to circulate among the U.N. delegates. One of the most heartrending accounts of the fighting came from the Budapest office of the Hungarian News Agency (MTI), which by some miracle was able to keep an open telex line to the Vienna Bureau of the Associated Press for almost seven hours after the attack began. These messages were turned over to U.S. Ambassador Lodge, and moved him to request an urgent meeting of the Security Council at 2:27 A.M.. The first message began with these words:

Russian gangsters have betrayed us. . . . I speak in the name of Imre Nagy. He asks help. . . . Please tell the world of the treacherous attack against our struggle for liberty. . . . Our troops are already engaged in fighting. . . . Help! Help! Help! . . . The tanks are getting nearer and there is heavy artillery. . . . What is the United Nations doing? Give us a little encouragement. . . . The tanks are coming nearer. Both radio stations are in rebel hands. . . . We will hold out to the last drop of blood. . . . Our building has already been fired on, but so far there are no casualties. The roar of the tanks is so loud we can't hear each other's voices. . . . They just brought us a rumor that the American troops will be here within one or two hours. . . . We hope the U.N. meeting won't be too late. Send us any news you can about world action in Hungary's behalf. . . . Just now the heaviest fighting is going on in the Maria Terezia Barracks. There is heavy artillery fire. . . .[5]

Then the connection was cut.

The Security Council met at 3 A.M. Not only was the hour of the meeting unusual, but the circumstances were unmatched. No one had ever envisaged a situation in which two permanent members of the council would be attacking a member state in one part of the world while a third permanent member was sending tanks and planes against another member state. Faced with the toughest assignment of his career, Arkady Sobolev tried to dull the diplomatic attack on the Soviet Union by pointing to the action of the British and the French. He also sought to blame the Hungarian uprising on reactionary elements instigated by the West. Sobolev told the council that

The people were deceived by propaganda containing nothing but lies. "It is therefore my submission that the United Nations and particularly the Security Council have nothing to do in this matter. Interference by the United Nations and by the Western countries in the Hungarian events might only lead to complications, and it goes without saying that such interference would be unlawful and contrary to the principles of the charter. We know why the United States, the United Kingdom and France are placing this matter before the Security Council. We know that the purpose is to conceal, behind speeches full of demagoguery, the action that has been taken by Israel, the United Kingdom and France against Egypt. They are trying to conceal these activities by raising this provocative question of Hungary in the Security Council.

It was apparent that the United States would have to stand alone in pressing for action against the Soviet Union. Britain and France were too vulnerable to take any sort of initiative. In fact, the United States was not prepared to propose anything stronger than censure. It was the feeling in Washington that the best approach would be an appeal to world opinion. Eisenhower sent a personal message to Soviet Premier Nikolai Bulganin, saying: "I feel that Western opinion, which was so uplifted only a few days ago by the news that the Soviet Union intended to withdraw its forces from Hungary, has now suffered corresponding shock and dismay at the Soviet attack on the people and government of Hungary."

In pressing for censure of the Soviet Union, Lodge called attention to a series of Soviet protests against the aggression of Britain and France. He then added: "How far can actions and words be apart?" As expected, Sobolev cast the Soviet Union's 79th veto to kill the proposed censure of its actions. Lodge said that the will of the United Nations had once more been thwarted by the Soviet veto. Therefore, he moved for an emergency session of the General Assembly to run concurrently with the emergency session on the Suez conflict. The vote was ten in favor, with only the Soviets opposing the proposal. Hammarskjöld immediately announced that the emergency session on Hungary would meet at 8 P.M. that night.

As a result of the emotional appeals of the Hungarian rebels and the brutality of the Soviet assault, public opinion was aroused throughout the world. The United States, especially, was concerned over widespread demands that the United Nations respond with military force. As far as Washington was concerned, such an approach had been discounted from the beginning; and without the leadership of the United States, it was out of the question. Andrew H. Berding, a former U.S. assistant secretary of state, quotes John Foster Dulles as saying: "This would be madness. The only way we can save Hungary at this time would be through all-out nuclear war. Does anyone in his senses want to start a nuclear war over Hungary? As for simply sending American divisions into Hungary, they would be wiped out by superior Soviet ground forces. Geography is against us. And in either event . . . the Hungarians would be the greatest sufferers." President Eisenhower wrote in his memoirs that the Soviet attack "almost automatically had posed to us the question of employing force to oppose this barbaric invasion." But, he added, "unless the major nations of Europe would, without delay, ally themselves spontaneously with us (an unimaginable prospect), we could do nothing. Sending U.S. troops alone into Hungary through hostile or neutral territory would have involved us in general war."[6]

Thus, when the emergency session of the General Assembly met on November 4 to take up the Hungarian question, it was clear that the best the United States could hope to do was to mobilize public opinion against the Soviet Union. Even the question of economic and diplomatic sanctions were not seriously considered. In the first of a series of resolutions, the assembly deplored the use of force and called on the Soviets to desist and withdraw their forces "without delay." Only the 8 communist countries voted against the proposal; but surprisingly, 15 countries abstained. The censure was an exercise in futility, anyway: The Soviet Union ignored the resolution and the new Kádár government—100 percent pro-Soviet—demanded that the United Nations drop the Hungarian question. The November 4 resolution called on the Soviet and Hungarian authorities to permit U.N. observers to enter Hungary. The Kádár government told Hammarskjöld that the events in Hungary were wholly within the domestic jurisdiction of the Hungarian government and that the sending of U.N. observers was unwarranted. On November 9, the emergency session again called on the Soviet Union to withdraw its forces, but this resolution too was ignored.[7]

The regular 1956 session of the assembly adopted a number of resolutions in which it condemned the Soviets for violating the charter "by depriving Hungary of its liberty and independence," called for an end of the Soviet intervention, urged the Hungarian authorities to permit the entry of U.N. representatives, and appealed for a halt in the mass deportation of Hungarian citizens. The resolution was ignored.[8]

On January 10, 1957, the General Assembly established a Special Committee on the Problem of Hungary. In September 1957, it appointed Prince Wan Waithayakon of Thailand as special representative on the Hungarian problem; and a year later, it named Sir Leslie Munro of New Zealand to this post. Both reported that the Hungarian government had rebuffed all efforts to obtain its cooperation.

Meanwhile, Soviet troops remained in Hungary, and the repressive measures of the prerevolt government were reinstituted. Some 200,000 refugees poured across the frontier into Austria. Many leaders of the insurrection were executed—including Imre Nagy and Pal Maleter, his defense minister, who were seized at the time of the Soviet attack. The General Assembly denounced the executions. It continued to discuss the Hungarian problem at every session until 1962, but without any positive results.[9]

The question has often been asked: Could the United Nations have done more? It has been suggested that the Western powers might have tried a tactic sometimes used by the Soviet Union: They could have threatened to send volunteers to help repel the intruders. Such a strategy might have had some validity if Britain and France had not been engaged in the Egyptian invasion at precisely this time. As it was, the Soviets probably would not have taken the threat seriously. Another factor was the general disenchantment of the Afro–Asian countries with both the Soviet action and the Anglo–French action. In fact, one could detect a tendency among the Afro–Asians to identify with the Egyptians—as one of their own group—much more closely than with the Hungarians. Lester Pearson was among those who believed that the United Nations had gone as far as it could, under the circumstances. To pretend that force might be used, he said, would have been a "cruel deceit." Ernest A. Gross has written: "The remission of the question of Hungary to the United Nations . . . exposed the organization itself to bitter calumny. Yet, the fact is that the United States and other leading Western powers held back from taking or suggesting more specific measures. Hence, the organization did no more, and no less, in the Hungarian case, than was asked of it by its members." Some have tried to draw a measure of comfort from the belief that the U.N. condemnation and public exposure may have inhibited the Kremlin's willingness to repeat the procedure. If so, the inhibition was short lived, for the Soviet performance was duplicated almost exactly 12 years later in suppressing a breakaway movement in Czechoslovakia.

10

The United States Intervenes in Guatemala and Lebanon

The U.S. position in the Hungarian crisis was weakened somewhat by Washington's role in the overthrow of the Guatemalan government in 1954. Although the latter case is more often remembered as a landmark in the trend toward the use of regional organizations to settle disputes, it also involved the intervention of a big power in the internal affairs of another U.N. member—including the use of force to bring down an unfriendly government. From the very beginning of the United Nations, the United States had taken what was sometimes described as a holier-than-thou attitude toward the veto, the walkout, and the use of force to settle disputes. With the Guatemalan case, however, it became apparent that the United States was not averse to bending the provisions of the charter when its own interests were involved. It had come close to doing so in Korea, but the Security Council had legitimized its military intervention by bringing it under the umbrella of the United Nations.

The Guatemalan case was different. For one thing, the U.S. role was concealed by deception. Ostensibly, the case involved nothing more than a coup d'etat launched by a group of Guatemalan exiles against the leftist government of President Jacobo Arbenz Guzmán. In fact, it was a U.S.-backed invasion planned by the Central Intelligence Agency and taking off from Honduras and Nicaragua under the leadership of Guatemalan Colonel Carlos Castillo Armas. The U.S. role was only thinly veiled. The invasion was supported by U.S. fighter-bombers and transports flown by the CIA, and Castillo Armas actually arrived in Guatemala City in the U.S. ambassador's private plane. Despite the transparency of its complicity, the United States insisted that the overthrow of the Arbenz regime was simply the result of a civil war. This version was viewed with skepticism at the time, and was later acknowledged by top U.S. officials to have been a fiction. President Eisenhower said in his memoirs, for example, that "we had to get rid of a communist government which had taken over."[1] Such well-known news correspondents as Joseph C. Harsch, Cyrus Sulzberger, and James Reston regarded the U.S. involvement as a matter of common knowledge. Reston said that "every official who knows anything about the fall of the Arbenz government . . . knows that the United States government through the Central Intelligence Agency, worked actively with, and financed, and made available the arms, with which the anti-Arbenz forces finally 'threw him out.' "

It is understandable that the United States wanted to keep the case in the hands of the Organization of American States (OAS) rather than have it debated in the U.N. Security Council. This might have been possible had the invasion succeeded as an overnight coup, as planned. Instead, it was so badly bungled that it dragged on for 12 days. This gave the Arbenz government time to appeal to the council—first on June 19, 1954, and again on June 22. The United States was forced to face two rounds of debate in the council, rather than one—or preferably, from Washington's viewpoint, none at all. The June 19 complaint alleged that an invading force had penetrated several miles into Guatemalan territory from Nicaragua and Honduras, and that aircraft, flying from the same direction had bombed Guatemala City and the port of San José. As president of the council for the month of June, it was Ambassador Henry Cabot Lodge who received the Guatemalan request for a meeting to deal with the invasion. He had no choice but to call the council into session—which he did on June 20—but the U.S. strategy was to avoid a full airing of the problem by referring it immediately to the OAS. With the support of the Soviet Union, the Arbenz government opposed the U.S. position by insisting that the issue be handled by the council. The stage was thus set for a debate on the legal and procedural role of regional organizations versus the United Nations.[2]

The debate placed the Western allies of the United States in an extremely embarrassing situation because of the generally accepted view that the CIA was behind the invasion. The Soviet Union declared that Honduras, Nicaragua, and the United States had conspired to organize the invasion and that it was unthinkable to send the dispute to the OAS since that organization was dominated by the United States. "Guatemala can expect nothing good from that body," said the Soviet representative, Semyon Tsarapkin. Brazil and Colombia— acting on behalf of the United States—sponsored a resolution calling for transfer of the Guatemalan complaint to the OAS. The vote was ten in favor and one against, but the one was the Soviet Union, so the proposal was defeated. The council then adopted a French resolution calling for the cessation of any action likely to cause further bloodshed, without prejudice to any measures the OAS might take. The vote on this was unanimous.[3]

This would have ended the matter if the invasion had not remained bogged down in incompetence. On June 22 Secretary-general Hammarskjöld received a new complaint from the Arbenz government, charging that the resolution of

June 20 was not being complied with and asking for another council meeting. This letter proved to have added significance since it provoked the first major controversy between Hammarskjöld and a permanent member of the Security Council. Hammarskjöld had been in office a little more than a year at the time. Already upset by the U.S. attempt to give the OAS precedence over the Security Council, he was disturbed further by what he felt was undue delay on the part of Lodge in calling the council meeting, as requested. When Lodge finally did call the meeting, he acted on a request by Brazil and Colombia, not the request of Guatemala and the Soviet Union—which had joined in the June 22 move by the Arbenz government. Largely as a result of U.S. pressure, the council refused to adopt the proposed agenda. However, this action was not much of a victory for the United States. The vote in favor of adopting the agenda was four in favor and five against, with Britain and France abstaining.

Meanwhile, Hammarskjöld drafted a statement on the relationship of regional organizations to the United Nations. One of his principal points was that the reference of a question to a regional organization in no way prevented a member from appealing to the United Nations. He intended to make his statement public, but was dissuaded by British Delegate Sir Pierson Dixon and U.S. Ambassador James J. Wadsworth. According to Brian Urquhart's account of the incident, Hammarskjöld's draft caused an uproar in the State Department. The United States strongly challenged the secretary-general's conclusions and questioned the wisdom of any intervention by him. His statement, the State Department said, was a "thinly disguised and tendentious attack upon the position taken by the U.S., the Latin American members of the Security Council and the OAS in the Guatemalan case." Hammarskjöld decided against circulation of the statement.[4]

Little more was heard of the Guatemalan question. Before the OAS foreign ministers could hold their meeting, which was scheduled for July 7, Castillo Armas was installed as head of the new government; and further discussions were cancelled. As for the controversy over the role of regional organizations, this was only the beginning. In the introduction to his 1954 annual report, Dag Hammarskjöld said:

The importance of regional arrangements in the maintenance of peace is fully recognized in the charter and the appropriate use of such arrangements is encouraged. But in those cases where resort to such arrangements is chosen in the first instance, this choice should not be permitted to cast any doubt on the ultimate responsibility of the United Nations. Similarly, a policy giving full scope to the proper role of regional agencies can and should at the same time fully preserve the right of a member nation to a hearing under this charter.[5]

No country was ever more frank than the United States in explaining its motives for the landing of U.S. marines in Lebanon on July 15, 1958. In a message to Congress, President Eisenhower stated that President Camille Chamoun had requested the stationing of U.S. forces there in order to enable his government to survive, and that he—Eisenhower—had complied because the preservation of Lebanon's independence and territorial integrity was "deemed vital to the United States' national interests and world peace." In further justification of the U.S. action, Eisenhower noted that the United Nations was already involved in the Lebanese problem, but asserted that "the measures thus far taken by the United Nations Security Council are not sufficient" to do the job. This sounded very much like the statements made by Britain and France two years earlier in explaining their reasons for invading Egypt. So did Eisenhower's statement that the United States would withdraw its forces just as soon as the United Nations "has taken further effective steps designed to safeguard the independence and integrity of Lebanon." Despite all the rationalization, the world was shocked by this intervention in a country thousands of miles away from the U.S. borders, and especially at a time when the matter was being dealt with by the United Nations.[6]

The situation in Lebanon had been going from bad to worse since May 1958 when the Lebanese government complained to the Security Council that Egypt was interfering in its internal affairs by infiltrating armed bands across the border from Syria to engage in terrorist activities against the Lebanese authorities. Egypt contended that the disturbances in Lebanon were purely internal manifestations inspired by Chamoun's desire to seek another six-year term as president. Nevertheless, on June 11, the Security Council decided to establish a U.N. Observer Group in Lebanon (UNOGIL) to make sure that there were no illegal infiltrations of personnel or military equipment into the country.[7]

There is no doubt but that the Lebanese dissidents were getting help and encouragement from Egypt and from Syria, which was then a part of the United Arab Republic (UAR). The entire Arab world was in a state of uncertainty and conflict at the time. Iraq was a member of the Baghdad Pact, which was bitterly opposed by the Egyptian president of the UAR, Gamal Abdel Nasser. The Lebanese unrest came only a year after the unveiling of the Eisenhower Doctrine, which promised military assistance to any nation in the Middle East that required such aid to preserve its independence. Lebanon was the only Arab country to accept the Eisenhower Doctrine publicly, although Jordan and Iraq privately welcomed it. When the Lebanese question came up in the Security Council, the United States voted for the establishment of the U.N. observer group, but the Eisenhower administration was by no means convinced that this would stop the alleged infiltrations.[8]

Stressing the urgency of the situation, U.S. Ambassador Lodge expressed the hope that the secretary-general would have "someone in Lebanon in twenty-four hours." Hammarskjöld replied that he had already taken the necessary preparatory steps and "I hope that it will be possible for us to live up to the expectations expressed by Mr. Lodge." He told a press conference the following day that the first group of observers—consisting of five officers—had arrived in Lebanon and that others would begin arriving within a few days. By June 26, there were 94 officers from 11 countries in UNOGIL; a regular patrol system had been set up, supplemented by two helicopters. Lebanon's President Chamoun was not satisfied, however. He insisted that an international police force similar to UNEF, was necessary. John Foster Dulles, the U.S. secretary of state, told a press conference in Washington on July 1 that "some results at least are being obtained" by the U.N. observer group. Dulles said that he doubted the practicality of an international police force for Lebanon, but he declined to rule out the possibility of collective defense measures in certain circumstances. Such a solution, he said, "would be a measure of last resort."

Dag Hammarskjöld made a personal visit to Cairo and Beirut during the latter part of June. He urged President Nasser to halt the infiltration and put a damper on Cairo Radio's propaganda campaign in support of the Lebanese rebel groups. Nasser did not deny that military aid was being supplied to the insurrectionists in Lebanon. In fact, he promised he would stop. Hammarskjöld's next task was to persuade Chamoun to moderate his actions, too. The secretary-general felt that the way would be opened for a negotiated settlement, if Chamoun would renounce his plans for a new term as president. This was a delicate matter, however, since it involved internal politics and Hammarskjöld could not approach Chamoun directly on it. Some of the Lebanese president's own supporters convinced him that this was indeed an essential step and in early July he publicly announced that he would leave office at the end of his term on September 23. The United States was not happy about the operations of UNOGIL because of the limited nature of its patrolling, but the situation began to ease off after Chamoun's announcement. Eisenhower said in his memoirs that, at the time, it appeared the Lebanese crisis "would pass without Western military assistance." Hammarskjöld had been deeply concerned about the possibility of Western intervention, and had warned Nasser that continued aid to the Lebanese rebels might provoke such action. On his return from the Middle East, the secretary-general wrote privately to both U.S. Secretary of State Dulles and British Foreign Minister Selwyn Lloyd, urging them to resist pressure for intervention.

The entire situation changed on July 14 when a group of army officers staged a coup d'etat in Iraq—assassinating King Faisal II, the crown prince, and Prime Minister Nuri es-Said. The new government of General Abdul Karim Kassem immediately announced the end of Iraq's pro-Western policy, withdrawal from its political union with Jordan, and adoption of a position of nonalignment. The Western powers were alarmed—but even more so were Chamoun and Jordan's King Hussein, who feared they might become the victims of pro-Nasser elements in their own countries.

Both Chamoun and Hussein appealed for Western military assistance. The U.S. Sixth Fleet, which was standing by in the eastern Mediterranean, headed immediately for Beirut. Within 24 hours after the Iraqi coup, U.S. marines began landing on the Lebanese beaches. On the morning of July 17, the first of two battalions of British paratroops were flown from Cyprus to Jordan. The United States requested an urgent meeting of the U.N. Security Council, which convened at about the time the marines were stepping ashore. Ambassador Lodge told the council that the revolt in Iraq and the continued infiltration of military equipment and personnel from the United Arab Republic had demonstrated a "ruthlessness of aggressive purposes which tiny Lebanon cannot combat without support from friendly nations." He promised that the marines would be withdrawn "as soon as the United Nations can take over."

As Lodge reported later, Secretary-general Hammarskjöld was angered by the U.S. action. In his book *The Storm Has Many Eyes*, Lodge tells it this way: "Dag Hammarskjöld's anger at a private meeting with me after the landing of the troops was indeed memorable. When I came into his office, his face first became pink and then flushed to red as he told me how much he deplored what we had done and how dangerous he thought it was." Hammarskjöld felt that the U.N. observer group had virtually succeeded in cutting off the infiltration and that, as a result of the U.S. intervention, Nasser would now cancel all restrictions. The secretary-general told Lodge that the United States was on very shaky legal grounds in basing its action on Article 51 of the charter—which provides for collective self-defense—because the action had been triggered by the coup in Iraq and not by developments in Lebanon. One important question raised by the U.S. landings was what effect they would have on future operations of the U.N. observer group. Hammarskjöld pointed out to Lodge that, if the U.S. forces attempted to seal the Lebanese border, the U.N. operation would become useless. Hammarskjöld did not want to remove UNOGIL on legalistic grounds, however, and he instructed it to stand pat until the situation was straightened out.[9]

But in fact, before anything could be done to help straighten things out, the secretary-general received a severe jolt from unexpected quarters. His former chief, Foreign Minister Osten Unden of Sweden, instructed Sweden's U.N. representative, Gunnar Jarring, to submit a formal proposal to the Security Council calling for the suspension of all activities of UNOGIL until further notice.

This was Unden's own way of showing his annoyance at the U.S. intervention. He had offered the original proposal for the establishment of UNOGIL. Now he was taking the position that, under the changed conditions, he did not want Sweden to be associated with it any longer. Jarring told Unden on the telephone that his proposal would get no support except from the Soviet Union, but Unden insisted on submitting it anyway. Jarring proved to be right. The Security Council rejected the Unden resolution by a vote of nine to two (Sweden and the Soviet Union). The United States—realizing that the presence of the marines in Lebanon created a delicate situation—quickly offered to establish liaison with UNOGIL, but Hammarskjöld was cool to this idea. On his instructions, the observer group issued a public announcement in Beirut declaring that only UNOGIL was in Lebanon under the auspices of the United Nations. "There is, therefore, no basis for establishing any contact or working relationship, formal or informal, between the United Nations Observation Group and any non-

Lebanese forces in Lebanon beyond what may be strictly required for independent fulfilment of its mandate from the United Nations Security Council without further action by the council."[10]

On July 16 Lodge submitted a U.S. resolution requesting that UNOGIL continue to develop its activities and asking the secretary-general to consult with Lebanon and other member states on additional measures, "including the contribution and use of contingents, as may be necessary, to protect the territorial integrity of Lebanon and to ensure that there is no illegal infiltration of personnel or supply of arms or other material across the Lebanese borders." The Soviet Union countered with a resolution calling on the United States "to cease armed intervention in the domestic affairs of the Arab states and to remove its troops from the territory of Lebanon immediately." The Soviet Union vetoed the U.S. resolution, and the Soviet proposal failed to get the required majority. The Soviets also vetoed a Japanese compromise resolution that called on the secretary-general to take any measures he might consider necessary to guarantee the political independence of Lebanon, "so as to make possible the withdrawal of United States forces from Lebanon." Soviet Ambassador Arkady Sobolev contended that, in effect, this language condemned the U.S. intervention.[11]

Having run into a dead end, the Security Council voted unanimously to shift the problem to an emergency session of the General Assembly—the third such session under the Uniting for Peace Resolution. By the time the assembly convened on August 8, the United States and Britain were anxious to get their troops out of Lebanon and Jordan. They were looking for a way out that would at least avoid condemnation, and preferably one that would sanction the troop landings as necessary to prevent the overthrow of the Lebanese and Jordanian governments by "indirect aggression." When President Eisenhower addressed the U.N. General Assembly on August 13, the United States had already withdrawn some of the 14,000 men that it had sent in to Lebanon. Eisenhower promised that the withdrawal would be completed either when the two host governments requested their withdrawal or when adequate U.N. action made their presence no longer necessary. The United States found little support for its thesis that Article 51 of the charter applied to "indirect aggression." The Asian and African countries were especially sensitive about the use of foreign troops to keep a government in power or to put down an insurrection. They were generally against any U.N. action that would appear to put a stamp of approval on the U.S.–British action.[12]

For a while it appeared that no resolution would get the necessary two-thirds majority. The impasse ended when the ten Arab states buried their differences and produced a joint resolution acceptable to all groups. The draft made no mention of "indirect aggression," but the Arab countries reaffirmed the pledges of the Arab League Pact against interference in each other's internal affairs. It contained neither a sanction of the Anglo–American action, nor a condemnation. A key paragraph repeated the earlier mandate of the secretary-general; it requested him to "make such practical arrangements as would adequately help in upholding the purposes and principles of the charter in relation to Lebanon and Jordan in the present circumstances, and thereby facilitate the early with-drawal of the foreign troops from the two countries." The emergency session ended on August 21, with unanimous adoption of the Arab resolution.[13]

The withdrawal of U.S. troops was completed on October 25; and the British withdrawal, on November 2. UNOGIL ended its operation on December 9, 1958.

11

The Soviet Union and the West
Clash over Decolonization

The signing of the U.N. Charter was a historic event for the millions of people who did not govern themselves—the people who lived in colonies, protectorates, mandates, and other dependent territories. The signatories themselves would have been incredulous, however, had they dreamed of the changes that were to take place in the next four decades. The founders obviously attached great importance to the problem, since they devoted three of the charter's 19 chapters to dependent peoples, but they were thinking in terms of gradual long-term evolution when they promised to promote the "progressive development" of all dependent peoples toward self-government or independence. Except for the handful of territories administered under League of Nations mandates, the charter left the problem pretty much in the hands of the colonial powers. They were simply required by the charter to report regularly—"for information purposes"—data on economic, social, and educational conditions in territories for which they were responsible. Nothing was said about reporting on political developments in the territories or about the creation of any U.N. machinery to keep watch over them.

In the beginning, the emphasis was almost exclusively on establishment of the Trusteeship Council, which was to work alongside the Security Council and the Economic and Social Council as one of the major organs of the United Nations. Limited as it was, the trusteeship system—as envisaged in the charter—was a vast improvement on the old League of Nations mandate system. The League Covenant, for example, said nothing about independence. It merely stated that the mandates should be administered for the "well-being and development" of the inhabitants. The U.N. Charter took a more positive approach by calling for the political development of the dependent peoples for independence or self-government. The trusteeship system was also much broader in that it provided for possible inclusion of three types of territories: (1) those held under mandate, (2) those detached from enemy states as a result of World War II, and (3) any other territories voluntarily placed under the system. In other words, it might conceivably have included all the dependent territories on earth—making the United Nations itself responsible for one of the world's great empires. The League mandate system had been established to provide only for those colonies and territories separated from Germany and Turkey as a result of World War I.

Indeed, the trusteeship system seemed to offer a bright promise; but it was clear long before the charter was approved that the nations ruling dependent territories would be in no hurry to give them up and that many of them were prepared to resist all efforts to accelerate independence, at least so far as their own territories were concerned. It soon became clear also that the charter was full of ambiguities, which would crop up repeatedly to plague the United Nations and hamper effective action on the colonial problem. The trusteeship system had much less territory under its supervision than the mandate system did at the start. No territory had been placed under trusteeship except former League mandates—and not all of them had been submitted. Syria and Lebanon had become independent and were among the founders of the United Nations. Palestine's future was still undecided, but it was not destined to be placed under the trusteeship system. Neither were the Kurile Islands, taken by the Soviet Union from Japan during World War II. And there appeared to be little chance that any other territory of any consequence would come under the system in the near future. The hard, cold facts were that the United Nations had supervision over only 15,000,000 of the 300,000,000 dependent people of the world, and it soon found that this supervision was severely limited. There were two basic difficulties. The first was the impotence of the United Nations in taking any binding action to improve conditions in territories administered by member nations. The second was the attitude of the administering nations themselves.

This may best be illustrated by a speech that Sir Carl Berendsen, a delegate from New Zealand, made before the Trusteeship Committee (Committee IV) of the General Assembly in November 1946. His statement is all the more significant because New Zealand's Labor government of that era was considered much more divorced from the old concept of imperialism than many other countries. New Zealand was the administering power in Western Samoa, under a League mandate; it was offering the territory for inclusion in the U.N. trusteeship system, with New Zealand continuing as administrator. Sir Carl began by painting an eloquent picture of conditions in Western Samoa. The people were happy, he said. They had no financial worries, and no problems such as unemployment. All they wanted was to be left alone. He went on to say that someone had made the "ridiculous suggestion" that the government of New Zealand should promote a policy of full employment in Western Samoa.[1]

Berendsen said,

In Samoa, a bountiful providence supplies all that the Samoans need, and a very large proportion of all that they want, with but the minimum of necessity for labor on the part of the people. There is no necessary employment at all in Samoa except the communal employment which is an age-long tradition of the people under which a certain group are allotted certain tasks in the preparation of foodstuffs, the catching of fish, the building of houses, etcetera. But the idea of employment for money is quite foreign to the Samoan tradition and to the Samoan philosophy, except that in recent years the Samoans have found that money was occasionally a pretty handy thing to have about the house in order to buy little luxuries—little Western luxuries—to which they have become accustomed. It is the exception rather than the rule that the Samoan takes employment for money. It is not a money economy, and I want to say I don't think any attempt should be made to alter what is a very admirable and ideal mode of life, one which I confess I envy from the bottom of my heart. Let us leave it alone; at any rate, do not let us, by artificial means, endeavor to bring about alterations before alterations are necessary and before they are acceptable to the people.

Despite this beautiful picture of life in Samoa, neither Sir Carl nor any other delegate left the United Nations to take up residence in this modern Garden of Eden. Sir Carl concluded rather sadly that "even such a happy people as the Samoans cannot be protected forever against the impact of what we at least call 'civilization.' " The truth of this was borne out a short time later when Western Samoa became the first territory to petition the Trusteeship Council for self-government.[2]

In fact, the Samoan chieftains were drafting their petition at approximately the same time Sir Carl was telling the United Nations how happy they were. The chieftains expressed their appreciation for what the New Zealand government had done for their people and asked New Zealand to continue as their protector and advisor, but nevertheless they said that they wanted to govern themselves. New Zealand informed the Trusteeship Council in advance that the petition was coming, but declared that the people were not ready for self-government and were not going to get it. They did not; but, like many other dependent territories, they did not have long to wait. Under U.N. supervision, a plebiscite was held in Western Samoa in 1961. The people voted 79 percent in favor of independence. Western Samoa became an independent state on January 1, 1962.

The main obstacle in this and some other cases was a provision in Article 79 of the U.N. Charter; it says in part that "the terms of trusteeship for each territory to be placed under the Trusteeship System, including any alteration or amendment, shall be agreed upon by the states directly concerned, including the mandatory power in the case of territories held under mandate by a member of the United Nations." In other words, no change in the status of the trust territory could be made without the consent of the mandatory power—in this case, New Zealand. The Trusteeship Council and the General Assembly could recommend independence, but could not order it.

How heavily the charter was weighted in favor of the colonial powers was demonstrated during debate on drafts of the first eight trusteeship agreements, which were submitted at the first New York meeting of the General Assembly. These drafts were submitted by Britain, France, Belgium, Australia, and New Zealand for the following League of Nations mandates administered by them: Tanganyika, British Togoland, British Cameroons, French Togoland, French Cameroons, Ruanda-Urundi, New Guinea, and Western Samoa. Efforts were made, particularly by the Soviet Union and India, to write important changes into each of the agreements—such as specific deadlines for the granting of independence—but the administering states firmly rejected all proposals except a few minor amendments. The agreements as finally approved by the assembly were substantially as they had been dictated originally by the administering states.

The weak position of the United Nations was emphasized again a few months later when the United States offered a draft agreement to place under the trusteeship system the Pacific Islands formerly mandated to Japan—the Marshalls, Carolines, and Marianas. Since these were to become "strategic area" trusteeships, the agreement went to the Security Council—instead of the General Assembly—for approval. Otherwise, however, the procedure was the same. In an unexplained move, the Soviet Union accepted the U.S. proposal in principle, and was content to seek a few amendments. Only one of these was important: a provision that the Security Council would have the power to amend the agreement at any time, whether or not the United States consented. Warren Austin—speaking for the United States—said that the Soviet proposal violated the U.N. Charter and that it could not be accepted by the United States under any circumstances. In effect, he told the council that it could either agree to the terms laid down by the United States of else Washington would continue to administer the islands outside the trusteeship system. The Security Council accepted the U.S. terms.

The only weapon that the United Nations could wield against an obstinate or arbitrary member in the trusteeship field was public opinion, and that was not always effective—as illustrated in the case of the Mandated Territory of South West Africa, which was administered by the Union of South Africa. At the London session, the General Assembly adopted a resolution calling on all mandatory powers to submit draft agreements as soon as possible to bring all former League mandates under the Trusteeship System. Instead of complying, Field Marshal Jan Christian Smuts, South Africa's prime minister, went to the New York session with a request for the outright annexation of South West Africa. In rather blunt language, he told the assembly that, if it failed to approve the request, he would continue to administer the territory under terms of the League mandate. Smuts said that he was acting in accordance with the wishes of the inhabitants of the territory and that he had no intention to act otherwise.

Smuts, was a veteran of many international conferences, dating back to the Versailles Peace Conference. He fought one of his most dramatic battles during that stormy assembly session, but it was an unpopular fight. In the end, the General Assembly adopted a sharply worded resolution declaring that annexation of territories held under mandate was inconsistent with the principles of the U.N. Charter, and stating that the inhabitants of South West Africa "are unable at the present stage of their political and educational development to express their considered opinion on such an important question as the incorporation of their territory." For these reasons, the resolution went on, "the Assembly rejects any solution involving the incorporation of the territory on South West Africa in the Union of South Africa, and recommends that the mandated territory of South West Africa be placed under the international Trusteeship System."

Before the 1947 assembly met, Marshal Smuts informed the United Nations that he would not comply with its request, but was going ahead with steps eventually leading to the incorporation of the mandated territory into the Union of South Africa. There was little that the United Nations could do except condemn the South African government. It has been doing so for four decades, while South Africa continues to administer South West Africa.

The Trusteeship Council—the last major organ of the United Nations to begin functioning, was born under circumstances that did not promise too much for its future. It was not established until December 1946, and did not hold its first meeting until March 1947—almost two years after the charter was signed at San Francisco. The setting up of the council had been delayed because of charter provisions that made its establishment impossible until enough trusteeship agreements were approved so that the council's membership could be balanced between administering and nonadministering states. For a while it appeared that the whole thing might be delayed indefinitely because of differences between the Soviet Union and the Western powers.[3]

The Soviet Union's interpretation of the charter—as set forth in a major speech by her able representative, Ambassador Nikolai V. Novikov—was so far from that of the other powers that, if Soviet views had been accepted by the assembly, every one of the eight draft trusteeship agreements awaiting approval would have to have been revised completely. In the Soviet Union's view, all the countries that had submitted draft agreements proposed to violate the charter in one respect or another. In fact, Novikov contended that the eight draft agreements under consideration were not agreements at all, but were "mere declarations of intentions to submit such draft agreements in the future."

Novikov's main argument was that none of the drafts had been approved by the "states directly concerned"—as required under the charter—since no one had ever determined exactly what was meant by this ambiguous phrase, which was written into the charter at the suggestion of the United States. This was a serious point. If it were decided, for example, that each of the five big powers was "directly concerned" in all the draft agreements, it would mean that any one of the powers could exercise a veto and block their approval by refusing to approve the agreements.

When the Trusteeship Council finally opened its first meeting on March 26, 1947, the Soviet delegate's seat was empty. In his opening remarks, Trygve Lie did not mention the Soviet boycott. He did note the political differences that had cast a shadow over the preparatory discussions. Lie told the delegates:

The road to the establishment of the council has been long and difficult. There have been many conflicts of ideas and interests. At times, because controversial political issues were involved, the debates may have raised the question in people's minds whether the interests of the nations or the interests of the inhabitants of the prospective Trust Territories were the paramount consideration. The administering authorities may have wondered on occasion whether they or the Trust Territories needed most the protection of the United Nations.

The Soviet Union boycotted the entire first session of the Trusteeship Council, but eventually took its seat at the beginning of the second session. The first speaker after Lie was Francis B. Sayre, the U.S. delegate who was later elected the Council's first president. Sayre expressed regret at the Soviet Union's absence, and said that it would be tragic if such a body as the Trusteeship Council "should not enjoy the participation of a country so great, so powerful and so important."

That first session of the council was disheartening. Here was an agency—originally envisaged as one of the major organs of the United Nations—beginning its work on a questionable legal status and with one of its main members refusing to take part. Even more discouraging was the final realization that this council was going to have little to do with the great problem of advancing the status of dependent peoples except to read annual reports from the administering states, make periodic visits to the trust territories—if, and when, the administering states agreed—and examine petitions from the inhabitants of the trust territories themselves. The Trusteeship Council had no authority to make any decisions on anything; it could only make annual progress reports to the General Assembly on each of the trust territories under the trusteeship system. With only 15,000,000 people under its jurisdiction, the challenge faced by the council was something less than breathtaking.

Initially the council's composition was such that the voice of the colonial powers was bound to be dominant. Under the charter, membership was supposed to be equally balanced between administering and nonadministering states, but this balance was upset at the outset by the absence of the Soviet Union. It was thrown still further off center by the presence of the United States as a nonadministering state. The classification of the United States was technically correct, since the Pacific Islands Trusteeship Agreement had not yet been ratified, but the sympathies of the U.S. delegation were clearly with the administering powers. This left only Nationalist China, Mexico, and Iraq on one side against Britain, France, the United States, Australia, New Zealand, and Belgium. And neither Nationalist China, Mexico, nor Iraq was noted for its militance on behalf of dependent peoples.

The dominant figure in the council was Sayre, a former assistant secretary of state and son-in-law of the late Woodrow Wilson. This soft-spoken ex-professor—as president of the council—introduced a new note in the U.N. proceedings: informality. He ran the council like a college seminar—calling on delegates to express their views, asking them questions, summing up what seemed to him to be the points of agreement and disagreement. He tried to avoid formal votes whenever possible by the simple expedient of saying "I take it we are in agreement" or "if there are no objections we will pass on to the next question." He liked to refer to the delegates as "my friend from France" or "my colleague from Australia," instead of using the stiffer expression so often heard in other U.N. bodies: "The honorable delegate from So-and-So."

It seemed surrealistic, however, to watch the council at work. The problem of the millions of dependent people was undoubtedly one of the most vital and urgent questions in the world, especially in this postwar period when people everywhere were striving for a greater degree of freedom. The time was ripe for great reforms in the colonial system. Instead, the delegates—who were mostly able and serious-minded men—devoted their first session to drafting an elaborate set of rules that would govern the council's procedure and to formulating a questionnaire that would serve as a basis for the annual reports of the administering states. The Trusteeship Council could not even touch the great problem of decolonization, because of charter limitations.

Trygve Lie hailed the creation of the Trusteeship Council as a historic event, and declared that it would "make a vital contribution to the foundations of world peace" if it fulfilled "the promise of both the letter and the spirit" of the charter. However, even Lie admitted that, in the final analysis, the success of the trusteeship system would depend largely on the "earnest intentions of the administering authorities."

It quickly became apparent that the important decolonization efforts would be made by the General Assembly and that they would deal with the millions not under the jurisdiction of the trusteeship system. The framers of the charter had not foreseen the imminent need for machinery to cope with the rising clamor for independence. They had not even made provision for handling the information reports required from the colonial powers. The colonial powers themselves had understood that the reports were for information only and that no U.N. action was necessary or expected. However, a majority of the General Assembly decided that there should be some sort of provision for examining the reports. So, in 1947, the first steps toward decolonization began. Over the bitter opposition of the colonial powers, the assembly established an Ad Hoc Committee on Information Transmitted under Article 73(e). The United States was one of the countries insisting that this was a violation of the charter. It was in this committee and in the assembly that the battle for decolonization began. Nearly a decade passed, however, before the floodgates were opened. At the end of 1954, U.N. membership had only increased to 60, from the original 51. The balance of power remained unchanged.

12

The United Nations in a Changing World

At the end of the United Nations' first decade, the balance sheet was far from good. Dag Hammarskjöld acknowledged at the tenth anniversary meeting in San Francisco that there had been disappointments, divisions, moments of danger, and almost despair. "There haven been reasons," he said, "good ones and bad ones, why the United Nations has not yet become the focus of world efforts for peace . . . that its founders intended." Sir Alexander Cadogan, the British representative, said: "Let us frankly admit that there is a widespread feeling of disappointment at the manner in which the Security Council has discharged its functions." The council had been all but paralyzed by the unrestricted use of the veto by the Soviet Union. Perhaps the biggest disappointment was the complete failure of the big powers to reach agreement on military enforcement machinery, as provided by Article 43 of the charter. There were no real negotiations of the issue after 1947. Theoretically, the discussions broke down over technical questions such as whether the major powers should make balanced contributions to such a force, or equal contributions; but the underlying reason was the inception of the Cold War and the suspicions between East and West. Each side was convinced that any military forces contributed by the other side would be inspired by ulterior motives. In addition, the West feared that the Soviet veto would nullify any value such a U.N. force would have, since its operations would be controlled by the big-power Military Staff Committee and its parent body, the Security Council. The Soviet Union, on the other hand, realized that it would be outvoted four to one in the Military Staff Committee if the veto were excluded. By the summer of 1947 it had become

apparent that neither the United States nor the Soviet Union wanted to implement Article 43.

Although it was obvious that the United Nations was in serious trouble
because of these failures, all the major powers continued to avow their confidence
in its future. From the U.S. point of view, there was one big plus: The United
Nations was completely dominated by the United States and its Western allies.
At that time the United States was Sugar Daddy. It was contributing just under
40 percent of the total U.N. budget, as against 6.34 percent by the Soviet
Union. It was by far the biggest contributor to the specialized agencies and such
voluntary programs as the U.N. Relief and Works Agency for Palestine
(UNRWA) and UNICEF. Even more importantly, it was able to command an
overwhelming majority in the General Assembly and other U.N. organs. As
chief participant and financial backer of the U.N. force in Korea, the United
States had established an image in 1950 as the leading champion of the United
Nations; and the Soviet Union—by its obstructionism—had become the villain.
No one seemed to mind if the United States was searching for alternatives such
as the Truman Doctrine, the Marshall Plan, and the formation of regional
defense alliances such as the North Atlantic Treaty Organization (NATO) and
the Organization of American States (OAS). Although the United States en-
deavored to identify these initiatives as steps strengthening the United Nations—and as being consistent with the U.N. Charter—they were in reality
intended to secure the United States against communism without having to
face Soviet obstacles in the United Nations. One of the founders of NATO,
Lester B. Pearson of Canada, described it as a "practical and regional means of
cementing cracks which had appeared in the charter security system." Echoing
this view, Paul Martin—another leading Canadian statesman—said that the
deadlock over Article 43 and the disunity of the big powers in the Security
Council had caused the NATO founders "to turn elsewhere for the satisfaction
of our security requirements." Some years later, President Eisenhower declared
in a letter to Soviet Premier Bulganin that Soviet abuses of the veto had destroyed
the hope of a universal collective security system as envisaged in the U.N.
Charter.

NATO came into existence on April 4, 1949, when the United States and
11 other countries signed the North Atlantic Treaty. They were all members
of the United Nations, and firmly insisted that NATO was not intended to be
a substitute for the United Nations but a military bulwark of the charter. In its
very first paragraph, the treaty reaffirmed the faith of the signatories "in the
purposes and principles of the charter of the United Nations." It made a number
of additional references to the United Nations—declaring that any military
action taken would be in accordance with Article 51 of the charter and that
the treaty did not affect the obligations of the signatories under the U.N. Charter
"or the primary responsibility of the Security Council for the maintenance of
international peace and security."

Although NATO is often cited as a symbol of the change in U.S. policy, it was not the first regional organization. The Inter-American Treaty of Reciprocal Assistance had been signed in Rio de Janeiro in 1947, and the charter of the Organization of American States had been drafted in Bogotá in 1948. NATO—like the Southeast Asia Treaty Organization (SEATO) and the Central Treaty Organization (CENTRO)—was primarily a mutual defense organization, while the OAS was concerned mainly with settling disputes among countries of the Western hemisphere. In fact, it was through the efforts of several Latin American countries that the U.N. Charter recognized a role for "regional arrangements." Throughout the discussions in San Francisco, the United States had stressed the supremacy of the United Nations over regional organizations; but by 1950, the United States was the leading exponent of "Try OAS First." In his treatise, "The O.A.S., the U.N. and the United States," Inis L. Claude, Jr., said:

This shift can only be understood as one aspect of the development of the United States policy of resistance to Soviet expansionism. The United States has led the fight for OAS jurisdiction in certain cases, not because it regarded them as local matters, but precisely because it believed they involved communist intrusion into hemisphere affairs; for the United States, the campaign on behalf of the OAS has been in reality a struggle against the Soviet Union.[1]

Critics often complain that the United States pays an unduly large percentage of the costs of operating the United Nations. The U.S. contribution to the OAS, however, was 66 percent of the OAS budget in the beginning; and initially, the U.S. assessment in NATO was 42.86 percent. In addition, the United States pays the full cost of the U.S. troops assigned to NATO. With the exception of the OAS, none of the regional organizations has played a role in the so-called fragmentation of the functions of the United Nations. More will be said about the OAS later, along with the role of two other important regional organizations—the Warsaw Treaty Organization and the Organization of African Unity. The Warsaw Treaty Organization (or Warsaw Pact), which was based on a 20-year mutual defense pact signed on May 14, 1955, was one of the first steps taken by Khrushchev and Bulganin to strengthen their hold over the communist states of Eastern Europe. The Organization of African Unity (OAU) did not appear on the scene until 1963, after the mass emergence of the new African states.

Despite the protests of the Western countries that NATO was intended to strengthen the United Nations, many observers—including Trygve Lie—watched with growing concern the hardening of the East–West division and the buildup of communist and noncommunist forces in Europe. As the secretary-general noted, the United Nations was being "relegated to a back seat in all the great power foreign offices." "I favored the North Atlantic Treaty Organization and other measures to strengthen the West," Lie said, "but not at the cost of allowing the United Nations to wither on the vine."[2]

At the San Francisco commemorative meeting in 1955, John Foster Dulles strongly defended the North Atlantic Treaty Organization and other regional organizations (while Vyacheslav Molotov blamed them for much of the trouble in the world). These organizations, Dulles said, were based on the spirit of the U.N. Charter, and it was Western strength—backed by these organizations— that had led to the solution of major problems. Dulles asserted that abuse of the veto by the Soviets had led to the creation of regional arrangements under Article 51. He said that the United States was a party to mutual defense treaties with no less than 44 countries. "These systems conform to the charter of the United Nations," he said. "They carry into effect the charter ideal of fellowship. They operate under the principles of the charter, and they are subject to the influence of the organization. They have attacked no nation. They have threatened no nation. And they thwart no nation that does not covet the land and peoples over which collective security stands guard."[3]

There is no doubt that the world was gripped by "pactomania" at that time, but changes were also being made in the United Nations itself to bridge the gaps caused by the Soviet veto and the failure of the Article 43 negotiations. One of these was the creation of the Interim Committee of the General Assembly in 1947, on the initiative of the United States.[4]

The Interim Committee—often referred to as the "Little Assembly"—was a committee of the whole established to provide continuous availability of the assembly on a year-round basis, just as the Security Council was available 12 months out of the year. The usefulness of the Interim Committee was limited, however, because of a Soviet boycott; and it soon passed into oblivion, although it was never formally abolished. The plan was for the Interim Committee to be composed of the permanent representatives of all member states and to deal with matters that came up between regular sessions of the assembly, which normally began each September and ran until just before Christmas. In the absence of the Soviet bloc, actions of the Interim Committee were little more than a rubber stamp for U.S. policies, as demonstrated by its actions on the Korean question before the outbreak of the war. The chief contribution of the Interim Committee during its brief period of activity was its attempt to liberalize the Security Council's voting system and to improve the machinery for the pacific settlement of disputes. Among other things, the committee recommended that the Security Council consider 35 specified types of questions as procedural— and therefore not subject to the veto. Another of the committee's proposals was that the Security Council adopt the League of Nations practice of using one of its members as a rapporteur to help in the conciliation of disputes. Although agreements came easily in the committee, they produced no results. From the beginning, the Soviet Union maintained that the whole operation was illegal. Consequently, the Soviets accepted none of its recommendations. The last meeting of the Interim Committee was held in March 1952.

In the fall of 1950, the United States had taken another—and more important—initiative to make sure that the United Nations could act in the event of a future act of aggression such as the attack on South Korea. It was assumed that the Soviets would not make the same mistake twice of being absent when such a case came before the Security Council. In the words of U.S. Secretary of State Dean Acheson, the purpose of his September 20, 1950, speech before the assembly was "to make further U.N. decisions possible by action" in the General Assembly whenever the Security Council was paralyzed by the veto.[5]

Acheson went ahead with his proposal—known as the "Uniting for Peace" plan—despite misgivings of the British and some other allies. When the British Foreign Office was consulted, it had warned of possible dangers in the future if the Western majority in the assembly should be replaced by a majority that held contrary views. In light of developments 20 years later, this warning seems prophetic. Most member states were acutely aware of the Soviet Union's performance in the Security Council since the end of its boycott on August 1, and agreed with Acheson that drastic steps were necessary. The result was an overwhelming approval of the Uniting for Peace Resolution on November 3, 1950, by a vote of 52 to 5 with India and Argentina abstaining. The five negative notes were cast by the Soviet bloc, which once more took the position that the whole thing was illegal. The four main provisions of the plan were as follows:

1. An emergency session of the General Assembly could be called within 24 hours if the Security Council were prevented from acting.

2. The establishment of a Peace Observation Commission would provide immediate and independent observation wherever international conflict might be threatened.

3. Member states would be asked to earmark military units to be continuously available for U.N. service.

4. A special committee of military experts would be established to develop the machinery for collective action.

Andrei Vyshinsky of the Soviet Union warned the assembly that "the basic principles of the charter are being thrown in the scrap heap." He objected particularly to point four, which provided for the Collective Measures Committee of military experts. Despite Vyshinsky's vigorous protests, he was unable to rally any support. The General Assembly president, Nasrollah Entezam of Iran, hailed the Uniting for Peace plan as the "most important decision of all those adopted during any session of the General Assembly since the inception of the United Nations."

John Foster Dulles, who represented the United States during the debate in the Political Committee (Committee I), said that the Korean experience had exposed organizational weaknesses which "must be corrected." One of the weaknesses to which he referred was the inability of the Security Council to meet its obligations. The main purpose of the Uniting for Peace plan was to facilitate the shifting of the peace-keeping machinery from the Security Council to the General Assembly. Under the charter, the assembly has the residual responsibility in this field, but it was prohibited from dealing with matters that were actively before the council. The new procedure made it possible for the assembly to act without delay in the event of a veto.

The change had psychological implications also, since it had the effect of giving the General Assembly more prestige, at the expense of the Security Council. In effect, it made the General Assembly the court of last resort. At the time, this seemed to be a major event, but actually no emergency session of the assembly was called under the Uniting for Peace Resolution until 1956— six years after its adoption. This was during the Suez crisis. And ironically, the resolution was not invoked to circumvent a Soviet veto, but the vetoes of Britain and France. Furthermore, it was not invoked by a Western power, but by communist Yugoslavia. The United States did initiate action under this pro- cedure a few days later, after the Soviet Union vetoed a resolution calling for the withdrawal of Soviet military forces from Hungary. Although the Soviet Union had insisted that the Uniting for Peace plan was illegal, the Soviets have voted in favor of using it on a number of occasions, and actually took the initiative in calling for the 1967 emergency session under this procedure during the Six-Day War in the Middle East.

While the Uniting for Peace Resolution is best known as the vehicle for convening emergency sessions, its sponsors felt that the other provisions were equally important—especially the establishment of two new bodies: the Col- lective Measures Committee and the Peace Observation Commission. Each of these bodies was to be composed of 14 members, including the five permanent members of the Security Council; but neither the Soviet Union nor any member of the Soviet block ever took a seat on either. The new bodies went ahead, nevertheless, with their efforts to bolster U.N. peace-keeping potentials. The principal achievement of the Collective Measures Committee was the formu- lation of a set of principles and procedures to meet aggression. One of the recommendations was that member states should earmark elements of their armed forces to be specially trained and made available to serve as U.N. units, if and when the need should arise. The assembly took note of these recom- mendations, including the earmarking of military units; and a few countries responded. Generally, however, the reaction was apathetic. Not one of the big powers—including the United States—agreed to designate the requested standby forces. This, for all practical purposes, was the end of the Collective Measures Committee. It still exists on paper, but has been inactive since 1954. The use of the Peace Observation Commission was no more spectacular than that of its companion. It maintained a subcommission in Greece from 1951 to 1954, but that was its lone operation. Like Article 43, the peace-keeping machinery under the Uniting for Peace Resolution was a victim of the Cold War.

On the tenth anniversary of the signing of the U.N. Charter, the member nations met in San Francisco to evaluate their performances and to take a look at the future. Typical of the comments was that of British Prime Minister Harold MacMillan. He said "Whatever its defects may be, however far it may have fallen short of the high hopes placed on it in 1945, it remains unique—the only place in the world where all the world's problems can be considered as a whole. The United Nations, as it stands today, probably represents the highest common factor of agreement that is possible amongst the nations. It is still evolving."

Some observers, like Associated Press columnist James Marlow, noted that one of the highlights of the San Francisco commemorative session was the private talks of the Big Four powers on arrangements for the summit meeting that was to take place the following August. Marlow asked,

Why since the governments speak to one another through the U.N. where all could hear and judge, do the Big Four attempt to get results in a closed-door meeting outside the U.N.? Perhaps, because the big powers, so accustomed in the past to doing business head-to-head, have not yet advanced to the point in civilization where they can work in an open, parliamentary way through the world's biggest parliament. To future generations this kind of personal diplomacy, a frank acknowledgment by the big powers that the U.N. isn't quite enough for them, may seem childish and primitive.

In this respect, nothing has changed. Four decades later, the big powers still find head-to-head talks a useful way to do business, while at the same time remaining active participants in the United Nations.

In all other regards, however, a great transition began in the mid–1950s. Between 1955 and 1965 the United Nations underwent a sweeping change of character, which saw the end of Western domination and the rise of the Third World as a significant international force. Even before the physical changes in the United Nations began in 1955, the psychological transition had begun. In the middle of the 1952 session of the General Assembly, Secretary of State Acheson reported to President Truman that the "outstanding fact of the assembly so far is its domination by the Arab–Asian bloc." This assessment must have been based on a substantial measure of intuition because at the time only nine new members had been admitted to the organization since the original 51 signed the charter. Six of the new members were in Asia—which, with the nine Asian and Arab founding members, brought the total to 15, or one-fourth of the total membership. What may have been in the back of Acheson's mind were the 20 Latin American countries and the three African members—not counting white-controlled South Africa—which had already shown a tendency to form links with the Asians and Arabs. This meant that even then, there were 38 future members of the Third World in the organization—although at that time most of the Latin American states could still be counted on to follow the U.S. lead, except on racial and colonial questions.

In 1950 nobody had given a thought to the Third World, but Eleanor Roosevelt reported to President Truman that she had encountered intense bitterness in the Social and Humanitarian Committee (Committee III) of the General Assembly "on the race problem and the 'haves' and 'have nots' and small nations against big nations." Her biographer, Joe Lash, quotes Mrs. Roosevelt as saying:

"My own feeling is that the Near East, India and many of the Asiatic people have a profound distrust of the white people. . . . The result is that in Committee III at least, there has been a constant attitude among a great bloc of these countries to oppose everything the United States has suggested."[6]

The real turning point came in 1955, beginning with the Bandung Conference in April of that year and climaxing with the so-called package deal in which 16 new members were admitted to the United Nations. This brought total membership to 76, and added 6 more Asian and Arab countries—as well as 4 more to the Soviet bloc. These were the first new members admitted in five years, although 22 applicants had been considered during that period. Of the 22 there had been 15 vetoed by the Soviet Union anywhere from one to six times. Up to December 14, 1955, the Soviets had used the veto 47 times on membership applications. On the other hand, seven communist countries had been kept out by the Western-dominated majority. Generally the Soviet argument was that Moscow did not have diplomatic relations with the applicants, and therefore would not approve their admission. The majority position was that the communist applicants did not qualify as "peace loving states which accept the obligations" contained in the charter.

In 1953 James F. Byrnes, the former secretary of state who was sitting as a member of the U.S. delegation, declared that a package deal was unacceptable to the United States because this would involve the tacit agreement, at least, that the communist applicants were peace-loving states. Several of them— including Albania, Bulgaria, Hungary, and Rumania—had in fact been condemned by the General Assembly for failure to fulfill their obligations under the peace treaties of 1947. In order to accept the package deal, therefore, both the United States and the Soviet Union had to make substantial concessions. One of the major factors in the shift of Soviet policy was the death of Stalin in 1953. It was then that the Soviet Union embraced the policy of peaceful coexistence and began wooing the newly emerged nations, as well as the Arabs— whom they had alienated in 1947 by their support of the Palestine partition plan. The United States, on the other hand, was anxious to bring in a large group of friendly countries, including Portugal, Ireland, Italy, Austria, Finland, Jordan, and Spain. To make the package deal more palatable to the United States, the resolution proposing the mass admission omitted any reference to "peace-loving" and merely noted the general feeling of the assembly "in favor of the universality of the United Nations."

The Bandung Conference had been inaugurated under the joint auspices of the Colombo Plan organizers: Burma, Ceylon, Indonesia, India, and Pakistan. Until this meeting there had been no organized collaboration among Asian and African countries, neither inside nor outside the United Nations. It was not a nonaligned affair since Red China's Chou En-lai not only was present but was a leading figure in the conference. Burma had sought to broaden the composition to include Israel and Yugoslavia (later a leader among the nonaligned countries), but had been outvoted. Foreshadowing things to come, the conference trained its guns on colonialism, which it condemned as an evil to be eliminated at the earliest possible moment. This was one objective that all the participants could always agree on, even though the Cold War might sometimes line them up on opposite sides of other issues. One of the results of the Bandung Conference was the creation of the Afro–Asian Group at the United Nations. It became active immediately as a consultative unit—seeking to present a united front on colonial questions especially, but also on any other issues in which they had a common interest.

No one was more aware of the new element than Charles de Gaulle, who was fighting a stubborn rearguard action to hold onto France's North African empire. It was a battle that finally brought Président de Gaulle to an almost complete break with the United Nations, and that ended in the first major victory for the Afro–Asians. The struggle had started in 1951 when six Arab states complained to the General Assembly that France was using repressive measures to curb the growing nationalist movement in Morocco. The assembly postponed action, but the question was raised again in 1952. France refused to take part in the discussions, on grounds that the Moroccan question was a domestic matter and, therefore, outside the competence of the United Nations. In 1952 the Tunisian problem was added, when 11 Asian and African countries complained to the Security Council that France was depriving the people of Tunisia of their right to self-determination. France boycotted this discussion also, on grounds of domestic jurisdiction. Despite French objections, the Afro–Asians continued to bedevil de Gaulle with U.N. pressure until Morocco and Tunisia gained their independence and were admitted to the United Nations in 1956. This was just a warm-up, however, for the battle over Algeria.

The question of Algeria first came up in the United Nations in 1955, and continued to be debated until 1962 when the North African country was admitted to the organization. One of the leaders of the Afro–Asian drive for Algerian freedom—it might be worth noting—was U Thant, who became Burma's permanent U.N. representative in 1957 and served as chairman of the working group set up to support and encourage the Algerian independence movement. Thant described de Gaulle's handling of the Algerian problem as "far from gratifying." He said that the French president had "emptied the word 'self-determination' of all its meaning." De Gaulle was not noted as one who forgave his critics; but, strangely, he did not oppose Thant's selection as acting secretary-general after Hammarskjöld's death in 1961. De Gaulle's dislike for Hammarskjöld was another matter. He had become increasingly hostile to both the secretary-general and the United Nations itself during the long controversy over the French North African territories. He not only reduced France's U.N. participation to token representation, but referred to the organization in derisive terms such as "this thing."

It is difficult to pinpoint the exact time at which the entry of the new nations in the United Nations began to cause concern among the founding members. From the mid–1950s on, however, it became more obvious that the membership explosion was having an impact on U.N. discussions. Hammarskjöld—for one—insisted that he saw nothing to worry about. At a press conference on June 2, 1960, the secretary-general was asked whether he was aware of rumors being spread at U.N. headquarters that the big powers were becoming reluctant to bring problems to the United Nations because of the flood of newly independent countries. Hammarskjöld replied that he was aware of the rumors, but saw no basis for them. "There is something very shocking in the idea that new states must take so-called irresponsible stands," he said. "I myself do not believe it for one moment. On the contrary, I believe that the new states are likely to approach problems with very great seriousness and with a very great sense of responsibility."[7]

Even as late as 1965, Ambassador Arthur J. Goldberg declared in an interview that "the position of the United States by and large continues to be supported by the overwhelming votes of the General Assembly." "So," he said, "I do not share the view that we have lost our position, that we are going to be outvoted. The facts do not sustain that."

The United States—like the Soviet Union—was not directly involved in the decolonization process since it had no dependent territories in the sense that Britain, France, the Netherlands, Belgium, and Portugal had. It was involved indirectly, nevertheless, as an ally of the colonial countries and—even more so—as the dominant force in the United Nations. If the emergence of the Third World countries was to result in a shift in the U.N. power structure, it would be at the expense of the United States. The United States had been nominally anticolonial since the time of Woodrow Wilson; but, in the United Nations, the State Department consistently seemed to support the "imperialist" position either to avoid offending NATO allies, to protect U.S. investments abroad, or to ensure the continuance of U.S. military bases on foreign territory. Up until the time of the Kennedy administration, at least, the prevailing feeling in the State Department was one of distrust for neutral and nonaligned countries. Dulles, for example, held that nonalignment was a sign of moral weakness. Even when John F. Kennedy was still a U.S. senator, he had become convinced that the Dulles doctrine was hurting the United States. Arthur Schlesinger, Jr., writes that Kennedy believed "the Third World had now become the crucial battleground between Democracy and communism and that the practical effect of Dulles' 'Bell, Book and Candle' against neutralism could only prejudice the American case and drive the developing countries toward Moscow and Peking." With Adlai Stevenson at the United Nations as U.S. representative and with this new outlook, it appeared that the United States was ready to make a serious bid for an alliance with the Third World. Unfortunately, there was no significant change in the U.S. voting pattern at the United Nations.[8]

Khrushchev had taken an important initiative in 1960 when he personally presented to the General Assembly his proposed Declaration on Decolonization. Coinciding, as it did, with the admission of 16 new African states, this declaration was clearly intended to place the Soviet Union on the side of the angels.[9]

The new group of members was not only larger than the 1955 package, but it moved Africa into the power struggle as number one in membership—ahead of both the Asian and Latin American groups. In going all out against colonialism, the Soviets had nothing to lose. They not only had no dependent territories; they had no friends ruling dependent territories. The United States did not want to oppose the proposed declaration, but it could not go along with the more radical terms of the Soviet draft—such as immediate independence of all dependent territories. The U.S. delegation, which was headed by Ambassador James J. Wadsworth, worked with the Afro–Asians in their efforts to tone down the language of the declaration, and succeeded to the extent that the State Department authorized the delegation to vote for it. The French and the British were bitterly opposed to the declaration, however, and Prime Minister Harold Macmillan prevailed upon President Eisenhower at the last minute to withhold U.S. support. Eisenhower sent instructions for Wadsworth to abstain. The ambassador and other members of the delegation were furious. Wadsworth tried to get through to the president to argue the case on the telephone, but his call was refused. The revised declaration was approved by a vote of 89 to 0. The United States wound up in the abstention column along with the traditional colonial bloc. Out of the nine abstainers, only the United States and the Dominican Republic had no dependent territories. The others were Australia, Belgium, Britain, France, Portugal, South Africa, and Spain. The feelings of the U.S. delegation were proclaimed by one member, Senator Wayne Morse, who said "on every major issue of colonialism at the 15th General Assembly our voting record shows that we rejected our own history, and allowed the communist bloc to champion the cause of these millions of people who are trying to gain their independence." Later in the session, the United States announced that it had changed its position and wished to be associated with the declaration, but many of the new countries never forgot that the United States had lined up with the colonial powers on what they considered a historic occasion.

The Declaration of Decolonization was historic in the sense that it formally recognized a transition that was already taking place with increasing momentum. Along with one-sided votes on such questions as Algeria's long struggle for independence and the 1961 Bizerte incident in Tunisia, the declaration demonstrated the growing influence of the Afro–Asians and foreshadowed more changes to come. By the end of 1960, U.N. membership had grown from the original 51 states to an even 100. By that time it was not uncommon for communications to the Security Council and the General Assembly—and for resolutions—to have the sponsorship of 35 or more members, mostly Asian and African. It was inevitable that such a change in the membership would be followed by institutional changes to take the power shift into account. In 1961, for example, the Ten-Nation Disarmament Committee was expanded to become the Eighteen-Nation Disarmament Committee, with the addition of eight non-aligned countries: India, Egypt, Ethiopia, Nigeria, Mexico, Burma, Brazil, and Sweden. Before the expansion, the committee had been a two-sided body, with five NATO members and five Warsaw Pact states. The new composition was negotiated by the Soviet Union and the United States, who continued to play a major role as cochairmen. One who did not like this arrangement was de Gaulle. The French president felt that disarmament decisions should be limited to the nuclear powers. For this reason, France—although a member—never participated in the Eighteen-Nation Disarmament Committee. The People's Republic of China refused in 1971 to take part in the committee because of the control exercised by the United States and the U.S.S.R. U Thant, who was newly elected as acting secretary-general at the time of the expansion, welcomed the addition of the nonaligned members, but would have preferred that there be a third cochairman from this new group. Thant said that disarmament was a subject in which all nations—big and small—were concerned, and that the nonaligned members had an especially important role to play in helping to bridge the gap between extreme positions on either side. His remarks might have applied just as well to the enlargement of the Committee on the Peaceful Uses of Outer Space. Although 9 of the committee's original 24 members were nonaligned countries, the General Assembly decided in 1961 to add four more—Chad, Mongolia, Morocco, and Sierra Leone—whose main qualification was that they were Asians and Africans.

Another 1961 action by the General Assembly—perhaps more far-reaching than these—was the establishment of the Special Committee for Implementation of the Declaration on Decolonization. In plain language, the job of this committee was to work for the speedy independence of the remaining dependent territories. In the beginning, the United States sided with the colonial powers in opposing the proposal, but it ended by voting with the 97–0 majority for the creation of the 17–nation body. Britain, France, Spain, and Portugal abstained. The colonial powers were justifiably unhappy with the new committee because of the Asian, African, and communist predominance among its membership. Of the original 17 members, 11 were in these three groups. The composition became even more one-sided when the committee was expanded in 1962 to include 24 members. During the next decade, the Special Committee—better known as the Committee of Twenty-four—was to become a thorn in the side of the few remaining colonial countries, particularly Britain, Portugal, and South Africa.[10]

One of the truly amazing institutional changes during this time was the expansion of the Security Council and the Economic and Social Council (ECO-SOC) through the first amendments ever made to the U.N. Charter. Many countries had urged revision of the charter to correct weaknesses—such as the abuse of the veto—but the Soviet Union had always insisted that no revisions would be accepted by the Kremlin until the People's Republic of China had taken its "lawful place" in the United Nations. This was still the Soviet position when Asian and African countries launched their move in 1963 for charter amendments to enlarge the Security Council and ECOSOC. In fact, neither the West nor the Soviet bloc was enthusiastic about the proposed amendments, but they bowed reluctantly to the overwhelming pressure of the Asians and Africans. The Untied States favored some expansion of the two councils, but felt that the proposed changes went too far. The Soviets at first opposed all amendments. The Soviet Union and France actually voted along with nine other countries against the amendments when they were offered initially. However, the Kremlin not only reversed itself; it became the first permanent member of the Security Council to ratify the amendments. Ratification by the U.S. Senate was the final act required to make the amendment effective. The Senate consented in June 1965; and the instrument of ratification was deposited on August 31 of that year—which brought the changes into effect. The Security Council would thereafter have 15 members instead of 11, and ECOSOC would have 27 instead of 18. The charter was also revised to require nine affirmative votes—instead of seven—for Security Council action. The avowed purpose of the amendments was to ensure "more equitable representation." What they meant from a practical standpoint was that the membership of the two councils would reflect the power shift from the West to the new countries of Asia and Africa. By 1965 the West had already lost its "mechanical majority" in the General Assembly and was now losing it in the two major councils, as well. Under the agreed geographic distribution, the Asians and Africans were guaranteed five of the ten elective seats in the Security Council—which gave them the balance of power for the first time in this key U.N. organ. In ECOSOC, the Asians and Africans were assured seven of nine new seats in addition to the five they already had. This meant that they would occupy 12 of the council's 27 seats—also enough to give them the balance of power.

The next two decades were to produce other radical changes in the character of the organization. The most important, perhaps, was the emergence of the so-called mini-states and their acceptance as members of the United Nations. No country was too small, and even the smallest was entitled to its vote in the General Assembly on a basis of equality with the great powers. The advocates of weighted voting had never found much support and had already acknowledged the futility of further efforts. Once the principle of universality had been accepted, the floodgates were opened. Between 1965 and 1985 the membership of the organization ballooned from 114 to 159. And, of these new members, 28 had populations smaller than the state of Rhode Island. The smallest had a population of 60,000. This was the Seychelles Islands. Three others had 100,000 or less. Many had strange and exotic names and were represented by diplomats who were making their first appearance on the international scene. It was a different world from the one that the United Nations saw in 1946 when 51 member nations met in London for the opening session.

13

The Congo Experience

The Belgian Congo became independent on July 1, 1960. Within a few days, chaotic conditions had developed. Soldiers immediately broke loose in a series of mutinies throughout the country; they began roaming the streets, manhandling Belgian civilians and raping women. Mineral-rich Katanga Province declared its secession from the central government. Without the consent of the Congolese leaders, Belgium flew in thousands of troops, including paratroops, in an attempt to restore order.

It was at this point that the new Congolese government requested the United Nations' assistance. In a telegram dated July 12, President Joseph Kasavubu and Prime Minister Patrice Lumumba accused Belgium of aggression and of "having carefully prepared the secession of Katanga with a view to maintaining a hold on our country." The telegram asked for the urgent dispatch of U.N. troops to the Congo. In a clarifying telegram the next day, the Congolese leaders stated that "the purpose of the aid requested is not to restore the internal situation in the Congo but rather to protect national territory against acts of aggression committed by Belgian metropolitan troops."

The Security Council acted quickly. It convened on the evening of July 13. During the early morning hours of July 14, the council adopted a resolution that began the United Nations' long and costly intervention. The resolution called on Belgium to withdraw its troops and authorized the secretary-general to provide the Congolese government with "such military assistance as may be necessary" until the national forces were able to handle the situation. Both the United States and the Soviet Union were among the eight council members voting for the resolution. Nobody voted against it, but three members—Britain, France, and Nationalist China—abstained.[1]

Hammarskjöld began implementing the resolution with almost unbelievable speed. Within hours he had appointed Swedish Major General Carl C. von Horn as supreme commander and had dispatched an appeal to Morocco, Tunisia, Ghana, Guinea, and Mali for troops to make up the proposed U.N. force. He asked the United States, Britain, and the Soviet Union for airlift assistance. On July 15—the day after the Security Council acted—the first contingent of Tunisian troops arrived in the Congo. By July 18, 3,500 U.N. troops had reached the site. Thanks to the secretary-general's experience in organizing the U.N. Emergency Force in the Middle East four years earlier, the establishment of U.N. Congo Force (ONUC) was accomplished without a hitch. So was a civilian assistance program set up under the direction of Ralph Bunche, the secretary-general's personal representative in the Congo.

It became apparent almost immediately, however, that clarification of the United Nations' role was needed. Just what was the U.N. force supposed to do now that it was in place? Its mandate was simply to assist the Congolese government until the government was able to do its own job. Did this mean that the United Nations could use force to expel the Belgians? Did it mean that it could use force to prevent the secession of Katanga? Could it use force to quell mutinous Congolese troops? Neither the Congolese government nor Hammarskjöld had definite answers. In fact, they differed in their interpretation of all these questions.[2]

On July 20, six days after the force was authorized, Hammarskjöld went back to the Security Council for guidance. Just after midnight on July 22, the council adopted a resolution that at least partially answered some of the questions. First of all, it commended Hammarskjöld for his prompt action in organizing ONUC. Then the council went on to authorize him "to take all necessary action" to implement the withdrawal of the 10,000 Belgian troops that had been flown in. It further spelled out that the U.N. objective was to preserve the territorial integrity and political independence of the Congo. The United Nations was thus committed to resist and prevent the secession of Katanga Province; but what measure of force—if any—could be used was still not clear. The Soviet deputy foreign minister, Vasily V. Kuznetsov, voted along with the other ten council members for the resolution, but he did not join in their praise of the secretary-general. He agreed that ONUC must "be entrusted with the task of safeguarding the territorial integrity" of the Congo, but declared that it had no right to assume responsibility for domestic law and order within the country.

Some concern was caused during the first days when Prime Minister Lumumba threatened to appeal to the Soviet Union for military help in getting the Belgian troops withdrawn. This was contrary to the original decision to use military contingents "only from neutral countries." Lumumba dropped his threat after adoption of the July 22 resolution. It was a foretaste, however, of Lumumba's future behavior and of the problems that would revolve around him. Hammarskjöld must have had a premonition of what was ahead: He declared that the organization had "embarked on its biggest single effort," and predicted that before the operation was concluded he might have to ask "for much, much more" in the way of military contributions from member nations. "There should not be any hesitation," he said, "because we are at a turn of the road where our attitude will be of a decisive significance, not only for the future of this organization, but for the future of Africa."

By mid-August—one month after the U.N. intervention—the entire U.N. effort was threatened by developments both inside and outside the Congo. The most pressing problem was the unexpected political chaos within the Congo's central government. U.N. officials were caught in a power struggle between Kasavubu and Lumumba. With the backing of the Soviet Union, Prime Minister Lumumba was turning more and more against the United Nations. U.N. officials were trying to remain neutral, but were being pressed by U.S. Ambassador Clare Timberlake to support Kasavubu. In Katanga Province, the rebel president, Moise Tshombe, was talking out of both sides of his mouth. He was being agreeable to U.N. officials while at the same time working with Belgium and the influential Union Minière to thwart U.N. antisecession efforts.

It is safe to say that no U.N. diplomat or U.N. observer could have anticipated the magnitude of the difficulties that the Congo Force encountered during the first months. To begin with, no one realized the extent of the Congolese military and civilian unpreparedness to take over the administration of a major African nation. The officers corps of the national army was almost 100 percent white Belgian. The same thing was true of the civil service, where Congolese nationals served only in subordinate positions. Rebellion against this situation was the underlying cause of the mutinies and disorders in the streets. Observers have described some of the Congolese leaders as unstable and undependable, but no one could have foreseen the quixotic behavior that U.N. officials had to face.

The U.N. operations were also experiencing unexpected obstruction from non-Congolese sources. When the Soviet Union voted for the U.N. intervention in July, no one foresaw that the Soviets would become a major problem a month later. Also, the attitude of the Belgian government turned out to be more difficult than expected. It had become clear that the Belgians were in no hurry to give up the rich mineral resources in Katanga Province. They found numerous excuses for delaying the withdrawal of their troops from Katanga; and, even after the troops were finally withdrawn on September 9, they were sending money and supplies to mercenaries organized by Union Minière.

These were serious difficulties—but the biggest proved to be the political personalities in the central government, and their power struggle. It became clear almost from the beginning that Hammarskjöld and Lumumba were on a collision course. The Congolese prime minister repeatedly pressed for the use of U.N. forces to crush the Katangese secession movement and later for U.N. intervention against rebellion in Kasai Province. Hammarskjöld explained that, as in the case of UNEF, the countries contributing military contingents had been assured the troops would be used exclusively for peace-keeping and would use their weapons only in self-defense. Lumumba either did not understand this concept or was not willing to accept it.

On August 15, Hammarskjöld received a letter from Lumumba that contained a list of demands, including the following:

—To entrust the task of guarding all air fields to the Congolese National Army, in place of the U.N. troops.

—To put aircraft at the disposal of the central government for the transportation of Congolese troops to restore order throughout the country.

—To seize all arms and ammunition supplied by the Belgians to the Katanga authorities and put them at the disposal of the National Army.

—To withdraw the Swedish U.N. units from Katanga and replace them with units from African countries.

In another letter, Lumumba denounced Hammarskjöld for his "maneuvers in sending to Katanga only troops of Sweden—a country which is known by public opinion to have special affinities with the Belgian royal family." He added that "the people of the Congo have lost their confidence in the secretary-general of the United Nations." Hammarskjöld referred these communications to the Security Council, and the council met on August 21 to consider these and other developments. Meanwhile, Lumumba declared a state of emergency and secretly appealed to the Soviet Union for transport planes and trucks to enable the Congolese National Army to invade Katanga. In the midst of this crisis—and probably inspired by Lumumba's tirades—Congolese soldiers attacked and seized members of a small Canadian communications unit at the Léopoldville airport. In a formal protest, Hammarskjöld warned that continued occurrences like this might make it necessary for the United Nations to reconsider its whole program of assistance. This was the first of numerous attacks on U.N. units.

In response to Lumumba's request, the Soviet Union undercut the U.N. position by secretly providing 15 Ilyushin transport planes as well as 100 trucks that had originally been promised to the U.N. force. These were used to transport National Army units to Kasai, en route to Katanga; but they became engaged there in ending tribal fighting and never reached Katanga. When Hammarskjöld complained, the Soviets admitted their intervention, but argued that the secretary-general had no right to control assistance rendered by any state at the request of the Congolese government. Another problem arose when Hammarskjöld learned that Belgium had misinformed him about the withdrawal of its last troops from Katanga. In fact, Belgium had assigned some of its officers to the Katanga forces that were opposing the policies of the central government. The Belgian government denied that these officers were operating under its authority or control. Hammarskjöld replied, "It would be hard to believe that officers of the Belgian army would have severed their connections with that army . . . without having obtained the approval of their military superiors." In another note, the secretary-general protested that a plane full of weapons had been unloaded at the Elizabethville airport from a civil aircraft of Sabena Airlines. He pointed out that this was contrary to the spirit and letter of the Security Council resolution of July 22—which called on all states to refrain from any action that might impede U.N. action in preserving the territorial integrity of the Congo.

It was approximately at this time that the Congolese government fell apart. For some weeks, relations between Prime Minister Lumumba and President Kasavubu had been strained. On September 5, Kasavubu fired Lumumba on grounds that he was leading the country toward civil war. Lumumba responded by dismissing Kasavubu as "a traitor to the state." The Chamber of Representatives declared both actions invalid, so both Kasavubu and Lumumba remained in office. While these events were happening, Andrew Cordier—who was acting as Hammarskjöld's representative pending the arrival of Rajeshwar Dayal—projected the United Nations into a new controversy by closing the Léopoldville radio station and airport for reasons of public order. His action brought a barrage of criticism, particularly from the Soviet Union, which called it an act of intervention totally beyond the United Nations' authority. Lumumba led a contingent of 20 soldiers in an attempt to seize the radio station, but was turned away by a platoon of U.N. troops from Ghana. One of the repercussions was the withdrawal of a United Arab Republic battalion assigned to the U.N. force.

The political situation was further complicated when 30-year-old General Joseph Mobutu, the Congo's newly appointed army commander in chief, suspended the elected leaders and appointed a "College of Commissioners" to take over the duties of the executive government and Parliament. Hammarskjöld and his representatives refused to recognize the Mobutu regime, and continued their efforts to reconcile Kasavubu and Lumumba. One of Mobutu's first acts was to order the embassies of all Soviet bloc countries to close within 48 hours. Hammarskjöld's representative, Rajeshwar Dayal, did his best to get Kasavubu to rescind this order but at the same time insist that all assistance be channeled through the United Nations. Kasavubu refused to intervene. On September 17, the personnel of the communist embassies—under a U.N. escort requested by them—were taken to the airport and flown out of the country.

It so happened that the Security Council was in session in New York at the time. Soviet Representative Valerian Zorin promptly introduced a resolution calling for removal of the ONUC command officers for "gross violation" of Security Council resolutions. In the Congo, Lumumba issued a statement demanding the total withdrawal of all U.N. personnel and declaring that they would be expelled by Soviet troops if they were not out in eight days. Four days later Lumumba sent a letter to Hammarskjöld stating that a reconciliation agreement had been reached between him and Kasavubu, and assuring the secretary-general of his full cooperation.

It is difficult to believe that these events were taking place only two months after the U.N. intervention had been authorized—but this was just the beginning. Because of a stalemate in the Security Council (caused by Soviet vetoes), an emergency session of the General Assembly was convened on September 17 to deal with the Congo problem. In the early morning hours of September 20, 1960, the assembly adopted an African-sponsored resolution giving Hammarskjöld an overwhelming vote of confidence. The vote was 70 to 0 with 11 abstentions.[3]

The Soviets, however, were not ready to accept this verdict. Premier Nikita Khrushchev—appearing in person at the regular fifteenth session of the assembly a few days later—made his famous speech not only demanding the resignation of Hammarskjöld, but proposing that the office of secretary-general be replaced by a committee of three. Many remember Khrushchev's U.N. appearance because of his bizarre behavior in pounding his shoe on the table, but this was less shocking than his unrestrained attacks on Hammarskjöld. In a speech lasting two-and-a-half hours, he accused the secretary-general of having "sided with the colonists," who—he said—had been "doing their dirty work in the Congo through the secretary-general of the United Nations and his staff." He broadened his attack to include abolition of the office of secretary-general and removal of U.N. headquarters from New York to Geneva or Vienna or even the Soviet Union. He proposed that the secretary-general be replaced by a "collective executive body" consisting of three persons representing the Western powers, the socialist states, and the nonaligned countries. This became known as the "troika" plan.[4]

Hammarskjöld replied three days later with a declaration that the secretary-general must adhere to a strict policy of independence, impartiality, and objectivity—even if his attitude "becomes an obstacle for those who work for certain political aims." He added, "I would rather see the office break on the strict adherence to the principle of independence, impartiality and objectivity than drift on the basis of compromise. That is the choice daily facing the secretary-general."

This was not the end of the exchange. Khrushchev renewed his attack on October 3 and capped it with a demand that Hammarskjöld resign. He said, "Mr. Hammarskjöld has always been prejudiced in his attitude toward the Socialist countries. He has always upheld the interests of the United States of America and the other monopoly-capitalist countries. The events in the Congo, where he played a simply deplorable role, were merely the last drop which filled the cup of our patience to overflowing. In order to prevent any mis-interpretation, I should like to repeat: we do not and cannot place any confidence in Mr. Hammarskjöld. If he himself does not muster enough courage to resign, so to say in a chivalrous manner, then we shall draw the necessary conclusions from the situation obtaining."

The secretary-general—seated beside the assembly president on the rostrum—was furious. He took the floor at the opening of the afternoon session to deliver a defiant reply in which he challenged the right of the Soviet Union or any other country to pass judgment on his behavior. He told the General Assembly that "you, all of you are the judges. No single party can claim that authority." In his brief but emotional speech, he proclaimed that:

I said the other day that I would not wish to continue to serve as secretary-general one day longer than such continued service was considered to be in the best interests of the organization. The statement this morning seems to indicate that the Soviet Union finds it impossible to work with the present secretary-general. This may seem to provide a strong reason why I should resign. However, the Soviet Union has also made it clear that if the present secretary-general were to resign now, it would not wish to elect a new incumbent but insist on an arrangement which—and this is my firm conviction based on broad experience—would make it impossible to maintain an effective executive. By resigning I would, therefore, at the present difficult and dangerous juncture throw the organization to the winds. I have no right to do so because I have a responsibility to all those member states for which the organization is of decisive importance—a responsibility which overrides all other considerations. It is not the Soviet Union or indeed any other big powers which need the United Nations for their protection. It is all the others. In this sense, the organization is first of all their organization and I deeply believe in the wisdom with which they will be able to use it and guide it. I shall remain in my post during the term of office as a servant of the organization in the interest of all those other nations as long as they wish me to do so.

The delegates at this point interrupted his speech by a standing ovation that lasted several minutes. It was clearly a vote of confidence for the secretary-general, while the Soviets sat unsmiling in their seats. Hammarskjöld resumed with this dramatic conclusion:

In this context the representative of the Soviet Union spoke of courage. It is not easy to stay on. It is very easy to bow to the wish of a big power. It is another matter to resist. As is well known to all members of this Assembly I have done so on many occasions and in many directions. If it is the wish of those nations who see in the organization their best protection in the present world, I shall now do so again.

As he sat down, Hammarskjöld received another standing ovation, which undoubtedly gave Khrushchev something to think about. At any rate, in his farewell remarks before leaving for home on October 13, the Soviet leader toned down his language somewhat. He said that there was nothing personal in his criticism of Hammarskjöld. "I have met him," he said, "and we have had very pleasant conversations. I consider that Mr. Hammarskjöld is in my debt because he exploited me, when he was our guest on the Black Sea. I took him around in a rowboat and he has not paid off that debt; he has not done the same for me." To this, Hammarskjöld replied, "I am very happy to hear that Mr. Khrushchev has good memories of the time when I had the honor to be rowed by him on the Black Sea. I have not, as he said, been able to reply in kind. But my promise to do so stands, and I hope the day will come when he can avail himself of this offer. For if he did I am sure he would discover that I know how to row—following only my own compass."

This declaration of independence did not improve the situation. The Soviet Union continued to criticize every U.N. move in the Congo. The final break came a few months later, following the arrest and murder of Lumumba. In a letter to the Security Council, Soviet Representative Zorin placed the blame directly on Hammarskjöld for Lumumba's death. He asserted that the secretary-general deserved "the contempt of all honest people" for his alleged participation in the Lumumba slaying. The Zorin letter concluded by saying that the Soviet government would have no further relations with Hammarskjöld. On February 23 a note from Hammarskjöld to the Soviet Mission was returned with the comment that the Soviet Union no longer recognized him as an official of the United Nations. It was a rerun of the Trygve Lie scenario after a lapse of 11 years. For the next six months the Soviet delegation addressed all communications to "The Office of the Secretary-General," rather than to Hammarskjöld.

Meanwhile, Rajeshwar Dayal had his hands full in the Congo. Relations between General Joseph Mobutu and the United Nations reached a breaking point during October because of what Mobutu called the United Nations' continued support of Lumumba and interference in attempts of the National Army to arrest him. It was true that, despite the U.N. policy of hands-off, some U.N. military contingents—particularly those from Ghana and Guinea—were supporting and protecting Lumumba. The United Nations took the position that Lumumba was still constitutionally the prime minister and was entitled to U.N. protection. He occasionally eluded his guards, however, and slipped out of his residence to harangue people in the streets. While Lumumba remained in Léopoldville, a pro-Lumumba group had set up headquarters in Stanleyville—the capital of Orientale Province—with Deputy Prime Minister Antoine Gizenga in charge and aided by General Victor Lundula, the former chief of staff. On the night of November 27, Lumumba quietly slipped out of his residence, apparently headed for Stanleyville. This proved to be a fatal mistake. Mobutu's men caught up with him in Kasai Province on December 1 and placed him under arrest. He and two companions were brought back to Léopoldville in an open truck—tied up like common criminals.

At the beginning of January 1961 Lumumba was transferred to Katanga into the hands of his archenemy, Moise Tshombe. What happened after that was the subject of a full U.N. investigation, and continues to remain in dispute. On January 12 it was announced by Katanga officials that Lumumba and his companions had escaped and that all three had later been captured and killed at an undisclosed village near Kolwezi. This story was generally discounted from the beginning. The U.N. Commission of Inquiry concluded that Lumumba and his companions were killed on the night of their arrival in Elizabethville, very probably in the presence of Moise Tshombe, Katanga Interior Minister Godefroid Munongo, and two Belgian army officers.

The worldwide reaction was extreme and sometimes violent. In Cairo the Belgian Embassy was sacked and burned. Demonstrations took place in other capitals and at U.N. headquarters. It happened that Adlai E. Stevenson was making his first speech on February 15 as U.S. representative in the Security Council and, while praising Hammarskjöld's Congo performance, he was interrupted by screams from the public gallery. In the ensuing melee, 20 of the United Nations' unarmed guards were injured by brass knuckles, spike-heeled shoes, and tire chains. The demonstration was led by about 50 black African nationalists from the Harlem ghetto who had received admission tickets from the Cuban delegation. One result of the disturbance was a decision by the U.N. administration that U.N. guards would carry billy clubs to protect themselves in the future. The Soviet Union seized on Lumumba's death to launch a new attack on the secretary-general. Valerian Zorin charged him with direct responsibility, and demanded termination of the United Nations' Congo operation.

From the very beginning, Dag Hammarskjöld had been plagued by staff problems, in addition to everything else. He had been criticized by the Soviet Union and some African countries for depending too much on his U.S. aides, especially Ralph Bunche and Andrew Cordier—both of whom played a key role in the initial phase of the Congo operation. When he named an Indian national, Rajeshwar Dayal, to succeed them as his personal representative, he still found some critics unhappy. In November the secretary-general had to face a crisis in the ONUC command itself. It had become clear by then that he had made a mistake in appointing his Swedish compatriot, Major General von Horn, as commander of the multination military force. Dayal told Hammarskjöld that he was worried about von Horn's performance—lack of proper coordination, lack of discipline, lack of foresight in planning, and unexplained delays. Hammarskjöld reluctantly recalled von Horn and replaced him with General Sean McKeown of Ireland. By then Dayal had left to be replaced by Conor Cruise O'Brien, another Irishman.

U.N. delegates have sometimes had a tendency to vote for peace-keeping operations and other expensive projects without considering the question of who was going to pay the bill. Despite the massive nature of the Congo military and civilian operations, no provision for financing was made in the initial stages. The only step taken was an appeal for voluntary contributions to create a temporary U.N. Fund for the Congo in the amount of $100 million, to be raised by passing the hat. The secretary-general reported to the General Assembly's Budgetary Committee (Committee V) on November 21, 1960, that only a disappointing $12.5 million had been pledged to the fund. Hammarskjöld, bluntly told the committee that "The organization cannot have it both ways. It must either pursue its policy, as represented by the force in the Congo, and make appropriate and speedy arrangements for covering the costs, or it must take the initial steps to liquidate the military operations and so reverse its policy."

Finally on December 20, the General Assembly approved a resolution authorizing an appropriation of $48.5 million to pay the costs for 1960 and another

$24 million for the first three months of 1961. To raise this money, the assembly voted to assess each member at the same rate of assessment assigned to each for the United Nations' regular budget. The entire Soviet bloc, France, and 12 other members voted against this assessment. The Soviets argued that only the Security Council had authority to raise money for the Congo costs. There were 44 countries that abstained on the 1961 appropriations—reflecting the erosion of Afro–Asian support for the Congo operation. Some of these countries, including the Soviet Union and France, never contributed one dollar to pay for the costly Congo intervention.

Continued Belgian involvement in Katanga was so blatant that, on September 20, 1960, the General Assembly called on "all states to refrain from direct and indirect provision of arms and other materials of war and military assistance for military purposes in the Congo" so long as the U.N. Congo Force was in the country. Belgium ignored the appeal. On October 8, Hammarskjöld complained to the Belgian government that unilateral Belgian assistance was still going to Katanga and South Kasai, in violation of the U.N. resolution. This was followed by another *note verbale* in which the secretary-general charged that 114 Belgian officers and 117 Belgians of other ranks were still serving in the Katanga gendarmerie and that 58 Belgian officers were serving in the Katanga police. He charged further that Belgium was recruiting Belgian nationals to join the Katanga government as experts and that these experts were obstructing and hampering U.N. technical assistance. Belgium rejected the secretary-general's complaints and continued to support the secessionist movement.

On April 15, 1961, the General Assembly adopted an Afro–Asian resolution deploring Belgium's actions and calling on the Brussels government to withdraw all military and paramilitary personnel, mercenaries, and political advisors not under the U.N. command. Belgium once more ignored the U.N. appeals. At one point, feelings were so intense that Foreign Minister Pierre Wigny declared Belgium might even consider withdrawing from the United Nations altogether. This outside interference of Belgium and other non-Congolese sources certainly made the U.N. task more difficult, but Hammarskjöld still had the confidence of most U.N. members, and was thus able to pursue the policies laid down by the Security Council and the General Assembly.[5]

In addition to his mandate to prevent the secession of Katanga, the secretary-general's main concerns were in: (1) supplying and controlling a multinational army of some 20,000 men scattered throughout the sprawling country, and (2) trying to live with and reconcile the quarrelling political factions that had brought the Congo to the brink of civil war. Trying to administer an army of so many different nationalities would have been difficult enough, but it was made more so when the contributing governments sided with one Congolese political faction or another. In a number of instances, participating governments actually recalled their contingents because of disagreement with U.N. policies. Other continued to take their place, however, and the force was maintained as the largest ever placed under U.N. command.

The internal political situation took a turn for the better on February 9, 1961, with the formation of a new provisional government in Léopoldville to replace Mobutu's College of Commissioners. Joseph Ileo was named prime minister; and Cyrille Adoula, minister of the interior. Kasavubu announced that the government would exercise legislative powers until Parliament could be recalled. Notably absent from the new government was Antoine Gizenga—Lumumba's deputy prime minister—along with Moise Tshombe and other dissidents. On April 15 the General Assembly in New York created a seven-nation Committee of Conciliation and urged all factions to cooperate in ending the political crisis. Hammarskjöld also was active through his representatives, Robert Gardiner and Mahmoud Khiari, in trying to bring the parties together. On June 19 agreement was reached on the modalities for convening Parliament. When the legislators formally got down to business a month later, all factions were represented, except Tshombe—who refused to send a delegation.

President Kasavubu named Cyrille Adoula as prime minister to head the government. Antoine Gizenga was named first deputy prime minister. These developments removed some of the main difficulties, but Tshombe and his Belgian supporters were more defiant than ever. Hammarskjöld decided to go to the Congo in September—before the opening of the 1961 General Assembly—to make a personal effort to end the secession. Unfortunately, serious fighting broke out in Katanga before the secretary-general arrived, and Tshombe did not show up for a scheduled meeting with the U.N. officials. Hammarskjöld sent a message to Tshombe; it called for an immediate cease-fire and proposed a meeting the next day at Ndola, in neighboring Northern Rhodesia. Assuming that Tshombe would be there, Hammarskjöld's party took off in his DC–6B plane at 5 P.M. (local time) on September 17. At ten minutes after midnight, the pilot informed the Ndola control tower that the airfield lights were in sight and that he was making his descent. No more was heard. Some 15 hours later a search party located the wreckage. Only one passenger was found alive— Harold Julien, one of the U.N. security men.[6]

During the 46 days between Dag Hammarskjöld's death and the election of U Thant as acting secretary-general, the situation in the Congo went from bad to worse. As U.N. representative of Burma, Thant had strongly supported Hammarskjöld's Congo performance; and, on assuming office, he gave top priority to the problem of completing the Congo operation. He was convinced that failure of the United Nations in the Congo could mean the end of the organization as a peace-keeping entity.

At the time of Hammarskjöld's death (14 months after the U.N. intervention) the entire Congo operation was in jeopardy not only in Katanga—where U.N. forces were under attack by mercenaries—but in other provinces where they were threatened by mutinous units of the Congolese National Army. Thant felt that part of Hammarskjöld's difficulty was the secretary-general's lack of authority to assist the central government in restoring and maintaining law and order.

The Security Council shared his concern. On November 24, just three weeks after Thant took office, the council broadened the mandate of the ONUC command—authorizing it not only to employ the requisite force for the expulsion of the mercenaries, but pledging "firm and full support" to the central government. No one objected when Thant read into the record his interpretation of the council's resolution, which—he said—in his opinion, implied "a sympathetic attitude on the part of ONUC toward the efforts of the government to suppress all armed activities against the central government" in addition to halting the Katanga secessionist movement.

Thant proceeded immediately to launch this new tough policy, by ordering U.N. units to defend and maintain their lines of communication and to attack sniper sanctuaries. The result was an acceleration of the fighting. Tshombe's response to the Security Council resolution was a wave of attacks on U.N. troops and a barrage of anti-U.N. propaganda. Four days after the council's action, two U.N. officials—George Ivan Smith and Brian Urquhart—were seized and beaten by Katanga paracommandos and gendarmes while attending a reception in Elizabethville in honor of U.S. Senator Thomas J. Dodd. The situation was aggravated by the erection of roadblocks by the gendarmes in Elizabethville and elsewhere in an effort to impede U.N. communications. A number of U.N. soldiers were killed before the conflict broadened to include bombings and strafing from the air. A Katanga plane dropped three bombs near U.N. positions at the Elizabethville airport, and U.N. planes responded by attacking airports at Jadotville and Kolwezi.

The new U.N. attitude quickly brought Thant into a diplomatic conflict with Paul-Henri Spaak, who had taken over the Belgian foreign ministry. Spaak challenged the legality of the U.N. military operations. In addition, he accused the U.N. Congo Force of violating the Geneva Convention by attacking civilians. Thant denied the latter charge and defended the actions of ONUC, as necessary. "The United Nations Force," he said, "is a peace force, but because of the hostile attitude of certain Katangese, and I must add of certain non-African civilians, including Belgians, it was obliged to resort to force in self-defense. I sincerely hope the fighting will not last long; but at the same time I am determined to take all necessary action to implement the action entrusted to me by the Security Council and the General Assembly." Thant also tangled with the president of the Congo Republic (Brazzaville), Abbe Fulbert Youlou, who notified the United Nations that U.N. aircraft transporting men and supplies to ONUC would be denied landing and overflight privileges. In a cable to Youlou, Thant said, "I find it inconceivable that a state which only so recently was . . . admitted to membership in the United Nations should now act in a manner which would inevitably have to be described as in contradiction with its declaration of being able and willing to fulfill its obligations under the charter."

It was around mid-December that the tide began to turn. On December 16, 1961, Thant informed the Advisory Committee on the Congo that he had received appeals for a cease-fire from the United Kingdom, Belgium, Greece, and Madagascar. At the same time he received word from President John F. Kennedy that Moise Tshombe had indicated a desire to negotiate with Prime Minister Adoula. By this time, fighting had ended except for small pockets in areas controlled by Union Minière, where mercenaries continued to direct mortar fire on U.N. forces.

With the assistance of U.N. and U.S. representatives, Adoula and Tshombe arranged a meeting on December 19 at Kitona, a former Belgian military base. On December 21 the parties reached an agreement that seemed at the time to offer some promise for the future. Under the agreement, Tshombe recognized President Kasavubu as head of state, recognized the authority of the central government over all parts of the Congo, and pledged respect for resolutions of the Security Council and the General Assembly. He also agreed to send representatives to Léopoldville on January 3, 1962, to take part in drafting a constitution for the country.

Unfortunately, it soon became apparent that Tshombe was not carrying out a pledge to rid Katanga of the mercenaries and was ignoring some other provisions of the Kitona Agreement. However, he did finally arrive in Léopoldville on March 15 to begin negotiations with the central government. The talks broke down on June 26 after 41 meetings, and Tshombe returned to Elizabethville.

Perhaps the most important development during the summer of 1962 was the announcement of the secretary-general's "Plan of National Reconciliation," which was submitted to the central government and the Katanga authorities on a take-it-or-leave-it basis. Cyrille Adoula accepted the plan on August 23; and Moise Tshombe, on September 2. U Thant welcomed the agreement, but said that the true significance "will be revealed only as the specific provisions of the plan are put into effect." Another important development took place in August 1962. At the suggestion of Prime Minister Adoula, Thant appointed four experts in constitutional law from Canada, India, Nigeria, and Switzerland to develop a federal constitution that would give the provinces greater autonomy. The draft of what later became the constitution of the Congo was completed and submitted to Adoula on September 27.

It seemed at last that real progress was being made, but there were still problems ahead. Again Tshombe was dragging his feet on implementing key provisions of the Plan of National Reconciliation. Among the stumbling blocks were: (1) assuring freedom of movement for U.N. troops, (2) sharing foreign exchange with the central government, and (3) ending Katanga's foreign representation abroad. There also was a new flurry of military activity as the Katangese gendarmerie launched an intense campaign of harassment against ONUC troops. In the midst of this, Tshombe suddenly left Elizabethville on January 12, 1963, for Kolwezi. Two days later Thant received a message from him and his ministers announcing their readiness to end the secession and grant U.N. troops full freedom of movement. Kolwezi was the last important mining center still occupied by the gendarmerie. On January 16, Tshombe agreed to the peaceful entry of U.N. forces into Kolwezi. This was done on January 21, and the Katangese gendarmerie ceased to exist as a fighting force.

Secretary-general Thant reported to the Security Council on February 4 that the Congo situation had improved to such an extent that an early withdrawal of the U.N. Congo Force was in sight. He said that a phasing-out schedule was being formulated. At a news conference in Geneva on May 3, the secretary-general said "My own personal feeling is that the primary function of the United Nations in the Congo has been fulfilled." Since mid–1962 the U.N. troop level had been reduced from 19,500 to 13,500. In his annual report issued August 20, Thant said, "The time has come when for various reasons, it is necessary to envisage the early withdrawal and winding up of the United Nations Force in the Congo." A few days later he disclosed that Prime Minister Adoula had asked him to leave 3,000 men in the Congo beyond the end of 1963—the anticipated cutoff date. Thant was anxious to liquidate the operation; but, on October 8, the General Assembly agreed to extend the stay of the U.N. forces until June 30, 1964. By the time the assembly acted, the size of the force had already dwindled to around 7,000 men.[7]

The United Nations ended its military operation in the Congo almost exactly four years after the Security Council authorized the intervention. Thant notified the council that U.N. objectives had in a large measure been fulfilled. These included the preservation of the territorial integrity of the Congo, the elimination of foreign military personnel and mercenaries, and the prevention of civil war. He noted that disorders continued in some parts of the country, but said that the question of maintaining law and order was the responsibility of the Congolese government.

Thus was concluded the largest peace-keeping undertaking ever embarked upon by the United Nations. During its four years, the ONUC operation cost the United Nations $381,505,000—not including expenditures for civilian assistance. By comparison, UNEF cost the United Nations $213 million over a period of ten-and-a-half years. The U.N. Congo Force suffered 235 casualties, and Dag Hammarskjöld lost his life in search of peace in the Congo.[8]

POSTSCRIPT

In 1965 Major General Joseph Mobutu was named president—a post he held throughout the 1970s and still held at the time of writing in 1987. He changed his name to Mobutu Sese Seko in keeping with his Africanization policy. The country changed its name in 1971 to the Republic of Zaire; and, in 1972, all Zairians with Christian names were ordered to change them to African names. Léopoldville became Kinshasa, and Katanga Province became Shaba.

14

France and Tunisia Clash over
the Bizerte Naval Base

French President Charles de Gaulle never kept secret his dislike of the United Nations, which he once called the "Tower of Babel." He was one of the few heads of state who never visited U.N. headquarters. When de Gaulle visited New York in 1960, Dag Hammarskjöld invited him to lunch, as was customary when such dignitaries were in the city. He was rebuffed coldly with a terse statement that "it is not my intention to visit the United Nations." With the beginning of the Congo crisis later in 1960, the situation worsened. De Gaulle believed that the U.N. intervention was an expensive mistake, and he was soon finding fault with the secretary-general and blaming him for every setback in the operation. It may be recalled that France had abstained when the Security Council authorized the Congo intervention and that France refused to pay any part of the operation's cost.[1]

It was not until the summer of 1961—during the so-called Bizerte crisis— that de Gaulle's hostility toward Hammarskjöld and the United Nations led France to flout Security Council decisions and openly snub the secretary-general. The Bizerte crisis grew out of France's refusal to withdraw its forces from the Tunisian naval base near the city of Bizerte. France had continued to occupy the base after Tunisia became independent in 1956. When negotiations broke down in 1961, Tunisia decided that it had waited long enough. It sealed off the naval base with a land blockade. France responded by flying in reinforcements. French armored units went on the offensive and occupied the city of Bizerte in bloody fighting that resulted in heavy casualties among Tunisian soldiers and civilians.

Tunisia called immediately for an urgent meeting of the Security Council.

At a meeting on July 21, Tunisia charged France with aggression. France replied that Tunisia had provoked the trouble and that France had been compelled to act to ensure the safety of its base and its freedom of communications. When the council resumed discussions the following day, reports from Bizerte told of continued fighting and mounting casualties. Without waiting for further debate, Hammarskjöld decided to use his prerogative as secretary-general in an appeal to the council that it consider, "without delay, taking an intermediary decision" requesting the two sides for a cease-fire and an immediate return to the military positions held before hostilities began. "This is an appeal," he said, "which is related exclusively to the immediate dangers and does not pretend to indicate the direction in which a solution to the wider conflict should be sought." Liberia immediately introduced a resolution along the lines suggested by the secretary-general, and the council approved it by a vote of 10 to 0. France refused to participate in the vote.[2]

The Security Council discussions continued, but failed to produce agreement on any further action. A resolution sponsored by Liberia and the United Arab Republic called for the immediate withdrawal of French reinforcements and for talks aimed at the speedy evacuation of all French forces from Tunisia. This resolution received only four affirmative votes, with seven members abstaining. The United States and Britain sponsored a resolution calling on both sides to refrain from any action likely to aggravate the situation and urging them to negotiate promptly a peaceful solution of the problem. This resolution received six affirmative votes, while five members abstained.

After the council adjourned, Tunisian Ambassador Mongi Slim asked the secretary-general if he could send U.N. observers to help implement the cease-fire. Hammarskjöld replied that such a decision would require a request from both sides and possibly further action by the council. He added, however, that he himself could go in the capacity of secretary-general if invited by President Habib Bourguiba for a personal exchange of views. On Sunday, July 23, Bourguiba cabled just such an invitation. Hammarskjöld replied; "Such a request on your part imposes upon me the clear duty to place myself at your disposal for such an exchange of views which, I hope, might help to lead toward peace." After informing the French U.N. mission of his intention, Hammarskjöld left for Tunisia that same night. He realized that he should have had a similar invitation from France, but he assumed that the French would not object. He soon found out that he was mistaken.

Hammarskjöld met with Bourguiba the next day. He learned that the French not only had occupied Bizerte, but had placed armored units in a threatening manner along the road to Tunis. France had proclaimed its own cease-fire, but ignored the Security Council demand that all troops be withdrawn to their previous positions. Hammarskjöld decided that the situation was so serious as to call for an immediate effort on his part to break the deadlock.

On the day after his meeting with Bourguiba, Secretary-general Hammarskjöld sent off a message to French Foreign Minister Couve de Murville in which he expressed concern that the French had made no move either to establish contact with the Tunisian authorities or to withdraw their troops as demanded by the Security Council. "I consider it my duty," he said, "to explore the possibilities of improving this disturbing situation by an effort, at least, to establish immediately the necessary contact between the two parties." He stated that he had heard the Tunisian account of the developments and "I should now like to have corresponding information of the French attitude."

While waiting for Couve de Murville's reply, Hammarskjöld drove from Tunis to Bizerte the next day for a firsthand look at the military situation. His car was stopped and searched on the outskirts of the city, despite his protests. Once he got into Bizerte, Admiral Amman—the French commander—refused to see him. By that time Hammarskjöld had realized that de Gaulle was deliberately obstructing his initiative in an effort to make his trip look foolish. The French leader confirmed this in his memoirs. He said that Hammarskjöld's visit to Bizerte "redounded to his discomfiture. For following instructions, our troops paid no attention to the comings and goings of the self-appointed mediator and Admiral Amman refused to see him."

Couve de Murville's reply was still another slap in the face. It accused Hammarskjöld of taking the side of the Tunisian government and ignored the secretary-general's request for information on the French views. The letter also dismissed the Security Council's resolution as irrelevant. Hammarskjöld decided to return immediately to New York to report to the Security Council. Before leaving Tunis, however, the secretary-general dispatched his reply to Couve de Murville. Obviously angered, but using the language of diplomacy, Hammarskjöld said that Couve de Murville's letter "might be interpreted as meaning that I have acted as the spokesman of one of the parties to the present conflict. I am sure, however, that such was not your intention, and it must have been apparent to you that my attitude, as presented in my letter, is based solely on the interpretation of the duties of the secretary-general ... and also on the intentions, I venture to believe, of all the members of the council who voted for the resolution of July 22, 1961."

When the Security Council resumed consideration of the Bizerte affair after Hammarskjöld's return, France boycotted the meeting. At the request of the representative of Liberia, Hammarskjöld give an oral report on his visit to Tunisia and noted that the council already had copies of the letters exchanged between him and Couve de Murville.

He did not comment directly on his treatment by the French. He left no doubt, however, about his concern over France's attitude. "The implementation of the Security Council resolution of last Saturday remains so far incomplete," he said. "It is true that the cease-fire has been established, but that does not seem to have led to an immediate cessation of all actions which, under such a cease-fire, should be ruled out; nor, as the council knows, does it mean that the integral demand by the council for a return of the armed forces to their original positions has been met." He added that the main problem was the failure of the various efforts to establish a contact between French and Tunisian authorities. "It is not for me to pass any judgment on the situation," he stated. "It is for the members of the Security Council to make comments and draw conclusions.

However, the council found itself divided as to what should be done, and was unable to agree on any action. Three resolutions were submitted, but none received the seven affirmative votes required for approval. Two were sponsored by Ceylon, Liberia, and the UAR; they reflected the anticolonial point of view. The first called on France to comply immediately with all the terms of the July 22 resolution. The second directed France to resume negotiations with Tunisia on the evacuation of French troops from the Tunisian naval base. Each of these resolutions received only four affirmative votes. The United States and the United Kingdom were among the abstainers. Turkey introduced the third resolution—not aimed at France, but calling only for full implementation of the July 22 resolution. This received six affirmative votes, including those of the United States and the United Kingdom; but Ceylon, Liberia, and the UAR joined the Soviet Union in abstaining because they felt that the proposal did not put the blame where it belonged—on France.

The problem was left hanging there until a special session of the General Assembly was convened on the initiative of Asian and African members. The assembly met between August 21 and 25. France again refused to take part. The assembly was able to produce a substantial majority for an Afro–Asian resolution recognizing Tunisia's sovereign right "to call for the withdrawal of all French armed forces on its territory without its consent" and calling on both governments to enter immediately into negotiation on the troop withdrawals. The vote was 66 to 0 with 30 abstentions; among the abstainers were the United States, the United Kingdom, and most of the other Western members.[3]

Despite France's boycott of the Security Council and General Assembly meetings, it quietly began five weeks later to withdraw its troops from the city of Bizerte to the naval base. Diplomatic relations between France and Tunisia were resumed in July 1962, and French withdrawal from the naval base was finally completed on October 15, 1963—more than two years after the conflict erupted in 1961. Dag Hammarskjöld did not live to see the evacuation. His death came less than a month after the General Assembly's action. By that time he was deeply involved in the Congo operation and more problems with France.

15

The Bay of Pigs and the Cuban Missile Crisis

The Bay of Pigs project may well have been one of the most ill-conceived, poorly organized, confused, dishonest, and legally insupportable actions ever undertaken by the U.S. government. It was authorized with total disregard to the obligations of the United States under the Charter of the United Nations. It was undertaken after the U.S. representative to the United Nations had denied that it was being planned. In fact, it was undertaken without any advance knowledge or consultation with this representative—who happened to be Adlai Stevenson, one of the most experienced and respected public officials in the country. The project was doomed in advance, whether intended as an outright invasion or as a projected rallying point for guerrillas. Even if it had proved a military success, it would have been another serious blow to the U.N. Charter, which prohibits the resort to force to settle disputes.

How did it begin? On March 17, 1960, President Eisenhower set the stage when he agreed to a CIA recommendation that the United States train a force of Cuban exiles at secret bases in Guatemala—and perhaps elsewhere—for possible use against Cuba's victorious revolutionary leader, Fidel Castro. Richard Nixon, who was then the vice-president, had proposed such a force as far back as the spring of 1959; and the CIA had been quietly working on a plan. Eisenhower's approval was cloaked in the deepest secrecy, as were all covert operations of the CIA. The timing of the decision was especially significant, since it came some eight months before the November elections when Eisenhower's successor would be chosen. Whoever was elected would inherit the project. The Cuban problem was not a major issue during the campaign, although U.S.–Cuban relations continued to worsen—especially after Premier Castro negotiated economic agreements with Red China and the Soviet Union, and the United States retaliated by suspending the balance of Cuba's 1960 sugar quota.

It was at about this time that the differences between Cuba and the United States first came to the United Nations. In a complaint to the Security Council that was dated July 18, 1960, the Cuban minister of foreign affairs, Raul Roa, accused the United States of "harboring war criminals, aiding counter-revolutionary forces, violating Cuban air space and carrying on a campaign of economic strangulation." Roa declared that, as a consequence "of repeated threats, harassments, intrigues, reprisals and aggressive acts," a grave situation existed "with manifest danger to international peace and security." As it later became clear, these charges were substantially accurate, but the United States flatly denied them at the time. It countered by placing before the council a memorandum that it had transmitted to the Inter-American Peace Committee of the Organization of American States (OAS) in which it accused Cuba of carrying on a campaign of distortion, half-truths, and outright falsehoods against the United States. The training of Cuban refugees by the United States was apparently still a well-kept secret, since no mention was made of it in the U.N. debate that was concluded on July 19 with a decision to refer the dispute to the OAS.[1]

John F. Kennedy—the Democratic nominee for the presidency—was as much in the dark about the CIA's Cuban project as everyone else. As late as October he was limiting his remarks on Cuba to blaming the Eisenhower administration for the deteriorating situation. In a speech in Cincinnati, Kennedy said: "For the present, Cuba is gone. . . . For the present, no magic formula will bring it back." He had been briefed by Allen Dulles, director of the CIA, about Cuba but had not been told about the secret army already in training in Guatemala. Richard Nixon—the Republican nominee—was aware of the Dulles briefing, and he assumed that Kennedy had been told the whole story. Not only that, but a chance reference to "freedom fighters" in a Kennedy headquarters statement led him to believe that the Democratic candidate was getting ready to claim credit for the refugee army. As a result, in their fourth television debate, Nixon accused Kennedy of advocating what in fact was the Eisenhower administration's ongoing project. What is even more strange, Nixon attacked the idea as dangerous and irresponsible. "If we were to follow that recommendation," he said, "we would lose all our friends in Latin America, we would probably be condemned by the United Nations and we would not accomplish our objective. . . . It would be an open invitation to Mr. Khrushchev to come in, to come into Latin America." Kennedy must have been puzzled by Nixon's attack, since he had never made any such recommendation or thought of making one. Not knowing what it was about, he simply ignored Nixon's remarks.[2]

It was not until after the election that Kennedy learned for the first time about the Guatemala operations. By that time, word was beginning to leak out to the public about the secret activities. The first published report appeared in the Guatemala City newspaper *La Hora*; it said that an invasion of Cuba was being organized, and hinted at U.S. involvement. In November, articles by

Ronald Hilton of Stanford University appeared in the *Hispanic American Report* and the *Nation*, bringing the Guatemala happenings to the attention of U.S. readers. It was obvious by then that Fidel Castro must be aware of the operations—from the published reports, if not from his own information sources in Guatemala.

It was an odd situation. Eisenhower was getting ready to leave office on January 20. Kennedy was beset with the problems of transition, but was not yet in authority. The project was going ahead, although its final shape and timing had not been determined; and, in fact, no final decision had been made as to whether it would still not be abandoned altogether after the Kennedy administration took over.

While discussions were proceeding between representatives of the outgoing and incoming administrations, Castro attempted once more to get U.N. action. On December 30, 1960, Cuba asked for an urgent meeting of the Security Council; it charged that a U.S. attack was imminent. When the council finally met on January 4, Raul Roa accused the United States of setting up training camps in Guatemala, Honduras, and Florida in preparation for an invasion of Cuba. Again he was partly correct; but the United States once more denied the charges, and the council again took no action. Members of the Security Council could agree neither on the existence of a threat nor on the terms of a resolution. So they adjourned without taking a vote.[3]

Meanwhile, back in Washington, the wheels were grinding steadily toward the point of no return. Long before Inauguration Day, John F. Kennedy had been persuaded by Allen Dulles and some of his own advisors that he had a tiger by the tail. He was told that the hundreds of Cuban refugees who had been armed and trained in Guatemala could not be disarmed and disbanded either where they were or in the United States without creating terrible problems. So he had reluctantly concluded—without any formal commitment—that the refugee army had to be employed one way or another against Castro. There was still argument back and forth as to how it should be used. Some thought that, once the force had landed, there would be a popular uprising against the Castro regime. Others thought the invading force would be able to establish a beachhead at least and hold enough territory so that a provisional government could move in and call for U.S. assistance. Efforts were actually being made by the CIA to organize such a shadow government. No one talked any more about the original concept of simply infiltrating the refugees into the countryside as guerrillas. The one thing both Eisenhower and Kennedy had insisted on from the beginning was that no U.S. nationals would be used in the fighting. Kennedy also wanted to keep the visibility as low as possible so that U.S. complicity would not be too obvious, particularly in the event that the adventure ended in failure. As plans progressed, however, it became obvious that there was no way to make anyone believe that a force of 1,500 men could be armed and trained and then transported by ship to Cuba without U.S. involvement.

During the discussions in Washington, little mention was made of possible international repercussions of the sort that Richard Nixon had predicted in his television statement. The only serious challenge was made at the last minute by Senator William Fulbright—chairman of the Senate Foreign Relations Committee—who protested to President Kennedy in a memorandum on March 30, 1961. Fulbright argued that any attempt to overthrow the Castro regime would violate the spirit—and probably the letter—of the OAS Charter, of other hemisphere treaties, and possibly of U.S. legislation. Fulbright said that the operation would cause problems in the United Nations and would commit the United States to the responsibility for making a success of the U.S.-sponsored government. He warned that, if the invasion seemed to be failing, the United States might be tempted to use U.S. military forces to achieve its objectives. "To give this activity even covert support," he said, "is of a piece with the hypocrisy and cynicism for which the United States is constantly denouncing the Soviet Union in the United Nations and elsewhere."

The president asked Fulbright to attend a crucial meeting on April 4 in the office of Secretary of State Dean Rusk, where the senator once more denounced the whole idea. He declared that an invasion would compromise the moral position of the United States in the world and make it impossible to protest treaty violations by the communists. Senator Fulbright was the only one in the group to oppose the project, on moral or any other grounds. Strange as it may seem, Adlai Stevenson was not present at this meeting or at other discussions of the operation. Although Stevenson had been U.S. representative at the United Nations since the inauguration of the Kennedy administration, he had never even been told of the project—much less asked for his views.

Stevenson's first official knowledge of the plan came on April 8 when he was briefed by presidential advisor Arthur Schlesinger, Jr. and Tracy Barnes of the CIA. This was just nine days before the landing attempt. Schlesinger and Barnes were told by Kennedy to give Stevenson full information so that nothing said at the United Nations would be less than the truth, even if it could not be the full truth. Writing later, Schlesinger quoted the president as saying: "The integrity and credibility of Adlai Stevenson constitute one of our great national assets. I don't want anything to jeopardize that." Schlesinger acknowledged in his book that the briefing was "probably unduly vague."[4]

The best available accounts of the briefing agree that it left much to be desired. Stevenson was told that the attack was to be carried out solely by exiled Cubans—who would comprise the landing parties, fly the air cover, and be on their own once they hit the beaches at Bahia de Cochinos ("Bay of Pigs"). He was further assured that there would be no U.S. military involvement. In fact, he was informed that none would be needed, since the landing would trigger an uprising in Cuba and that the Castro regime would quickly be toppled. Stevenson's deputy to the U.S. mission to the United Nations, Francis T. Plimpton, said that what they were told "bore no resemblance to what happened."

There is no doubt that Adlai Stevenson was stunned by the briefing. He was appalled that it should now fall on him to stand before the world and defend the U.S. action. Stevenson made it clear to Schlesinger after the briefing that he wholly disapproved of the plan, regretted that he had not been given an opportunity to comment on it, and believed that the action would cause infinite trouble.

Schlesinger was simply serving as a messenger. He was as apprehensive as Stevenson. But although he had strong reservations on the proposed invasion, Schlesinger was somewhat overawed by the high-ranking pro-invasion faction, which included the CIA leaders, the secretary of defense, the joint chiefs of staff, and the secretary of state. As he later wrote: "Had one senior adviser opposed the adventure I believe that Kennedy would have canceled it. No one spoke against it." Schlesinger himself had presented two memorandums opposing the invasion plans. His main points were that the project could possibly turn into a prolonged civil war, which might lead to pressure for U.S. military intervention to assist the rebels, and that such intervention would result in anti-U.S. feelings in the United Nations and elsewhere. He believed, however, that because of his position as special assistant to the president it would not be appropriate for him to speak out in high-level White House meetings where the sentiment was solidly in favor of the Bay of Pigs plan.

One thing that might have averted the disaster would have been premature disclosure by the media. This did not happen. The recruiting and training operations had received only a limited amount of publicity; but as the invasion date approached, Miami buzzed with rumors. Several correspondents—including Tad Szulc of the New York *Times*—were able to confirm that the invasion was imminent. Publication of the facts could have blown the whole operation. Szulc actually did file such a story from Miami; but—after consulting with the Washington Bureau Chief James Reston—Turner Catledge, the executive editor of the *Times*, decided to withhold publication. Schlesinger commented in *A Thousand Days* that "this was another patriotic act, but in retrospect I have wondered whether if the press had acted responsibly it would not have spared the country a disaster."

Despite his opposition to the plan, Adlai Stevenson assured Schlesinger that he would do his best to defend U.S. policy during the debate that was scheduled to open in the General Assembly's main political committee on April 17. During the briefing, Stevenson had been given the impression that nothing would happen until the U.N. debate was concluded. But he was in for more surprises. On Saturday, April 15, eight of the old World War II B–26 bombers attacked three important Cuban airfields. These were U.S. planes, with U.S.-trained pilots. Although bearing Cuban insignia, they had flown from a base in Nicaragua. Cuban Foreign Minister Raul Roa, who was in New York for the scheduled U.N. debate, asked to have the political committee convened immediately, and he was able to have the meeting rescheduled for that same afternoon. Adlai Stevenson had no idea what the air attacks were all about. He spent a hectic day on the telephone with Harlan Cleveland, assistant secretary of state, trying to shape up some sort of defense. The CIA informed Cleveland that the pilots of the B–26s were genuine defectors from the Cuban air force, and Cleveland passed the information along to Ambassador Stevenson, who prepared his defense on this basis.

When the political committee met, Roa led off with an emotional speech charging that the United States had planned and financed the air raids as a "prologue" to a large-scale invasion of Cuba. He said that seven Cubans had been killed in the attacks. When Stevenson took the floor to reply, he innocently told the delegates that the planes and pilots were not U.S. nationals, but Cubans who had taken off from Cuban airfields. The planes bore Cuban markings, he said. He then presented a photograph of one plane that had landed in Florida after the raids. It did in fact carry the insignia of the Cuban air force. What Stevenson did not realize was that the picture was a CIA fake.

Before the committee had time to pursue the debate, the Bay of Pigs invasion had begun. The air raids had indeed—as Roa said—been a prologue to the attack. They had been intended to neutralize the Cuban air force by destroying its planes on the ground, but this—like other parts of the plan—failed. The Cuban air force had been left largely intact and was able to inflict severe damage on the invading force. The raids also served to give Castro advance notice that the seven slow-moving ships were on their way with some 1,400 Cuban exiles. Castro's army of 200,000 was ready to greet the invaders. The ill-conceived project never had a chance. The entire landing force was either killed or wound up in Cuban prisons.

When the General Assembly's political committee met that morning in New York, Raul Roa reported that Cuba had been invaded "by a force of mercenaries, organized, financed and armed by the government of the United States." Stevenson knew that these charges were true, but he replied evasively that there were "no Americans in action inside Cuba." This was not one of the great moments in either Stevenson's career or the history of the United States. The United Nations did not exactly cover itself with glory either. On April 21— four days after the Bay of Pigs landing—the General Assembly adopted a resolution sponsored by seven Latin American countries; it referred to the Security Council resolution of July 19, 1960, which did nothing more than urge all member states to use all peaceful means to resolve existing tensions. The United States did not even get a slap on the wrist.[5]

It was inevitable that U.S.–Cuban relations would worsen. It was not until early 1962, however, that they once again became critical. Perhaps the crucial development during this period was the action taken at the second conference at Punta del Este, Uruguay, from January 22 through January 31. It was here that the foreign ministers of the American republics, under the leadership of the United States, adopted a group of resolutions aimed at isolation of the Castro regime. Among the resolutions in the so-called Final Act were: (1) a declaration that communism was incompatible with the principles of the Inter-

American system, (2) exclusion of Cuba from the Inter-American Defense Board, (3) immediate suspension of trade with Cuba in arms and other implements of war, and (4) a directive to the OAS to study the feasibility of extending the trade embargo to other items.

Castro responded immediately with allegations not only that the actions violated the U.N. Charter but that the exclusion of Cuba from OAS activities violated the principles of nonintervention. The Soviet Union threw its support behind the Castro government. In a letter dated February 19, Moscow told the General Assembly that Cuba would not have to stand alone, but that it could rely on assistance from the Soviet Union. It was not clear at the time what form this aid would take; but, as it turned out, this was not an idle threat. On February 22—despite his previous lack of success in the United Nations— Premier Castro asked for a meeting of the Security Council to consider the situation created by the Punta del Este resolutions. He was rebuffed once more when the council refused to place his complaint on its agenda.[6]

Castro went back on March 8 with a request for another meeting of the council. This time he wanted the Security Council to ask the International Court of Justice for an advisory opinion on the legality of the Punta del Este actions. Again the Cuban delegation went home empty-handed after the proposal was rejected.

On July 2, 1962, Raul Castro—Cuba's minister of armed forces—flew to Moscow for talks with Soviet officials on possible military assistance against what the Cubans called U.S. threats. It was during these talks that agreement was reached secretly on the installation of nuclear missiles in Cuba. Who initiated the idea has been clouded somewhat by conflicting claims. Khrushchev told the Supreme Soviet in December 1962 that "We carried weapons there at the request of the Cuban government." He also stated that these included a "couple of score" of intermediate-range missiles, which were manned by Soviet military personnel. Raul Castro gave contradictory versions. He told some interviewers that the missiles had been a Soviet idea and others that they were Cuba's idea. In any event, the agreement appeared to be an implementation of the Soviet statement that Cuba would not stand alone.

The first shipments began arriving in late July. These included mainly materials for construction of the missile installations. Within a few days, the CIA detected unusual activities in Cuba. It was believed initially that the construction work was aimed at reinforcing the Cuban air defense system. At that time it was assumed that the Soviet Union would certainly not install offensive weapons. Late in August, the CIA concluded that surface-to-air missile sites were being constructed, and so reported to President Kennedy. It was on the basis of this information that the president told a news conference on September 13 that the Soviet installations were not a serious threat. He pointedly warned—however—that, if Cuba were to become "an offensive military base of significant capacity for the Soviet Union, then this country would do whatever must be done to protect our own security and that of our allies."

While declaring that there was no reason for serious concern, the president did order an increase in U–2 surveillance flights. These finally paid off on October 14 when a U–2 plane brought back photographs clearly showing that offensive missile sites were under construction and that intermediate-range missiles were actually on the ground at the bases. Kennedy had warned that this would not be permitted. He now had to face the responsibility of how he would respond. The decision was not reached until the end of seven days of high-level discussions. The first impulse was to take the missile sites out, by a surprise air attack. Another alternative was to go to the United Nations for action. This, however, found little support. The discovery of the offensive missiles was still a secret during this period, and Kennedy wanted to keep it so until he was ready to act.

The U.N. General Assembly was in session at the time, and Soviet Foreign Minister Andrei Gromyko—in New York as a delegate—requested an appointment to see President Kennedy to review problems of mutual concern. The question of Cuba was one of the subjects discussed. Gromyko assured the president that Soviet aid to Cuba was solely for the purpose of strengthening the island's defenses against possible U.S. aggression. Kennedy was infuriated by what he considered an outright lie, but he chose not to confront Gromyko with the evidence of the offensive missiles. Instead, he simply reminded the Soviet foreign minister of the September 13 warning.

Not until October 22 was the U.S. response to the situation announced to the world. It had been finalized in intensive White House discussions during the 48 hours before the president made his appearance on a nationwide television evening broadcast. Kennedy began by declaring that the Soviet Union was constructing offensive missile sites in Cuba that were capable of striking most of the major cities in the Western hemisphere. Kennedy said that he had ordered a number of measures, including a naval and air quarantine on the shipment of all offensive military equipment to Cuba. He further announced that he was asking for an urgent meeting of the U.N. Security Council to consider measures to end the Soviet threat.

This time, Adlai Stevenson had been a participant in the White House discussions. He had already prepared his speech for delivery in the Security Council and had it approved by the president. Stevenson had insisted that the United States should take no military action until every peaceful means had been tried to remove the missile threat. The ambassador had an ally in Attorney General Robert Kennedy, who is quoted by Theodore Sorensen as saying that a sudden air strike at dawn on Sunday without warning would be "a Pearl Harbor in reverse and it would blacken the name of the United States in the pages of history as a great power who attacked a small neighbor."

As soon as President Kennedy concluded his broadcast, Ambassador Stevenson sent his request for a Security Council meeting to the council president for the month, who happened to be Ambassador Zorin of the Soviet Union. Stevenson also submitted a draft resolution calling for the immediate dismantling of the Soviet missiles and their prompt removal from Cuba under U.N. obser-vation. Stevenson led off the debate as the drama shifted to New York. With his usual eloquence, he presented the U.S. demands and was able to announce that the OAS had just unanimously adopted a resolution in Washington em-powering OAS member states to take all measures individually and collectively, including the use of armed forces, which they may deem necessary." Stevenson concluded with these words: "Since the end of the second world war, there has been no threat to the vision of peace so profound, no challenge to the world of the charter so fateful. The hopes of the world are concentrated in this room."[7]

When Stevenson finished, Zorin took the floor to challenge the right of the United States to "attack vessels of other states on the high seas" and to "dictate to Cuba what policy it must pursue . . . and what weapons it may possess." He insisted that Soviet aid to Cuba was for defensive purposes only. He then submitted his own resolution condemning "the actions of the government of the United States . . . aimed at violating the United Nations charter and in-creasing the threat of war." The representative of Cuba also spoke, calling the quarantine an "act of war."

After these opening remarks, the situation seemed to be stalled. There was no movement at the United Nations the following day. Soviet ships had not turned back, but still there had been no confrontation at sea.

It was then, on October 24, that Secretary General U Thant intervened at the urging of "a large number of member governments." Without waiting for the outcome of the Security Council debate, Thant dispatched an urgent appeal to Khrushchev and Kennedy in which he asked them to "refrain from any action which may aggravate the situation and bring with it the risk of war." He proposed specifically "the voluntary suspension of all arms shipments to Cuba and also the voluntary suspension of the quarantine measures involving the search of ships bound for Cuba." He added; "I believe such voluntary suspensions for a period of two to three weeks will greatly ease the situation and give time to the parties concerned to meet and discuss with a view to finding a peaceful solution of the problem."

In a statement to the Security Council, Thant reported his action and read the text of his message. "Today," he said, "the United Nations faces a moment of grave responsibility. . . . If today the United Nations should prove itself in-effective, it may have proved so for all time." In retrospect, this seems to be somewhat melodramatic, but it did not seem so at the time. The atmosphere at the United Nations had never been more apprehensive. "During the seventeen years that have passed since the end of the second world war," the secretary-general declared, "there has never been a more dangerous or closer confrontation of the major powers. . . . I hope that at this moment, not only in the Council chamber but in the world outside, good sense and understanding will be placed above the anger of the moment or the pride of nations."

While Thant was engaged in his behind-the-scenes exchange of messages with Kennedy and Khrushchev, the Security Council continued the debate. On

Thursday, October 25, Adlai Stevenson made one of his most dramatic and widely quoted speeches. This was in response to an intervention by the Soviet ambassador, who continued to insist that there was no evidence of Soviet offensive missiles in Cuba.

"Let me say something to you, Mr. Ambassador," Stevenson said. "We do have the evidence. We have it and it is clear and incontrovertible. And let me say something else—Those weapons have to be taken out of Cuba. . . . The other day, Mr. Zorin, I remind you that you did not deny the existence of those weapons. Instead, we heard that they had suddenly become defensive weapons. But today again, if I heard you correctly, with another fine flood of rhetorical scorn, you now say they do not exist, or that we haven't proved they exist. All right, Sir, let me ask you one simple question: do you, Ambassador Zorin, deny that the USSR has placed and is placing medium and intermediate-range missiles and sites in Cuba? Yes or no? Don't wait for the translation." (There was no need to wait for the translation, since all Security Council proceedings are also heard in simultaneous translations.)

Zorin declined to answer. "I am not in an American court of law," he said, "and therefore do not wish to answer a question put to me in the manner of a prosecuting counsel. You will receive your answer in due course in my capacity as representative of the Soviet Union."

Stevenson resumed the attack. "You are in the courtroom of world opinion," he declared. "You have denied they exist and I want to know if I have understood you correctly. I am prepared to wait for my answer until hell freezes over, if that is your decision. And I am prepared to present the evidence in this room, now." He then turned to his aides and directed them to set up an easel in the back of the room, where they proceeded to display a number of greatly enlarged photographs one after another showing the missile sites and missiles.

Although this confrontation was certainly dramatic, it was to have little bearing on the situation, as it turned out. On October 26, Thant received Khrushchev's message, stating "We . . . accept your proposal, and have ordered the masters of Soviet vessels bound for Cuba but not yet within the area of American warships' piratical activities to stay out of the interception area, as you recommended." The same day Kennedy informed the secretary-general that "if the Soviet government accepts and abides by your request . . . you may be assured that this government will accept and abide by your request that our vessels in the Caribbean will do everything possible to avoid direct confrontation with Soviet ships in the next few days in order to minimize the risk of any untoward incident."[8]

This still left the question of dismantling the Cuban missile sites and removing the missiles. The Security Council left this to be negotiated by Ambassador Stevenson and Soviet Deputy Foreign Minister Vassily V. Kuznetsov—which they proceeded to do. Kuznetsov, who was one of the most charismatic of the Soviet diplomats, had been sent to supercede the fiery Zorin after the Stevenson–Zorin clash. The forgotten element in all this was Fidel Castro. The representatives of the United States and the Soviet Union agreed to permit U.N. inspection to verify the removal of the missiles, but nobody bothered to ask Castro for his consent. When the Cuban leader expressed a willingness to receive Thant, the secretary-general assumed not only that Castro had been consulted, but that he had agreed to the inspection plan.

Actually Castro had told Thant that, "should you consider it useful in the cause of peace, our government would be glad to receive you in our country as secretary-general of the United Nations with a view to direct discussions on the present crisis." In the same letter, the Cuban leader rejected "the presumption of the United States to determine . . . what kind of arms we consider appropriate for our defense." He said that Cuba would do whatever it was asked to do except "to renounce the rights which belong to every sovereign state."

Thant replied on October 28, accepting the invitation and expressing the hope that "a solution would be reached by which the principle of respect for the sovereignty of Cuba would be assured and it may also be possible for action to be taken which would reassure other countries which have felt themselves threatened by recent developments in Cuba." What Thant had in mind was U.N. inspection of the missile withdrawal. In a letter to Khrushchev, Thant reported that he planned to visit Cuba at the invitation of Castro and that he would discuss the "modalities of verification by United Nations observers to which you have so readily agreed."

Two days later, prepared to set up inspection machinery, the secretary-general flew to Havana. He was accompanied by several aides who had brought along equipment to establish some sort of U.N. observation post. Much to Thant's surprise and embarrassment, Castro flatly rejected any outside inspection and refused to discuss it. Thant left the next day with his aides and their equipment. In a statement at the New York airport, he made no mention of Castro's rebuff. Instead, he said, "During my stay in Havana I was reliably informed that the dismantling of the missiles and their installations was already in progress and that this process should be completed by Friday. Thereafter there would come their shipment and return to the Soviet Union, arrangements for which are understood to be at hand." After Thant's return to New York, Cuba's position was spelled out in a letter to the secretary-general in which Castro declared, "We have given you—and have also given publicly and repeatedly—our refusal to allow unilateral inspection by anybody, national or international, on Cuban territory."

This was all academic, anyway. As far as the United States and the Soviet Union were concerned, the matter had been concluded. Stevenson and Kuznetsov finally wound up their two months of negotiations early in January 1963. In a joint letter to Thant, they expressed their appreciation for his efforts and declared that "in view of the degree of understanding reached between them on the settlement of the crisis and the extent of progress in the implementation of this understanding, it is not necessary for this item to occupy further the attention of the Security Council at this time."[9]

The Soviets had begun dismantling the missile installations on October 28, even before Stevenson and Kuznetsov started their discussions. Some sort of agreement must have been reached secretly as a basis for the Soviet action. Some details of the tense behind-the-scenes maneuvering have since come to light through publication of the Kennedy papers and in a letter from Dean Rusk to James G. Blight made public in March 1988. Blight is executive director of the Center for International Affairs at Harvard University. Among other things, it was disclosed that Robert Kennedy had offered a three-point ultimatum to the Soviet Union through Ambassador Anatoly Dobrynin. Under this proposal, the Soviet missiles would be withdrawn from Cuba, the United States would agree not to invade Cuba and the United States would pull its Jupiter missiles out of Turkey according to previous plans—but not as part of any deal with the Soviets. The Soviet Union had wanted an explicit trade on the withdrawal of the Jupiter missiles, but the United States had refused. Dean Rusk disclosed that President Kennedy had been prepared to make a concession on the trade-off, but this proved to be unnecessary when the Soviets agreed to accept Robert Kennedy's terms. According to the Rusk letter, Rusk himself had dictated to Andrew W. Cordier—executive assistant to U Thant—a statement that would be made by the secretary-general proposing the removal of both the Jupiter missiles and the Soviet missiles in Cuba. The statement, Rusk said, was to be put in the hands of Thant only after a further signal from Washington. He added, "That step was never taken and the statement I furnished to Mr. Cordier has never seen the light of day. So far as I know, President Kennedy, Andrew Cordier and I were the only ones who knew of this particular step."

In an interview with David Surek that was published in the *Saturday Evening Post* on September 21, 1963, Thant reiterated his earlier statement that the Cuban crisis represented the most dangerous confrontation since World War II. No doubt, his personal intervention was a major factor in easing the tension— if only because his appeal to the two superpowers provided an opportunity for them to back down without loss of face. He modestly declined to claim credit, except to state that "the debate in the United Nations and the intervention which I felt it necessary to undertake are generally recognized as having contributed to reduce the crisis at its critical point." The main lesson of the Cuban crisis, Thant said, was two-fold:

(a) that the United Nations is not just a debating society, but can play a crucial role in the solution of important issues; and (b) that some give and take on the part of all concerned is required to solve major issues. It was the spirit of willingness to give and take on the part of all the parties concerned and the usefulness of the United Nations as a mediator that made it possible in the first instance to avert the confrontation and in due course to ease the crisis itself.

16

West Irian, Yemen, and Malaysia

From the beginning of his administration, U Thant demonstrated that he would be an activist secretary-general, in the sense that he used his office as an agency for settling disputes—often without waiting for a directive from the Security Council or the General Assembly. The Congo situation was already critical when he assumed office, and the Cuban missile crisis was on the horizon; but even in this period (1961–64), a number of lesser known disputes were also threatening the peace. One of these was a border dispute between Thailand and Cambodia; another was a territorial dispute between Indonesia and the Netherlands; another was a controversy over the future of North Borneo (Sabah) and Sarawak; and a fourth was developing out of a civil war in Yemen. Thant became involved in all of these. His role varied from preventive diplomacy to intervention with peace-keeping forces, but it is significant in that it was innovative and that it demonstrated the flexibility of the United Nations in dealing with potentially explosive situations. Each of these cases was similar in two respects: In each instance the parties concerned requested the intervention of the secretary-general; and in each instance the parties concerned paid the costs.

When the Republic of Indonesia attained independence in 1949, one of the questions left unsettled was the future of West New Guinea—or West Irian, as it was called by Indonesia. This territory was at the eastern extremity of the 3,125-mile string of islands in the Netherlands East Indies. The transfer agreement provided that the future of West Irian would be determined within a year through negotiations between Indonesia and the Netherlands. No such agreement was reached, however; and the issue continued for the next decade as a source of continuous friction between the two governments.

Two proposals advanced by the Netherlands were turned down: (1) that sovereignty be invested in a short-lived Netherlands–Indonesian Union; and (2) that the issue be submitted to the International Court of Justice. Meanwhile, Indonesia turned to the U.N. General Assembly for help. It appealed to the assembly in 1954, 1955, and 1957. Each time it failed to obtain a two-thirds majority for its resolutions, which urged settlement through negotiations and assumed that sovereignty had already passed to Indonesia. The situation became critical in December 1961. President Achmed Sukarno—losing patience—ordered a total mobilization of his armed forces and declared that he was prepared to take the territory by force.

U Thant, who had been in office as acting secretary-general for only a month, decided to make a personal effort to head off the threat of violence. On December 19 he dispatched messages to the leaders of the two countries in which he expressed deep concern and urged a peaceful solution. The situation became urgent in mid-January when Dutch and Indonesian naval vessels clashed off the shores of the disputed territory. Thant sent off new appeals, and at the same time launched private talks with the U.N. representatives of the two countries. Meanwhile, he asked the Netherlands to release the Indonesians who had been taken prisoner during the naval clash—as a humanitarian gesture "which might help ease tension." Prime Minister Jan de Quay promptly agreed. He also accepted a proposal by the acting secretary-general that a U.N. representative be sent to West Irian to arrange for the release and repatriation of the prisoners.[1]

At a press conference on March 27, 1962, Thant disclosed that he had been engaged in secret talks since the middle of January with the U.N. representatives of the two governments. "About two weeks ago," he said, "it was agreed that the discussions would be staged in two phases: the first phase would be secret and informal and the second would be formal. It was also agreed that for the first phase, in order to avoid publicity and in order to avoid unnecessary speculation, somebody outside the United Nations should offer his good offices. With my knowledge and consent these preliminary talks took place outside New York in the presence of Mr. Ellsworth Bunker." Bunker—an experienced U.S. diplomat—had volunteered his services, as he had in other similar situations.

It was learned later that the talks were taking place at Camp David in Maryland. They were interrupted from time to time as the participants required instructions from their respective governments.

On April 24 Thant disclosed that Bunker had submitted his own formula for a settlement and that he was awaiting the reaction of the Dutch and Indonesian governments. Thant said that he was fully aware of the substance of the formula, but that he had not given Bunker his reaction because, "if that particular formula happens to be unacceptable to one party or the other, it might damage the office of the secretary-general." He went on to say that, if the formula did prove acceptable, he would have to ask for a special meeting of the General Assembly to authorize the implementation of the agreement.

Thant followed the negotiations closely and intervened personally when they broke down in May. He sent messages to both governments in which he urged "the immediate ending of all hostilities" so that negotiations might be resumed under the most favorable conditions.[2]

It was not until June 20 that the Netherlands and Indonesia accepted Bunker's proposals in principle, and it was not until August 15 that the agreement was finalized. The agreement called for a phased transfer of the West Irian territory from the Netherlands to Indonesia, with the United Nations taking over administration of the territory for the first stage and an eventual plebiscite before 1969 to permit the people to decide their own future. The formula was approved by the General Assembly on September 21 by 89 votes to none, with 14 abstentions.[3]

The settlement was significant for several reasons. It was the first time that a territory had been placed under the direct administration of the United Nations. The territory was administered by a newly created unit called the United Nations Temporary Executive Authority, headed by Dr. Djalal Abdoh and staffed by 32 international civil servants. A detachment of Pakistani troops under U.N. command helped the administration to maintain law and order. The U.N. administration took over responsibility on September 28, 1962, and carried on until May 1, 1963, when it transferred authority to Indonesia.[4]

The operation was hailed as an important success, but it had one embarrassing aspect. Once Indonesia took over the administration of the territory, it decided that it would not conduct the agreed plebiscite. Such a plebiscite has never been held.

The fall of 1962 was a busy time for the acting secretary-general. The major concern was the Cuban missile crisis. Another event during that period was Thant's appointment of a personal representative to Thailand and Cambodia— at the request of the two governments—to help solve their border dispute. The United Nations had first become involved in this problem in 1958 after Thailand occupied the temple of Preah Vinear, which Cambodia regarded as part of its territory. At the request of the two governments, Dag Hammarskjöld had designated Johan Bech-Friis as his special representative. Bech-Friis visited Cambodia and Thailand in January and February 1959; and during his visit, the two governments agreed to reestablish normal diplomatic relations. On July 15, 1962, the International Court of Justice ruled by a vote of nine to three that the temple was situated on Cambodian territory and that Thailand should withdraw any forces stationed there. This opened the whole controversy once more. Tension increased, and again the two countries asked the United Nations for assistance in settling the dispute. U Thant informed the Security Council that he was sending Nils G. Gussing to the area as his personal representative.

Gussing—like Bech-Friis—was a Swede. He served from October 1962 until the end of 1964, when the two governments agreed on the termination of his mission. By that time the governments had resumed friendly relations.[5]

It was also in the fall of 1962 that Secretary-General Thant quietly intervened in the Yemen civil war, which had developed into an international struggle between the United Arab Republic and Saudi Arabia. The UAR was backing the new republican government in Yemen, headed by Colonel Abdullah el-Sallal; and Saudi Arabia was supporting the royalists, who had rallied around the deposed Imam Badr. Thant's role was revealed by him in a report to the Security Council on April 29, 1963. He reported that he had been carrying on consultations with the U.N. representatives of Yemen, Saudi Arabia, and the UAR since the previous October and that he had sent Under Secretary Ralph Bunche to Yemen and the UAR in late February and early March on a fact-finding mission. At the same time, Ellsworth Bunker was on a similar diplomatic mission under the auspices of the U.S. government, and the results of his talks had been reported to Thant. These initiatives were undertaken with the consent of the three countries concerned, without any directive or authorization by the Security Council. By the time Thant made his April 29 report, he had received a separate communications from the three governments confirming their acceptance of identical terms of disengagement and agreeing to have impartial observers check on the implementation of the disengagement, which included some 125,000 UAR troops.[6]

Thant then informed the Security Council that he had appointed Major General Carl von Horn, chief of staff of the U.N. Truce Supervision Organization in Palestine (UNTSO), to work out the modalities and make recommendations as to the size of the observation force needed. On May 27 Thant reported that not more than 200 men would be required; and in another report on June 7 he told the council that the cost would be borne by Saudi Arabia and the UAR.

It was at this stage that the Soviet Union requested a meeting of the Security Council. The Soviet representative, Nikolai T. Federenko, said that the reports submitted by the secretary-general contained proposals on which only the Security Council could make decisions. Although Thant had not asked for council authorization, he had foreseen the possible need for such action. In a press conference on May 3 he had said that the council might perhaps be involved in reaching a final decision—which would depend "on the nature of the United Nations operations based on General von Horn's report." When the Security Council met on June 10 Thant did not object to council action, but stressed the urgency of the situation. At the conclusion of the two-day debate, the council adopted a resolution "noting with satisfaction" the initiative taken by the secretary-general and formally requesting him to go ahead with the formation of the proposed observation mission. The vote was ten to zero, with the Soviet Union abstaining.[7]

The United Nations Observation Mission in Yemen (UNYOM) began its operation on July 4, 1963. It was a small force with only 200 men, and its mandate was for only four months. Everything went against it from the start. The parties to the disengagement agreement failed to honor it. The UAR made only token withdrawals of its troops, and even replaced some of those it had withdrawn. Saudi Arabia continued to assist the royalists, with men and weapons.[8]

The mission had barely begun when word leaked out that von Horn was engaged in a serious controversy with U.N. headquarters in New York over his insistence on additional logistical support, particularly transport planes to airlift personnel and supplies. The dispute led to the resignation of von Horn on August 20 and to a subsequent press conference in which he attacked the United Nations and asserted that headquarters officials had "foggy ideas about reality." In a book published in 1966, General von Horn said that the blowup was precipitated by a message from him advising headquarters that the U.N. reconnaissance squadron would have to be withdrawn from Yemen unless he received an additional Caribou plane within the next few days. He said that the tone of the reply from New York was "dictatorial." "I was advised in so many words," he said, "to stop bellyaching and to get on with my job." He replied with a private message to Thant—"telling him exactly what I thought about the administrative failure that was strangling the mission." Thant told von Horn that his "somewhat offensive remarks" were unwarranted and told him to tighten up his own administrative procedures. That was when von Horn sent in his resignation.[9]

The intensity of the backstage drama was not generally known at the time, nor was it fully disclosed in the secretary-general's report on von Horn's resignation. At a press conference on September 12 Thant said headquarters had met all of von Horn's requests that had been considered reasonable, but had not been able to comply with all of them because the Yemen operation had to be confined within the financial resources available.[10]

The matter ended with General von Horn withdrawing his resignation, and Thant rejecting the withdrawal. "Since I had given sufficient thought to the matter," Thant said, "it became my painful duty not to be able to accept his withdrawal." It may be recalled that von Horn had been removed earlier as commander of the U.N. Congo Force for alleged mismanagement, but had been reassigned as commander of UNTSO.

The Yemen Mission was terminated on September 4, 1964, after the UAR and Saudi Arabia informed the United Nations that they were not prepared to continue paying for the operation and that they had no objection to its termination. Thant agreed that there was not much justification for continuing the mission, in view of the situation. He said that special representative, Pier Spinelli of Italy, had met with UAR and Saudi officials in August and had found no reason for encouragement. In a report to the Security Council, Thant said that the mission had observed "only a disappointing measure of disengagement." He added that "the hoped-for direct high level discussions between Saudi Arabia and the United Arab Republic with a view toward further progress toward disengagement had not taken place and there is no certainty that they will."

More than 150,000 people died during the fighting, before the conflict ended. There was a bloodless coup in 1967, and another in 1974. The People's Democratic Republic of Yemen and the Yemen Arab Republic went to war with each other in 1979, but the conflict was ended quickly by an agreement sponsored by the Arab League, which called for unification of the two countries. The unification, however, did not take place; and the two countries continued as separate entities.

On August 31, 1957, the Federation of Malaya attained full independence within the British Commonwealth. Four years later the prime minister of the new country proposed the formation of an expanded federation to consist of the Federation of Malaya and North Borneo, Sarawak, and Singapore. Britain—as the administering power of North Borneo, Sarawak, and Singapore—agreed in principle that the expanded nation, which was to be known as the Federation of Malaysia, should be established by August 31, 1963. The proposal ran into trouble, however, when both Indonesia and the Philippines tried to block its implementation.

The Philippines challenged the British sovereignty over North Borneo (Sabah), which had belonged to the Filipino Sultan of Sulu until 1878. President Sukarno of Indonesia denounced the proposed federation as a "neo-colonial concept." He met with President Diosdado Macapagal of the Philippines and Prime Minister Abdul Rahman of Malaya in Manila on July 30, 1963, to seek a compromise. Six days later they sent a cable to U Thant—asking him to dispatch a mission to North Borneo and Sarawak to ascertain whether or not the people of those territories wanted to join the federation. On August 8, Thant agreed to undertake the mission, on the condition that the British must consent. He stipulated that his conclusions would not be subject to ratification by any of the governments concerned, even though they would be permitted to observe the survey.

The terms were accepted. Laurence V. Michelmore, a member of the U.N. Secretariat, was appointed to head an eight-member team, which arrived in the territories on August 16. It quickly completed its survey and departed on September 5. The secretary-general's conclusions, which were made public on September 14, stated that the people of both North Borneo and Sarawak were in favor of joining the proposed Federation of Malaysia. Two days later the federation was proclaimed. The matter was not closed, however. Both Indonesia and the Philippines expressed strong reservations on the findings of the U.N. mission.[11]

(Singapore—incidentally—had already voted in 1962 in favor of federation. Later on, in 1965, it withdrew because of friction between the Chinese and Malay residents, and became an independent state.)

The situation deteriorated during the weeks following federation until it developed into actual armed conflict between Malaysian forces and infiltrators from Indonesia. The Philippines broke relations with Malaysia more gently, but Indonesia cut off all communications and trade links and openly announced a policy of military confrontation. It sent guerrilla troops into North Borneo and mobilized its naval forces in Borneo waters. Open warfare appeared certain to erupt; but the conflict remained limited to intermittent armed clashes, without any formal declaration of war. Malaysia brought the situation before the Security Council in September 1964, with charges of Indonesian aggression. The council debated the question during a number of meetings, but was unable to agree on a resolution.

In his annual report issued on November 20, 1964, Secretary-general U Thant said,

Tension in the area . . . continues to be a source of concern to me. I wish to express the hope that the endeavors of statesmen in the area to solve this difficult question peacefully will be steadfastly continued and that the leaders of the countries involved will spare no effort to bring about a peaceful settlement of their differences.

Unfortunately, the peace efforts did not succeed. On the last day of 1964, the permanent representative of Indonesia informed the secretary-general that his country was going to withdraw from the United Nations if the Federation of Malaysia were seated as a member of the Security Council. Thant sent a personal appeal to President Sukarno immediately, but he did not touch on the substance of Indonesia's complaint. The condition laid down by Sukarno had, in fact, left no room for reconsideration. The General Assembly had already agreed without objection that, in accordance with a 1963 understanding, Malaysia and Czechoslovakia would split the two-year term, with Malaysia serving the second year. Malaysia took its seat in the council on January 7, 1965.[12]

The formal notification of Indonesia's withdrawal was received by Thant on January 20. A letter from Indonesia's foreign minister, Dr. Roden Subandrio, declared that Malaysia had been pushed into the United Nations on September 17, 1963, by a deliberate avoidance of voting procedures, although Indonesia and some other "anti-colonial" countries had opposed the action as a "maneuver of neo-colonial powers." Malaysia contended that no vote was needed for the admission of the expanded federation since it was already a member of the United Nations as the Federation of Malaya. Subandrio declared that Malaysia's selection as a member of the Security Council was the result of another colonial maneuver. Indonesia had remained silent at the time, he said, because it did not wish to obstruct the work of the United Nations at a time when it was faced with a possible breakdown over Article 19 (which will be discussed in Chapter 19).

Thant did not reply to the Indonesian letter until February 26, after a careful legal study of the situation and consultation with member states. There were new questions raised here since it was the first time that a member nation had withdrawn from the United Nations. Although there was no express provision in the charter for withdrawal of members, those who drafted it had foreseen such a possibility and had stated in a formal declaration that it was not the purpose of the organization to compel a member "to continue its cooperation" in the United Nations if that member "because of exceptional circumstances" desired to withdraw. Thant concluded that he had no choice but to implement Indonesia's decision.

Many considered Indonesia's action to be a serious blow to U.N. prestige, especially as the organization was preparing to observe its twentieth anniversary. However, the withdrawal was accepted without any official acknowledgment by either the General Assembly or the Security Council. In the introduction to his annual report issued on September 20, 1965, Thant noted the concern over Sukarno's decision. "Inevitably," he said, "there were comparisons with the history of the League of Nations, but subsequent events have shown that some of those gloomy prognostications reflected undue pessimism. I sincerely hope that Indonesia's withdrawal is only a temporary phase and that, before long, Indonesia will find that its long-term interests can be best served by resuming its membership." His hope was fulfilled on September 19, 1966, when—without fanfare—Indonesia resumed its place in the United Nations after Sukarno was ousted by a military coup.

17

Vietnam and the United Nations' Hands-off Policy

The early 1950s were notable years for the United Nations not only because of the organization's involvement in the Korean War, but because of developments in French Indochina that would widen the East–West schism and eventually raise serious questions as to the United Nations' competence in the field of peace-keeping. It was evident by 1950 that Cambodia, Laos, and Vietnam—the components of French Indochina—would become part of the decolonization explosion that followed the end of World War II. However, it was not foreseen that the attainment of independence by the three states would almost immediately open a new Cold War front in Southeast Asia, and trigger three decades of bloodshed.

The main problem lay in Vietnam, where the pro-French government headed by Prince Bao Dai was being challenged by Ho Chi Minh—whose Vietminh forces occupied the northern segment of the country. Ho was already in revolt against France in January 1950 when the French National Assembly ratified the Elysée Agreements accepting Vietnam, Laos, and Cambodia as independent states within the French Union. And, as the conflict continued, it was the French army that had to do the fighting for the Bao Dai regime since the new government was not able to defend itself. On the other hand, Ho was receiving military support from the Soviet Union and the People's Republic of China. This was clearly more than a civil war. Its international character became even more obvious as the United States began providing military assistance to the hard-pressed French forces. By the end of 1952 the United States was contributing one-third of the costs of the French campaign. It was generally recognized by then that the U.S. participation was part of the Truman Doctrine, whose objective was to stop the expansion of communism. It seemed to be a losing battle, however. By the end of 1953 France was showing signs of withdrawing from the costly and politically unpopular war. Finally, facing a crushing defeat at Dien Bien Phu after a long and costly siege, France decided that the time had come to seek a negotiated armistice. However, there was no inclination to take the problem before the United Nations, since none of the participants in the conflict except France was a member of the organization—and France had never had much faith in it. Certainly neither Peking nor Hanoi would accept any U.N. role. Recognizing this situation, the foreign ministers of France, Britain, the United States, and the Soviet Union met in Berlin in February 1954 to consider the problem. It was agreed that the best course was to arrange a conference that would bring all the parties together face to face to consider armistice terms.

Actually, the conference that began in Geneva on April 26, 1954, was a two-tiered meeting; one part devoted to seeking the reunification of Korea, and the other attempting to end the fighting in Vietnam. The meetings were held at the Palais des Nations—the European headquarters of the United Nations— and were staffed by U.N. personnel, but were completely independent of the world organization and outside its jurisdiction. The Korean problem had been dealt with by the United Nations since 1948, but both the Panmunjom armistice negotiations and the Geneva unification discussions were seen by most observers as bypassing the organization. Secretary-general Hammarskjöld was sensitive on this subject. He insisted that the Geneva Conference was in the U.N. "orbit," although not actually under U.N. jurisdiction. "I feel solidly that we are in the picture," he said. He added, however, that "if the habit developed to treat major issues outside the United Nations . . . it would build up an entirely false view in people's minds concerning the role of the United Nations." None of the participating countries were overly concerned about the absence of a U.N. role. The agreed format was accepted as the only realistic way to bring together all the parties to the conflict, including the nonmembers of the United Nations.

After weeks of wrangling, a cease-fire agreement was signed on July 21; it divided Vietnam along the 17th parallel—with North Vietnam getting an area of 62,000 square miles and a population of 13 million, and South Vietnam getting an area of 65,000 square miles and 12 million people. The agreement further provided for elections to determine the future of the divided country. Neither South Vietnam nor the United States signed the agreement. The situation remained relatively quiet until 1956, when the communist Vietcong began guerrilla operations in the south. This was the beginning of what was generally known as the Vietnam War.

This conflict—the largest and most costly in money and lives since World War II—never became a problem for the United Nations, in the usual sense of the word. It was a problem in that it cast a shadow over other U.N. activities, and in the sense that the organization's credibility was damaged; but, technically, the United Nations was never "seized" with the question, since none of the participants or other U.N. members ever asked to have the Vietnam conflict placed on the agenda of either the Security Council or the General Assembly. It has been said that the United Nations stood by with folded arms and did nothing to end the fighting in Vietnam. U.S. Ambassador Henry Cabot Lodge said that "the U.N. did nothing about Vietnam partly because it lacked the tools, but fundamentally because it lacked the will."[1]

Secretary-general U Thant frankly acknowledged that the organization was not competent to deal with an East–West conflict such as this, even if any of the members had wanted to try. When U Thant became acting secretary-general on November 3, 1961, the Vietnam situation had begun to cause some concern because of the increasing role of the United States. However, the conflict was basically still a Vietnamese affair, with only 2,000 U.S. military personnel in the country (and these not combat troops). Thant's first press conference held a month after he took office, was devoted mainly to the Congo problem and to U.N. finances. It was only at the end of the conference that a correspondent asked whether the United Nations could do anything about "the tense situation in Southeast Asia, particularly in Laos and Vietnam." Thant replied briefly that the subject had not been brought before the General Assembly, and "I do not know whether it will ever come up. It is up to any member state to bring it to the attention of the assembly or the Security Council as it deems fit." This never happened.[2]

Despite the absence of formal U.N. involvement, it is safe to say that no one individual played a more active role from 1964 through 1968 than U Thant in seeking a way to end the Vietnam conflict. For him, it was a thankless and frustrating experience. His interventions were seldom welcomed by any of the parties. They were frequently resented. The main catch was that all the parties were counting on a military victory to solve the problem, and no one was ready for a negotiated solution. This was not a good atmosphere for a peace-maker; and, on top of that, Thant was fully aware of his limitations as a mediator on the Vietnam problem. He felt that Washington did not trust him because of his outspoken criticism of U.S. policy. President Lyndon B. Johnson and Secretary of State Dean Rusk had made it clear that they regarded him as a meddler. On the other hand, neither North Vietnam nor the People's Republic of China would deal with the United Nations or with him as secretary-general. His contacts with them had to be in a nonofficial capacity as a fellow Asian. His peace efforts were uphill all the way.

His first intervention in the Vietnam situation was on behalf of Buddhists who allegedly were being mistreated by the Catholic Ngo Dinh Diem government. The secretary-general—himself a devout Buddhist—disclosed at a news conference on June 28, 1963, that he had taken "certain steps, very discretely, to see that the alleged discriminations be remedied." On August 31, he made a formal appeal to President Diem on the subject. This was during the period when Buddhist monks were publicly burning themselves to death in protest against government measures. Thant had never made any secret of his feelings

toward Diem; but he told a news conference on September 12 that he had asked
Adlai Stevenson to see if the Kennedy administration could do something to
remedy the chaotic situation in South Vietnam, which—he declared—was completely lacking in "the great virtues of democracy." Events were moving fast in
Vietnam, however. On November 1—just three weeks before John F. Kennedy
was assassinated—the Diem regime was overthrown by a military coup; and both
Diem and his brother, Ngo Dinh Nhu, were killed. The situation became really
chaotic as one coup followed another, with a succession of military leaders
taking over for brief periods. On June 12, 1965, a National Leadership Committee headed by Major General Nguyen Van Thieu took control; and Nguyen
Cao Ky, commander of the air force, became premier. Ky's appointment sparked
even more unrest among the Buddhists. By the spring of 1966, their protests
and demonstrations in the vicinity of Hue and Da Nang came close to outright
rebellion.

As early as the spring of 1964, Thant had begun his peace efforts. At a news
conference in Paris on April 24 of that year, he said that the Vietnam problem
"is not essentially military: it is political and, therefore, political and diplomatic
means alone can solve it." He also expressed doubts once more as to the United
Nations' competence to deal with the situation. Instead, he proposed that the
Geneva Conference be reconvened. This, however, did not find acceptance
among any of the concerned parties. Adlai Stevenson, for example, declared
in the Security Council on May 21 that there was no need for another Geneva
Conference. Such a conference, he said, "if it reached any agreement at all,
would prove no more effective than the agreements we have already."[3]

In August of 1964 Thant again attempted to bring the parties together for
private talks; but President Lyndon Johnson was cool to the idea, and Ambassador Stevenson advised the secretary-general to wait until after the November
elections.

Early in January 1965, Stevenson suggested privately to Thant that he go
ahead and arrange a place for a meeting. The secretary-general immediately
went to the Burmese ambassador, James Barrington, and asked him to approach
the Burmese government on the possibility of playing host to private peace talks.
The Burmese government readily agreed to arrange facilities in Rangoon if both
sides agreed. Thant notified Stevenson that a site had been arranged. He was
stunned on January 30 when Stevenson advised him that the United States
would not send a representative to Rangoon after all, because it feared that—
if news of such a meeting were to leak out—the effect would be demoralizing
to the South Vietnam government. Shortly before his death in July 1965, Adlai
Stevenson was quoted as telling Eric Severeid in an interview that Secretary of
Defense Robert McNamara was responsible for this U.S. decision. Stevenson
also reported that Thant was furious over the surprise rebuff. Different versions
of the incident continued to surface from time to time.[4]

In June 1967 Secretary of State Rusk poked fun at the Thant peace effort in what was supposed to be an off-the-record talk with a group of U.S. educators. "You've heard about the end of '65 beginning of '66 business when peace was about to break out in Rangoon," he said. "The only contact there was a Russian member of the secretariat. During that period I had several long talks with Mr. Gromyko. So it is not surprising that I would consider Mr. Gromyko more relevant than anything that came from a relatively junior member of the secretariat. In any event, Hanoi denied there was ever any such contact and other denials came into the picture." This version reflected the U.S. feeling at that time that Thant was not to be trusted. The secretary-general had, in fact, conferred with Andrei Gromyko on New York on November 29, 1964; and the Soviet foreign minister had verified the report that Hanoi was interested in establishing contact with the United States. The "Russian" whom Rusk referred to as a junior member of the Secretariat was Vladimir Suslov, under secretary for political and security affairs—the highest rank in the Secretariat next to the secretary-general himself.

The public had no inkling of these behind-the-scenes exchanges, and there is reason to believe that not even President Johnson was aware of the Rangoon initiative. White House Spokesman Bill D. Moyers said that he could find no evidence that the matter had come to the attention of the president. Johnson himself told Thant in October 1966 that he had never been informed of the Rangoon aspect of the secretary-general's efforts, and declared that the arrangement had been aborted without his knowledge. Several authoritative accounts published since that time indicate that Stevenson may have approached Thant on the proposed arrangements without authorization from Washington.

By then, the war was accelerating rapidly. The South Vietnamese army was being reinforced by combat units of the U.S. army and marine corps. The Vietcong were getting increasing help from North Vietnam, Red China, and the Soviet Union. In February 1965 the U.S. air force began bombing strategic targets in North Vietnam. By mid–1966 more than 250,000 U.S. troops were in South Vietnam and were already engaged in search-and-destroy operations. Thant disclosed at a news conference on February 24, 1965, that he had initiated private efforts to bring about a negotiated peace. He said he had "presented concrete ideas and proposals" to some of the parties directly concerned in the conflict, including the United States.[5]

Although the White House spokesman—George Reedy—denied at the time that the secretary-general had made any proposals to the United States, President Johnson gave a different version in his memoirs. Johnson said that Thant came to the White House on February 21—three days before the news conference— and reported receiving indications from unofficial sources that the North Vietnamese would be willing to begin talks if the United States halted the bombing of North Vietnam. Johnson commented that Thant's report was "interesting but hardly conclusive."[6]

This was neither the first time nor the last that the secretary-general's efforts were rebuffed; and he plainly showed his impatience when he told correspondents that, if the U.S. people only knew the facts, they would agree with him that further bloodshed was unnecessary.

As the war accelerated, more and more of the public—and especially the media—asked why the United Nations was doing nothing. Thant had insisted from the beginning that this was not a problem for the United Nations. He explained his reasons at length during a news conference on April 5, 1966. Thant said,

I have been consistently opposed to Security Council intervention in the Vietnam question for reasons which you know. One of these reasons is that in 1954 the parties directly involved in the conflict decided that the matter should be brought to Geneva outside the framework of the United Nations because of the simple fact that only France, of all the participants, was a member of the United Nations. The same consideration should apply today; only one, the United States, is a member of the United Nations. . . . But it is not only for the reason that Hanoi is not a member of the United Nations or that Peking is not a member of the United Nations. . . . Another reason from the point of view of Peking—rightly or wrongly—Peking feels, as you all know, that in the Security Council there is a usurper. . . . Of course, my attitude regarding Security Council involvement is guided by one single consideration. If the council has to take action on any dispute, the first prerequisite is that it must be in a position to hear both sides of the question; this is a must. . . . If both sides were to come and plead their respective cases before the Security Council, I will be the first to advocate immediate Security Council involvement. But, as you know, this is not the case. There are no prospects of Peking or Hanoi coming to the council because of the reasons I have stated.[7]

Despite explanations such as this, it was difficult for the public to accept the idea that a peace-keeping organization such as the United Nations had to watch a major war from the sidelines. Not only was this passive role doing tremendous damage to the image of the organization, but it was having a chilling effect on other work of the United Nations as well. In his annual report issued on September 20, 1965, the secretary-general declared; "I cannot emphasize too strongly the profound and dangerous effect which . . . the present situation in Vietnam is having on the atmosphere in the United Nations." He noted that the war had put an end to the East–West détente that had begun to develop. "The conflict over Vietnam," he said, "has cruelly set back that trend and has served to revive, to intensify and even to extend some of the attitudes of the Cold War." A year later Thant said, "The chances of fruitful international cooperation on many crucial issues. . . . have been steadily and seriously impaired over the past two years by a situation over which [the United Nations] had not been able to exercise any effective control." He described the conflict as a "formidable barrier" to cooperation.[8]

At the end of April 1966, Thant visited London and Paris where he held private talks with Prime Minister Harold Wilson and President Charles de Gaulle. Afterward, he had little to say about these discussions; but it was during his European visit that he first unveiled his three-point formula for bringing the Vietnam combatants to the conference table. He outlined the plan in a broadcast on French radio and television in which he set forth the following three conditions: (1) cessation of the bombing of North Vietnam, (2) de-escalation of all military activities in South Vietnam, and (3) a willingness on the part of some of the parties primarily concerned to speak with other parties to the conflict. The latter point referred to the reluctance of the United States and the Saigon government to negotiate with the National Liberation Front, which was the political arm of the Vietcong. The secretary-general told a news conference in Geneva on July 6 that he had not met with "any positive response" to his three-point plan.

Thant paid a five-day visit to Moscow later that month. On his return to New York, he told correspondents that "inevitably, the Vietnam war dominated our talks." But he said that he had not presented his peace proposals since he did not believe they had "any relevance to the Soviet Union." Thant said that he came away from the Soviet capital more apprehensive than ever that the war might spill over the frontiers. "If the present trend continues," he declared, "I feel that the Vietnam war is likely to develop into a major war."[9]

During the ensuing months, the secretary-general continued to press for his three-point proposal. In a letter to Arthur J. Goldberg, who had succeeded Adlai Stevenson as U.S. representative to the United Nations in 1965, Thant again advanced the three points "to which I still adhere." "I strongly believe," he said, "that the three-point program, of which the cessation of bombing of North Vietnam is the first and essential part, is necessary to create the possibility of fruitful discussions."[10]

At his first news conference of 1967—held on January 10—Thant disclosed that the United States had attached conditions to any acceptance of a bombing halt and that Hanoi had taken exception to point two, which called for de-escalation of military action in South Vietnam. Thant spoke frankly about his differences with the United States on some aspects of the war. For one thing, he challenged the U.S. claim that the National Liberation Front was a "stooge" for Hanoi. Without elaborating on the status of his relations with Washington, Thant said that "There are basic differences in our approach, in our concepts, and even in our assessment of the situation."[11]

There was a brief truce during the Lunar New Year (*Tet*) observances in 1967, but fighting was resumed with a new intensity despite appeals from Thant and Pope Paul VI for an indefinite extension of the cease-fire. Not only did the United States resume its bombing of North Vietnam; but its naval guns were shelling areas north of the demilitarized zone, and mines were being laid in North Vietnamese waters. President Johnson told a news conference that he had ordered the new actions to hasten the end of the war.

U Thant was in Burma at the time, presumably on vacation. While he was there, however, a North Vietnamese diplomatic mission arrived in Rangoon unobtrusively and without explanation. The North Vietnamese made no immediate contact with Thant, but he was contacted a few days later while at the Burmese seaside resort of Ngapali. The result was a secret meeting with the North Vietnamese consul general in Rangoon on March 2. The meeting was not to remain secret for long. On the following day, the North Vietnamese consul general, Le Tung Son, said, "U Thant came here and I received him as an Asian and we exchanged views on the Vietnamese problem." Taking part in the talks also were Colonel Ha Van Lau—North Vietnam's chief representative on the International Control Commission in Hanoi—and Nguyen Tu Nguyen. Thant left for New York on March 4. He told newsmen that he had met the North Vietnamese representatives in his "private capacity and not as secretary-general of the United Nations." He declined to go into details about the talks, but said that he had presented his own assessment of the situation and had listened to their assessment.

On March 14, after his return to New York, he submitted to the concerned parties a revised three-point peace proposal. The new plan was sent to the United States, North Vietnam, South Vietnam, and the National Liberation Front as an aide-mémoire. It called for: (1) a general standstill truce, (2) preliminary talks, and (3) reconvening of the Geneva Conference. When Thant made the aide-mémoire public at a news conference on March 28, he had already received in writing the replies of the involved parties. He did not make the replies public; but by that time, North Vietnam had already reacted publicly with sharp criticism. A broadcast from Hanoi Radio on March 19 charged that the U.S. government was trying to "use the United Nations to interfere in the Vietnamese questions." This was followed by an official news agency broadcast, which declared that "to call on both sides to cease fire and hold unconditional negotiations . . . is to make no distinction between the aggressors and the victims of aggression, to depart from reality and to demand that the Vietnamese people accept the conditions of aggression." The United States and South Vietnam raised strong objections to the provision in point two of the proposal that the preliminary talks be limited to the United States and North Vietnam. This provision had been put in deliberately by Thant to avoid the question of inviting the National Liberation Front. A South Vietnamese spokesman said, "We resent being treated like a puppet. It is unthinkable that the recognized government of South Vietnam should not be included in talks which so vitally affect its interests." The United States agreed "the government of South Vietnam will have to be appropriately involved throughout the entire process." It was clear that this initiative by the secretary-general had run into a dead end, although Thant said that he did not consider any of the published reactions "a categorical rejection." In response to a question, Thant said that he still considered his earlier three-point proposal "the best solution." On April 1 the secretary-general issued a statement calling on the United States—as a predominant world power—to put the proposed standstill truce into effect by unilateral action. Nothing came of this.[12]

After the failure of his March 14 effort, Thant had become convinced that nothing could be achieved until the bombing of North Vietnam was halted. He stepped up his demands for such a move. At a luncheon of the U.N. Correspondents Association on May 11, Thant acknowledged that his proposal for a general standstill truce had been shelved since "neither side had fully and unconditionally accepted the proposals." His immediate efforts—he said would be to continue seeking a bombing halt, "which alone, in my view, can create conditions for meaningful talks."

As the war dragged on into 1968, signs began to appear that the Vietnam problem might at last be headed toward the conference table. Both Hanoi and Washington had been making conciliatory gestures. After a suspension of his peace efforts for almost a year, Thant began a new round of consultations. In February the secretary-general used a visit to India to meet with Nguyen Hoa, Hanoi's consul general in New Delhi. The North Vietnam official told Thant that his government was ready to "hold talks with Washington on all relevant matters at an appropriate time after the unconditional cessation of bombing and all other acts of war against North Vietnam." Thant handed Nguyen Hoa a list of questions to be transmitted to Hanoi. He received the answers in Paris, where Thant met Mai van Bo—North Vietnam's representative in France—as he stopped over on his way back to New York. The secretary-general was told that talks between Washington and Hanoi could begin just as soon as a bombing halt became effective. Mai van Bo said that either side could bring up any matter, but he mentioned two subjects specifically: a reduction of fighting in the south, and the reconvening of the Geneva Conference.

Thant returned immediately to New York where he gave a full report to U.S. Ambassador Goldberg and to Saigon's U.N. observer, Huu Chi. On February 21, during a brief trip to Washington, he also gave a report to President Johnson and Secretary of State Rusk. The president assured Thant that he sincerely desired peace. He reaffirmed the continued validity of the "San Antonio Formula," which he had presented in a speech the previous September at San Antonio, Texas. The two sentence formula reads as follows: "The United States is willing to stop all aerial and naval bombardment of North Vietnam when this will lead to productive discussions. We, of course, assume that while discussions proceed, North Vietnam will not take advantage of the bombing cessation or limitation."

This opened the way for the breakthrough. On March 31, Johnson announced that U.S. bombing of North Vietnam would cease "except in the area north of the demilitarized zone where the continued enemy buildup directly threatens allied forward positions and where the movement of their troops and supplies are clearly related to that threat." This did not meet Hanoi's demand for a complete and unconditional cessation of the bombing, but on April 3 Radio Hanoi stated that North Vietnam was ready to meet with representatives of the United States to consider an end to the fighting. All seemed to be settled except the time and the place. Thant suggested four possible sites: Warsaw, Geneva, Paris, and Phnom Penh. He told newsmen in Paris that he had been in touch with Washington continuously on the question of site selection; but Thant made it clear that he did not expect to take part in the peace talks, once they got underway. The preliminary talks finally began in Paris on May 10, 1968, while the fighting continued.

It quickly became apparent that the war was not over. The Paris talks bogged down on questions of format and procedure. They dragged on. Because of the delays, the first substantive discussions did not take place until January 1969. From then until 1973, it was a case of verbal battles in Paris and continued fighting in Vietnam. Thant made his last serious peace initiative on May 5, 1970. Even then he could find no reason to bring the problem to the United Nations. Instead, he proposed another international conference—this one to be composed of 15 members including all the parties involved in the war, the five big powers, and the three members of the International Control Commission (Canada, India, and Poland). In July, Thant conceded that his proposal had failed to win any substantial support.

The most significant development during this period was the decision of Richard M. Nixon—the new U.S. president—to begin a phased withdrawal of U.S. troops under his plan to Vietnamize the war. The first contingents began leaving Vietnam in September 1969; and by October 1972, less than 33,000 men remained of the 475,000 Americans who were there at the end of 1967. Meanwhile, President Nixon had sent his special assistant for national security affairs, Henry Kissinger, to Paris to negotiate secretly with the North Vietnam representative, Le Duc Tho. These talks, too, had their ups and downs. After they broke down in 1972, the United States unleashed a massive aerial offensive against the Hanoi and Haiphong areas. The talks were resumed in January 1973, and Nixon announced on January 23 that a peace agreement had finally been reached. The agreement—signed on January 27—called for the release of all U.S. prisoners of war, full accounting for those missing in action, withdrawal of all U.S. forces from South Vietnam, and the right of the people of South Vietnam to determine their future without interference. Kissinger and Le Duc Tho were later awarded the Nobel Peace Prize for their work; but unfortunately the war was soon on again—each side accusing the other of violations.[13]

The U.S. pullout was completed by the end of 1973, however; and the South Vietnamese were on their own, except for continued military supplies and financial aid. Fighting was intense throughout 1974 and the first part of 1975. It was a losing battle all the way for South Vietnam. The provinces fell one by one as the North Vietnamese armies drove ahead. The final dramatic chapter came on April 30, 1975, when Saigon capitulated to communist forces and South Vietnam resistance collapsed. Since the days of the initial rebellion against French rule, the conflict had lasted 30 years. The war had cost the United States 45,000 lives and $150 billion and had left some 1,500,000 Vietnamese dead on both sides. It left deep political, social, and psychological scars in the United States—which lingered for years after the fighting ended. Neither Ho Chi Minh, Lyndon Johnson, nor U Thant lived to see the end.

18

Cyprus

The island of Cyprus attained its independence in 1960 just a few weeks after the Belgian Congo. The two situations were different in almost every respect, however, except for the fact that they both became serious problems for the United Nations. In the Congo one of the problems was the reluctance of the former colonial ruler to let go, but in Cyprus the British were ready and willing to get out. Britain faced the same sort of situation here that it had faced in Palestine a dozen years earlier—internal turmoil and outside pressures—and saw no easy solution. In Palestine, it had been a struggle between Arabs and Jews; in Cyprus it was a conflict between Greek Cypriots and Turkish Cypriots.

The island, with its population of just over half a million, had been under British colonial administration since 1878 and had been relatively quiet until the 1950s when a guerrilla force led by a retired Greek army colonel, George Grivas, began a campaign of terrorism and intimidation aimed at union of Cyprus with the Greek mainland. Britain brought in 10,000 troops to try to maintain internal security while efforts were being made to find a formula for Cypriot independence that would safeguard the rights of the Turkish minority. While Grivas was exerting pressure internally, the Greek government was carrying on a diplomatic campaign at the United Nations to win support for application of the principle of self-determination for the island. The assumption was that the 77 percent of the population who were of Greek origin would vote for union with Greece—or *enosis*, as it was popularly called. The Greek government brought the question before the General Assembly in 1954, 1956, 1957, and 1958 without success. The opposition came mainly from the newly emerged nations, who felt that the Greek proposal would be nothing more than trading British rule for Greek rule.

Cyprus became independent on August 16, 1960, after Britain, Greece, and Turkey drafted a Cypriot constitution in Zurich and London and the three countries signed a treaty guaranteeing its independence. However, the constitution had a number of controversial provisions, and tensions soon developed between the Greek Cypriots and Turkish Cypriots. Real trouble began when the Cypriot president, Archbishop Makarios III, proposed a series of amendments, taking away some of the rights originally granted to the Turkish minority. Both Greek Cypriots and Turkish Cypriots began organizing secret fighting units for what threatened to become open civil war.

The first clash occurred on December 21, 1963, when two Turkish Cypriots were shot dead and another Turk and Greek were wounded. From then until Christmas the fighting became heavy throughout the capital city of Nicosia, where the Turks barricaded themselves in their own quarter. Both Greek and Turkish authorities had lost control of their own forces. The fighting was ended temporarily by British forces, which had remained in Cyprus under the guarantor treaty permitting the three signatories to maintain military contingents on the island after independence. At the request of President Makarios, the three countries agreed to supervise a cease-fire and assist in maintaining law and order. This task fell entirely on the shoulders of the British, since the Greek and Turkish contingents left their neutral camps and joined their Cypriot brothers in the field.

Throughout January 1964, sporadic fighting continued in various parts of the island, as both sides pursued their military buildup. From mainland Turkey—only 40 miles away—came weapons and troops slipped at night into a few small harbors controlled by the Turkish Cypriots. The Greeks controlled most of the ports, and were using them openly to bring in reinforcements.

The British troops were hard pressed to contain the fighting. February opened with violent anti-American demonstrations by Greek Cypriot students who felt that the United States was pro-Turkish. Two bombs exploded in the U.S. embassy in Nicosia, and the U.S. ambassador ordered 600 U.S. dependents flown out. A full-scale battle broke out in the port of Limassol when the Greeks attacked 6,000 Turks in their quarter of the town. Turkish Premier Ismet Inönü once again threatened to send his army into Cyprus. Greece responded by alerting its forces and vowing to fight to defend the Greek Cypriots.

That was the situation when President Makarios met in London with representatives of Britain, Greece, and Turkey and the four agreed to ask for a U.N. peace force to deal with the problem. On that same day U Thant addressed an urgent appeal to the president of Cyprus and the foreign ministers of Greece and Turkey in which he called on the three governments to "refrain from any acts which might lead to a worsening of the situation." The Security Council began a series of meetings on the Cyprus question on February 17 while the secretary-general engaged simultaneously in private consultations with council members and representatives of the parties directly concerned. The result was the adoption of a resolution on March 4—launching the United Nations on another peace-keeping operation. Under terms of the resolution, Thant was given the responsibility for determining the size of the Cyprus Force (UNFICYP), obtaining the troops from member nations, choosing a commander, directing the force, and raising the money to finance it. He was also authorized to appoint a mediator and direct his work. The sponsors of the resolution acknowledged that Thant himself had worked out the provisions of the proposal during his private consultations. Although the resolution was approved unanimously, some countries expressed misgivings about the powers given to the secretary-general. Czechoslovakia, France, and the Soviet Union abstained in the preliminary voting on the key paragraph creating the force, but they voted for the resolution as a whole. One of the surprising provisions of the resolution was the stipulation that the force was being authorized for a fixed period of three months. It did not seem very realistic to believe that order would be restored within such a short time.[1]

Thant immediately went into action to implement the resolution by requesting military contingents from Austria, Brazil, Canada, Finland, Iceland, Sweden, and Britain. As one of the guarantor powers, Britain agreed to provide 3,500 of the 7,000 men envisaged for the force. The secretary-general informed the council that he had appointed Lieutenant General P. S. Gyani of India as force commander. He also sent an appeal to all members of the United Nations for voluntary cash contributions to pay the estimated cost of $2 million a month to finance the operation. His implementation of the resolution was not without its problems. The first setback was the rejection by the Turkish government of his proposed appointment of his deputy cabinet chief, José Rolz-Bennett of Guatemala, as mediator. After a ten-day delay, he received the agreement of Cyprus, Greece, Turkey, and Britain on the appointment of his second choice, Sakari S. Tuomioja of Finland. He encountered one unforeseen problem when Turkey—as one of the guarantor powers—threatened to send in Turkish troops unless President Makarios complied with certain requests for the security of the Turkish minority. The secretary-general headed off this action by an urgent appeal to the Turkish government to reconsider its decision, which—he said—was "fraught with such grave possibilities." "The best hope for emerging from this dangerous crisis," he said, "is to allow time necessary for the implementation of the Security Council resolution of March 4, 1964, however much patience this course may require from the parties concerned, and for all parties to refrain in the meanwhile from adding to this explosive situation new elements which could only make the problem more insoluble and increase the danger."[2]

On March 17 Thant reported to the Security Council that sizable elements of the Canadian contingent had arrived in Cyprus and that advance parties of the Swedish and Irish contingents were due shortly thereafter. "On this basis," Thant stated, "I am able to say that the United Nations force in Cyprus is in being." The force became officially operational on March 27, when Lieutenant

General Gyani assumed command. The authorized three-month mandate thus began on this date, and would expire on June 26 unless extended.[3]

On June 15 Thant was able to report to the Security Council that, due largely to the presence of the U.N. force, "quiet prevails and there has been no fighting of consequence for quite some time." He recommended a three-month extension of the force, however, on grounds that its withdrawal might trigger a new round of fighting. The council agreed, and extended the force until September 26. The secretary-general reported that Tuomiojo had carried on continuous consultations with representatives of the Cyprus communities and with the governments of Britain, Greece, Turkey, and Cyprus—but with little positive results. "Given the circumstances which have prevailed in Cyprus," he said, "the task of the mediator could not have been expected to be an easy one."

Despite the lull in the fighting, tension was still high. Thant's concern over the clandestine buildup of military forces by both Greek and Turkish Cypriots led him to send identical messages on July 16 to leaders of the Cypriot, Greek, and Turkish governments in which he urged them to "halt this perilous trend." He was particularly disturbed by the attitude of the Cypriot vice-president, Fazel Kucuk—leader of the Turkish minority—toward U.N. officials. Kucuk had charged that "the apparently biased attitude of some senior United Nations officials in Cyprus" was making the United Nations a tool of Greek elements of the Cypriot government. He said further that Thant's reports to the Security Council were "anti-Turkish" and were written in "full ignorance or in total disregard of the contents of my numerous communications to you." The secretary-general sent a sharp telegram to Kucuk in which he emphatically denied any bias on the part of the U.N. officials in Cyprus and affirmed the "absolute integrity" of the U.N. operation.

The situation in general was deteriorating rapidly. For one thing, the Cypriot government was denying U.N. forces access to certain areas, despite its agreement to permit freedom of movement. By late July, 10,000 Greeks had infiltrated into the island to join Greek Cypriot fighters, and the Turks were stepping up their buildup. On July 22, Thant appealed to Kucuk to put an end to the infiltration of men and weapons into the areas controlled by the Turkish Cypriots. "The United Nations force," he said, "cannot ignore activities which are clearly in contravention of the resolutions of the Security Council as well as the laws of the land. It is for this reason that I am asking you to take all steps available to you to put an end to them."

Without waiting for the United Nations to deal with the problem, Makarios opened an offensive against the fishing village of Kokkina, where the Turkish forces were assembling. The Turkish government responded on August 8 by sending waves of Sabre jets across the forty-mile stretch of water, in scores of sorties—bombing and strafing Greek-held villages near the north coast. A Greek gunboat in the Xeros harbor was shattered and sunk. The Greek government failed to back Makarios. He appealed to the Soviet Union, which also ignored the appeal. On August 9 the president of the Security Council intervened with an urgent appeal to the governments of Cyprus and Turkey for a cease-fire. Both governments quickly agreed to halt the fighting. The next few weeks did little to ease the tension, however, partly because of an economic squeeze the Cypriot government imposed on the Turkish communities. In a report to the Security Council, U Thant declared that the economic restrictions in some instances had been severe enough to amount "to a veritable seige." "The policy of economic pressure," he said, "has definitely caused much hardship to the Turkish population; it has greatly increased tension and would no doubt lead to a new eruption of fighting, if continued." He declared further that the Turkish air raids in August had made a peaceful solution more difficult. "These raids on defenseless people killed and maimed many innocent civilians," he asserted, "destroyed much property and inevitably led to a stiffening of the position of the Cypriot government, as might have been anticipated."

On top of all these negative developments, Thant had the unhappy task of announcing the death of his Cypriot mediator, Sakari Tuomiojo, who had died in Helsinki as a result of a stroke on August 16. Thant named the former president of Ecuador, Galo Plaza, to succeed Tuomiojo as mediator.

As expected, the Security Council voted on September 25 to extend the mandate of the Cyprus Force for an additional three months. By now it had become a routing decision. Thant seized the occasion to express his unhappiness over the council's continued reliance on voluntary contributions to finance the operation. He called the arrangement "most unsatisfactory," and warned that he would be forced to "withdraw the force before the end of the three-month period" if voluntary contributions failed to provide the funds required. He noted that the financial burden "has been carried up until now by the supporting spirit and generosity of a limited number of member states." Britain and the United States—as usual—were the most generous contributors. Some of the Security Council members who had voted to send the U.N. force to Cyprus and continued to vote for the extensions of its mandate were contributing nothing to its support.

By the end of 1964 it had become obvious that the United Nations was facing a long-term involvement, even though the council stuck to its practice of three-month extensions. In his annual report, Thant described the situation as "a grim and formidable one." "As regards the efforts to resolve the long-term problems of Cyprus through the United Nations mediator," he said, "it is not possible at this stage to report any significant advance." Nevertheless, the island was quiet all through 1965 and 1966, except for a few minor clashes. In a report to the Security Council on March 11, 1965, the secretary-general declared that, while the situation had remained relatively peaceful for the past few months, "this should not blind anyone to the equally significant fact that both sides in Cyprus are now better prepared to fight, from a military point of view, than before and consequently the results of any renewed fighting are likely to be more severe than heretofore."

Efforts at a long-term solution received a severe setback when Turkey angrily notified the United Nations that it would no longer deal with Galo Plaza. In no uncertain terms, Turkey's announcement said that "Mr. Galo Plaza's functions as a mediator have come to an end upon publication of the present report." The Turkish government objected to parts of the mediator's report—which, they claimed, "go beyond his terms of reference." Thant appealed to Turkey not to insist "on the extreme position that the services of the mediator have come to an end." The appeal was ignored, however. A year later Thant notified the Security Council that the mediation efforts remained in suspension. Actually, the post of mediator had been vacant since December 22, 1965, when Galo Plaza resigned.

The situation began deteriorating again in mid-November 1967, after a three-year period of quiet. Fighting broke out at several points on November 15. In the little village of Ayios Theodoros, 24 Turkish and 14 Greek Cypriots were killed. The situation was all the more serious because Cypriot National Guard troops manhandled personnel of the U.N. force and deliberately damaged U.N. equipment during the fighting. On November 20, members of a U.N. patrol were beaten and disarmed by Turkish Cypriot fighters. Turkish jet fighters repeatedly flew over Cypriot territory. The Greek and Turkish governments were exchanging angry notes. On November 24 Thant declared the two NATO members "were on the brink of war." He appealed to the prime ministers of Greece and Turkey to "use the utmost restraint." In Washington, President Lyndon Johnson sent Deputy Secretary of Defense Cyrus Vance on a marathon mediation trip to assist Thant's representative, José Rolz-Bennett, and NATO Secretary-general Manlio Brosio of Italy. These efforts succeeded in ending the fighting and resulted in an agreement for the withdrawal of all non-Cypriot forces except those under U.N. command.

In a report to the Security Council on June 11, 1968, Thant stated that "the relaxation of tension in Cyprus which set in at the beginning of the year has continued." He added, "There are recent indications that both the Greek and Turkish Cypriots have at last begun to realize that they cannot solve their dispute by force. . . . On the other hand, the basic issues dividing the two communities have remained unresolved." He found one development "most encouraging." That was the opening of direct talks between representatives of the two warring communities for the first time in four and a half years. "I attach great importance to these inter-communal talks," Thant said. The situation continued to remain quiet through the remaining years of Thant's second term as secretary-general. In his final report to the Security Council on the subject of Cyprus—dated November 30, 1971—Thant expressed concern over the failure of the United Nations to find a solution to the problem. "After nearly eight years," he said, "the solution of the Cyprus problem is still not in sight, conditions in the island remain precarious, and I have come once more before the Security Council—in fact for the twentieth time—to recommend a further extension of the mandate of UNFICYP. It is obvious that the situation cannot continue indefinitely, to the detriment of the people of Cyprus and as a lingering threat to international peace and security." The Cyprus problem was one of the legacies that U Thant left to his successor, Kurt Waldheim of Austria.

As Thant implied when he left office, the situation was too good to last. The real trouble started in the summer of 1974 when the Greek military dictatorship, which had seized power in 1967, decided to get rid of President Makarios. Diehard *enosis* supporters on the mainland were infuriated with the black-bearded spiritual and political leader because he had given up the goal of uniting Cyprus with Greece. Makarios had finally decided that Cyprus should remain an independent nation. On July 5, 1974, he publicly accused the Greek junta of plotting to overthrow him. He was right. On July 14, the Cypriot National Guard—a 10,000-man force led by 650 mainland Greek officers—made its move. Backed by 40 tanks, the rebelling troops occupied key locations in the major cities and then moved on the presidential palace. They quickly announced that Makarios had been killed. It turned out, however, that the president had escaped through a back door and made his way through the mountains to a British base. From there he was flown to safety in London.

The man named by the Greek military leaders to succeed Makarios as president was Nikos Sampson—a man once sentenced to death by the British as triggerman of the Greek Cypriot guerrilla group EOKA. The Turkish community was horrified by the choice of Sampson, who was known for preaching extreme solutions and was expected to carry out union with mainland Greece as soon as possible. Rauf Denktash, the leader of the Turkish Cypriots, warned that "Turkish military intervention will be necessary and will be done" unless Makarios was returned to power immediately. This was not an idle threat. Five days after the coup, the Turks attacked from the air and across the water. Paratroops dropped from the sky, and Turkish soldiers waded onto the beaches. Waves of jets dropped bombs on key locations, while Turkish ships shelled seaports.

Sampson resigned three days after the Turkish invasion, and named in his place as president a moderate acceptable to the Turks, Glafcas Clerides. Despite a cease-fire, fighting continued as the Turks widened their bridgehead along the northern coast. Sampson was not the only loser in the ill-fated coup. The military junta in mainland Greece collapsed; and former Premier Constantine Caramanlis returned to Athens to form a new government, after 11 years in exile. Peace talks were begun immediately in Geneva by representatives of the guarantor powers—Britain, Greece, and Turkey—but when the talks collapsed, the Turks struck again. Before a new cease-fire could be arranged, Turkish forces had occupied one-third of the island. Caught in the middle of the conflict was the U.N. force, which could do little but watch.

The United States was also trapped in a tight corner by the conflict, which was between two of its NATO partners. The Greek government announced that it was pulling out of NATO. Anti-American riots broke out in Greek cities. In such a demonstration in Nicosia on August 19, 1974, a mob smashed the iron gates of the U.S. embassy and opened fire on the building. Ambassador Roger P. Davies and an embassy secretary were killed in the attack. The anti-American violence was sparked by resentment over what the Greeks believed to be a U.S. bias in favor of Turkey during the fighting. The issue was raised in the U.S. Congress, where a majority decided it was Turkey that was at fault. Both the Senate and the House of Representatives decided that Turkey had violated the terms under which U.S. military aid was given, and voted to cut off further aid to Turkey. The Turkish government responded by closing some U.S. bases. Turkish Premier Suleyman Demirel rejected a plea by President Gerald Ford for the reopening of the bases in return for a grant of $50 million in U.S. weapons. On March 26, 1976, the United States and Turkey patched up their differences. They reached an agreement that would permit the reopening of the bases in exchange for $1 billion in U.S. grants and loans. On April 12, Greece and the United States also settled their differences in a four-year accord permitting continued use of U.S. military bases in Greece.

Meanwhile, back in Cyprus, a number of significant developments had taken place. Makarios returned from exile late in 1974, and resumed the presidency. On January 18, 1975, thousands of Greek Cypriots ransacked British offices in Nicosia and burned a wing of the U.S. embassy in protest against London's decision to let 10,000 Turkish Cypriot refugees leave the British military base for Turkey. On February 13, Turkish Cypriots proclaimed the establishment of a separate state in the Turkish-occupied northern part of Cyprus. They offered to join Greek Cypriots in a federation. Makarios quickly denounced the pro-clamation, and said that Greek Cypriots were prepared to resist and—if nec-essary—to sacrifice themselves to prevent partition of the country. The Turkish Cypriots, however, went ahead with their plans for a separate state. A con-stituent assembly drew up a constitution, which was approved by the Turkish community in a referendum on June 8. A year later—on June 30, 1976—Rauf Denktash was elected president of the Turkish Federated State of Cyprus. Soon afterward, leaders of the Greek Cypriots and Turkish Cypriots agreed on a general transfer of minorities to their respective sectors of the island. Despite this ap-parent settlement of the problem, talks continued off and on among the inter-ested parties. Archbishop Markarios—wearied by the constant pressures—died in Nicosia following a heart attack on August 3, 1977. Spyros Kyprianou, president of the Cypriot House of Representatives, was elected president to serve out the remainder of Makarios's term, and was reelected in 1978 and again in 1983 for five-year terms.

In April 1986, U.N. Secretary-general Javier Perez de Cuellar of Peru pre-sented a draft framework agreement for solving the Cyprus problem, and the Soviet Union proposed a representative international conference on Cyprus within the U.N. framework. But as of this writing, the situation has remained unchanged. The Security Council still finds it advisable to continue the U.N. peace-keeping force in Cyprus, after more than two decades. And the end is not in sight.

19

Confrontation on Peace-keeping Assessments

Despite the importance of peace-keeping, the United Nations has never found a satisfactory way to pay for such costly operations as UNEF and the Congo Force. The Soviet Union, France, and a dozen other members have challenged the legality of allowing financial assessments to be made by the General Assembly, and have refused to pay for peace-keeping activities. Not only has this resulted in a serious financial problem for the United Nations, but it also led to a frightening confrontation between the United States and the Soviet Union—a quarrel that at one point threatened to break up the United Nations. The crisis actually did cause a state of virtual paralysis in the assembly during the final months of 1964 and the first part of 1965.[1]

At the center of the dispute was a question as to how certain articles of the U.N. Charter should be interpreted. The Soviet Union contended that only the Security Council had the authority to assess members for peace-keeping operations, but the International Court of Justice rendered an advisory opinion on July 20, 1962, holding that the expenses of peace-keeping operations were the same as other expenses of the United Nations and could be met by General Assembly assessments. The Soviet Union and France refused to accept this ruling, however, and continued to withhold payments even after the assembly voted 76 to 17 to accept the court's opinion as binding.

It was obvious that, if the Soviets and others continued to withhold payments long enough, they would run afoul of another charter provision. This was Article 19, which provides for possible loss of voting rights under certain conditions. This article says:

A member of the United Nations which is in arrears in the payment of its financial contributions to the organization shall have no vote in the General Assembly if the amount of the arrears equals or exceeds the amount of contributions due from it for the preceding two full years. The General Assembly may, nevertheless, permit such a member to vote if it is satisfied that the failure to pay is due to conditions beyond the control of the member.

By its refusal to pay peace-keeping assessments, the Soviet Union came within the scope of this article when its debt amounted to $54,768,188 on June 30, 1964. France was in arrears $17,752,565—enough to make her also subject to the penalty. "We will not pay one single kopek, not one single cent," declared Soviet Ambassador Nikolai Federenko. He said that, if the United States tried to suspend the Soviet right to vote, it would be regarded as "an unfriendly act" and could cause the Soviet Union to withdraw from the United Nations.[2]

The situation appeared grim, in view of the rigid position taken by the United States that the penalties under Article 19 would automatically become effective when the General Assembly opened its 1964 session on December 1. On October 8 U.S. Ambassador Adlai Stevenson sent a memorandum to the assembly in which he expressed the hope that the countries in arrears would meet their obligations, but added that if "the plain and explicit terms of Article 19 become applicable there is no alternative to its application." Harlan Cleveland, U.S. assistant secretary of state, said, "There are lots of ways of breaking up a club, but enforcing the rules on delinquents is not one of them." In Washington, the U.S. House of Representatives had already endorsed the tough State Department stand by a vote of 351 to 0.

Secretary-general Thant and many U.N. members were trying desperately to head off a confrontation, but found both the United States and the Soviet Union firmly dug into their positions. Stevenson made a final effort on November 13 to avoid a showdown by suggesting that "voluntary payments could be made without prejudice to the Soviet's or anyone else's legal views." He added that "any payments consistent with the charter and satisfactory to the secretary-general will be satisfactory to the United States." The Soviet Union did not take up the suggestion.

In the introduction to his annual report issued on November 20, Thant said that "valiant efforts have been and are being made to avoid a confrontation." These efforts resulted in a last-minute agreement among the United States, the Soviet Union, France, and the United Kingdom on an arrangement that would permit the assembly to transact business on essential items without formal voting. The president of the assembly would simply ask if there were any objections to whatever was being considered and—if none were heard—he would declare the matter decided. For the scheme to work, it was essential for each member to acquiesce. This would limit action to noncontroversial items. One objection could prevent action on any item of business. Thant explained the agreed procedure when the General Assembly convened on December 1. "I have been in consultation with several delegations for the past week," he said, "for the sole purpose of avoiding a confrontation. In this connection, I may mention that there is an understanding to the effect that issues other than those that can be disposed of without objection will not be raised while the general debate proceeds. I hope that all delegations will agree with this procedure." His reference to the general debate meant that the delegates would go ahead with the general policy statements normally made at the opening of each annual session of the assembly. They did this, and were also able to elect Alex Quaison-Sackey of Ghana as president, to admit three new members—Malta, Malawi, and Zambia—to adopt a budget for 1965, and to fill some vacancies in the Security Council and the Economic and Social Council without a formal challenge to the nonvoting arrangement.[3]

The session recessed on December 30 until January 18 in the hope that things would be better by then. It turned out, however, that nothing had changed during the recess, despite the fact that the United States was under increasing pressure to agree to some sort of compromise. The Third World countries— realizing that the Soviet Union would not back down—felt that the only solution would be a shift in the U.S. position. Stevenson himself was trying to find a way to back away, but he found both President Lyndon Johnson and Secretary of State Dean Rusk adamant. On January 26, Stevenson told the assembly that there was no way to reinterpret the language of the charter and that the issue was "whether or not we intend to preserve the effective capacity of this organization to keep the peace." The assembly adjourned for a week to permit more talks. It met on and off during the first half of February to dispose of some additional essential housekeeping items. It was too much to hope, howver, that this situation could continue indefinitely—although some felt that the assembly ought to adjourn the session altogether until September.

One delegate had other ideas. When the assembly was called to order on February 16, Albanian Ambassador Halim Budo raised a yellow pencil above his head to signal that he wanted to speak. Many delegates sensed that time had run out for the nonvoting arrangement, and that trouble was ahead. They were right. Budo declared that his delegation could not permit itself any longer to be "blackmailed" by threats of the United States to deprive certain members of their voting rights. He presented a formal request that the General Assembly return to normal procedures without delay, and asked for an immediate roll call vote. This would have brought on the dreaded confrontation. The assembly president appealed to Budo not to press his proposal because of the "overwhelming desire" of the members to avoid a showdown on Article 19. But Budo— who was known to represent the views of communist China—not only insisted on the roll call vote, but asked that it be given "priority over all other questions." A number of delegates went to the podium with appeals that Budo withdraw his request or at least permit them a day or two to get instructions from their governments. The assembly president ended the crisis—at least for the moment—by adjourning the meeting for 48 hours.[4]

Despite the overwhelming pressure to the contrary, Budo rose to press his demands for a vote when the assembly reconvened on February 18. He interrupted a statement by Assembly President Quaison-Sackey to demand the floor on a point of order. When the president told him that he would be permitted to speak at the proper time, Budo ignored his ruling and rushed to the podium. The president turned off the podium microphone, but Budo attempted to make himself heard by shouting into the dead microphone. The president pounded his gavel and insisted that Budo return to his seat. He continued to speak, however, until a veteran delegate, Ambassador Jamil Baroody of Saudi Arabia, stepped to the podium and pleaded with him to sit down.

When order was restored, the president ruled that the assembly had agreed on the nonvoting procedure and "there is a consensus against reconsidering that decision." Budo was not ready to give up. He challenged Quaison-Sackey's ruling under assembly rule 73, which says that "A representative may appeal against the ruling of the president. The appeal shall be immediately put to the vote and the president's ruling shall stand unless overruled by the members."

Adlai Stevenson—trying to head off a vote on the Budo challenge—waved for attention and was recognized by the president, but Budo started shouting when Stevenson tried to speak. Budo insisted that Stevenson not be allowed to speak and that the vote on his challenge be taken immediately. At this point it looked as if the confrontation was unavoidable and imminent. In the midst of the confusion, an aide rushed to Stevenson's side and whispered in his ear—pointing to an opened rule book. The U.S. delegation had discovered a rule that permitted a delegate to speak on a point of order concerning the actual conduct of the voting. The president allowed Stevenson to continue.

The crisis was not yet over, because a way still had to be found to avoid the confrontation—not just delay it. Stevenson came up with a surprise solution. He said that he regarded the proposed vote on Budo's challenge as a procedural vote, and declared that such a vote would not involve Article 19. The United States, he said, would not raise any objection to the procedural vote. The president's ruling was then upheld by a vote of 97 to 2 with 12 abstentions. Only Albania and Mauritania voted against the ruling. All this still left the possibility of a confrontation on Article 19 hanging over the assembly when it adjourned until September. Fortunately, the threat had been removed by then, and the assembly once more was able to resume its normal procedures.

It was the United States that backed down, after it regretfully conceded that it could not muster the support needed to enforce the penalties under Article 19. Arthur J. Goldberg made the concession on August 16 in his initial speech as U.S. ambassador. Without waiting for the fall session of the General Assembly, he told the 33 members of the Committee on Peace-keeping that the United States accepted "a simple but inescapable fact": A majority of the 114 U.N. members was not prepared to apply Article 19 at the risk of a Soviet walkout. Another fact was that a majority of the members wanted the assembly to get on with its business, and "we will not seek to frustrate that consensus, since it is not in the world interest to have the work of the assembly immobilized in these troubled days." Goldberg made it clear, however, that if other members could arbitrarily decide which U.N. assessments they would pay, the United States would reserve the right to do the same. This the U.S. government has done on several occasions since then.

At the time the Article 19 crisis ended, the Soviet Union owed $62 million in peace-keeping assessments, France owed $17 million, and 11 other countries owed $28 million. Most of this resulted from the costs of UNEF and the Congo Force. The other major peace-keeping project involving large expenditures was the Cyprus Force, which was financed by voluntary contributions. Neither the Soviet Union nor France contributed anything for the Cyprus operation, although both voted for its authorization. The Korean War—a U.N. operation in name—cost the organization nothing. A number of countries made voluntary contributions in troops, weapons, and other materials, but the bulk of the fighting and the costs was borne by the United States.

The financial problems of the United Nations began soon after the establishment of UNEF in 1956, but did not become critical until member states began to default on their Congo assessments four years later. By the time U Thant assumed office in November 1961, unpaid bills amounted to $82.5 million, the U.N.'s Working Capital Fund was exhausted, and the organization owed $20 million in temporary loans from other U.N. accounts. On December 11—a month after he took office—Thant warned that "the consequences of insolvency will have to be faced seriously and soon" unless action was taken to meet the deficit and provide for the continuing costs of authorized activities.

One of Thant's first moves was to begin private consultations on the financial situation. At his first press conference on December 1, 1961, he disclosed that "certain proposals" were under discussion, but that they were still "highly tentative." He was referring to the still-secret plan for a U.N. bond issue. The plan in the form of a working paper—was to emerge a fortnight later as a resolution sponsored by Denmark, Ethiopia, Malaya, Norway, Netherlands, Pakistan, Tunisia, and Yugoslavia. Later, Canada joined as a sponsor. At his press conference, Thant had denied that the bond issue was his idea; but Tunisian Ambassador Zouhir Chelli, who made the presentation on behalf of the sponsors, told the Budgetary Committee (Committee V) that the resolution was produced in response to the acting secretary-general's appeal. It was no secret that the proposal not only had Thant's support, but had been drafted under his auspices. A U.N. press release stated that the resolution had been introduced after "extensive informal discussions in the early part of December between the acting secretary-general and most of the delegations of the United Nations." The release also said that Thant had consulted with Eugene Black, president of the International Bank, "who gave support and valued advice concerning the possible issuance of the United Nations bonds."

Although Ambassador Philip M. Klutznik, U.S. representative in the Budgetary Committee, denied Soviet charges that the United States was the secret originator of the bond issue, it was generally known that the bond concept originated in Washington and that, after Thant accepted it, U.S. experts worked with U.N. Comptroller Bruce Turner, a New Zealand national, in drafting the resolution. As finally approved, the plan called for the issuance of $200 million in U.N. bonds at 2 percent and repayable in 25 years by annual installments. The bonds were to be offered to member states, U.N. specialized agencies, and—if the acting secretary-general so decided—to private nonprofit organizations.

The Soviet Union opposed the bond issue as a dangerous precedent, which—it said—would involve a change in the nature of the United Nations. Soviet Representative A. A. Roschin declared that adoption of the proposal would be tantamount to mortgaging the organization and would place the "shareholders" in a position to influence its policies. He said that the plan was obviously inspired by the United States and that Washington was also responsible for its being sprung on the Budgetary Committee without warning. U.S. Ambassador Klutznik noted that the acting secretary-general had discussed the proposal at length with many delegations and had circulated an aide mémoire setting forth the concept of the bond issue.

The plan was finally approved by the General Assembly on December 20, but by a vote that made it all too apparent that many members were not happy with the idea. The vote was 58 to 13, with 28 abstentions. Both the Soviet Union and France voted against it and refused to buy ony of the bonds. Despite a pledge by President Kennedy that the United States would match the purchases of other countries, the bond sales were disappointing. Total sales reached $154.7 million out of $200 million authorized. Purchases were made by 65 countries, including 5 that were not U.N. members. This meant that almost half the member states failed to participate in the plan. The bonds were never offered to nongovernmental investors.

The bond issue did relieve the financial pressure for the moment, but it left the long-term problem unresolved. The response to the plan demonstrated that this was not the answer, and ensured that it would not be tried again. The situation then went steadily downhill until it finally hit bottom in the Article 19 crisis. As of the time of this writing, the United Nations was still searching for a formula to finance its peace-keeping operations.

20

On the Use of Force: The Dominican Republic and Czechoslovakia

On April 28, 1965, President Lyndon B. Johnson appeared on national television and announced that the United States had sent marines into the Dominican Republic to protect U.S. citizens endangered by political turmoil in that country:

The American government has been informed by military authorities in the Dominican Republic that American lives are in danger. These authorities are no longer able to guarantee their safety and have reported that the assistance of military personnel is needed for that purpose. I've ordered the Secretary of Defense to put the necessary troops ashore to give protection to the hundreds of Americans who are still in the Dominican Republic and to escort them back to this country.

Johnson disclosed that 400 marines had already been landed. Before the crisis was over, 20,000 U.S. soldiers and marines would join this initial group. The impact of the U.S. intervention on other Latin American countries was not so adverse as might have been expected in view of their traditional dislike of such action by Washington. The council of the OAS quickly decided to send a five-man committee to the Dominican Republic to help restore order. However, it was inevitable that the U.S. intervention would also come before the United Nations. On May 1 the Soviet Union called for an urgent meeting of the Security Council to consider the "armed intervention" by the United States. Once again it was Adlai Stevenson who had the task of defending the U.S. action, just as four years earlier he had to defend the Bay of Pigs fiasco. This time, at least, Stevenson had been included in the Washington discussions leading up to the intervention, but he had opposed it. By the time the question came before the

Security Council, President Johnson had added a second reason for the intervention: to prevent a communist takeover in the Dominican Republic. There
was no doubt that the interventionary forces did save U.S. lives during the
street fighting, but there was no substantial evidence that a communist threat
existed. In his book *The Vantage Point*, Johnson later said that he had reached
a decision on April 29 that "the danger of a Communist take-over in the
Dominican Republic was a real and present one" and that "a Communist regime
in the Dominican Republic would be dangerous to the peace and security of
the hemisphere and the United States."[1]

There was no known or avowed communist connection with either of the
military factions engaged in the struggle following the overthrow of the military
junta that had ruled since 1961. One group was headed by Colonel Francisco
Caamano Deno, who had emerged as a symbol of the current revolution; and
then there was the "Government of National Reconstruction," which was
headed by General Antonio Imbert Barreras. The U.S. State Department released the names of 57 individuals who were said to be communists associated
with the rebels. Another State Department release charged that Cuban-trained
guerrillas were involved in the uprising and that the rebels were receiving
financial aid from Fidel Castro. At the United Nations, Stevenson himself
named a number of men identified by the United States as communists among
the rebel leaders, but he did not stress this point. In a speech on May 5—three
days after Johnson had publicly raised the communism issue—Ambassador Stevenson declared that "It may be said—I think accurately—the bulk of the
participants in the rebellion are not Communists and that even in the present
leadership non-Communists are active." He added, however, "that only twelve
men went to the hills with Castro in 1956 and that only a handful of Castro's
own supporters were Communists."[2]

The main issue in the Security Council—despite Soviet criticism of the U.S.
intervention—was the continued fighting and what role the United Nations
should play in trying to stop it. Stevenson argued that the question was one for
the OAS, which was already at work in Washington and was preparing to take
its efforts to the scene in Santo Domingo. Nevertheless, the council unanimously
adopted a resolution on May 14 calling for a strict cease-fire and asking the
secretary-general to send a special representative to report on the situation. The
following day, Secretary-general Thant announced the appointment of José
Antonio Mayobre—executive secretary of the Economic Commission for Latin
America—as his special representative. Mayobre arrived in Santo Domingo on
May 18. His first task under the direction of the Security Council was to seek
an immediate suspension of hostilities so that the International Red Cross might
carry on the humanitarian work of searching for the dead and wounded.[3]

From the beginning, the Dominican problem had raised again the question
of regional organizations versus the United Nations—which had already come
up in the Cuban and Guatemalan cases. This time the situation was especially
delicate because, for the first time, both the United Nations and a regional

organization had peace missions operating in the same country simultaneously. This was bound to cause problems. The arrival of Mayobre brought a complaint from the special committee of the OAS that the United Nations was obstructing its peace efforts. The committee asked that the Security Council suspend all U.N. action until every regional procedure had been exhausted. After dispatching this request, the special committee resigned. The OAS accepted the resignations and reassigned the peace mission to its secretary-general, José A. Mora, who was asked to coordinate his efforts with those of the U.N. representative. OAS also added a new element with the creation of the Inter-American Peace Force, whose purpose was to guarantee public security and create an atmosphere of conciliation. This was the first peace force established and directed by a regional organization. From the U.S. point of view, it was important because it permitted a reduction of U.S. forces and—at the same time—gave the operation an international character, rather than being run by the United States alone. Troop contingents were provided by Brazil, Honduras, Paraguay, Nicaragua, and Costa Rica as well as the United States. On May 29 Brazilian General Hugo Panasco Alvim took command of the force.

On May 21 U Thant reported to the Security Council that an agreement had been reached with the two factions for a 24-hour suspension of hostilities. Although General Imbert refused to lengthen the truce formally, it did in fact end the fighting except for sporadic outbursts. At the United Nations, however, the battle continued as hot as ever in the Security Council all through June and July. The Soviet Union and Cuba pressed for the withdrawal of the Inter-American Peace Force, which still had 1,700 men in the country. Cuba was not a member of the council, but had intervened as an interested party and was allowed to take part without a vote. The Soviets and Cubans argued that neither the OAS nor any other regional organization had any right to take enforcement action. France, Jordan, and Uruguay also questioned the legality of the OAS intervention. Stevenson—speaking for the United States—maintained that the Inter-American Force could in no way be regarded as an enforcement body since its aim was simply to restore normal conditions and establish an atmosphere of conciliation. The debate finally ended without any decision.

Meanwhile, the United States was trying to build an interim government around General Imbert, who was identified with neither the rebels nor the overthrown military junta. Imbert's Government of National Reconstruction was sworn in on May 7, but it failed to win the support of the rebels and their favored standard-bearer in the proposed election, former President Juan Bosch (whose short-lived tenure in 1963 was overthrown by the military junta). Reconciliation efforts were continued throughout the summer by a three-man OAS group consisting of Ambassadors Ellsworth Bunker of the United States, Ilmar Penna Marinho of Brazil, and Ramon de Clairmont Duenas of El Salvador. They finally succeeded in winning agreement on a settlement called the "Act of National Reconciliation." The act created a provisional government led by lawyer-diplomat Hector Garcia-Godoy. The new government took office on

September 3, and the rival factions were dissolved to permit preparations for an elected government. One immediate problem facing the authorities was the thorny question of civilian disarmament. A weapons search-and-seizure drive was only mildly successful. Several thousand rifles and carbines taken from arsenals during the uprising remained unaccounted for. A brief outburst of violence occurred in October when a mob shouting communist slogans attacked a conservative political leader, Angel Severo Cabral. He was wounded and then killed in an ambulance that was taking him to a hospital. The disturbance was quelled when OAS troops backed by U.S. tanks moved into the heart of Santo Domingo on October 25. The demonstrations had failed to draw any broad support from the people.

Under the Act of Reconciliation, elections were to be held in nine months, which meant sometime in the spring of 1966. In April, Juan Bosch decided to be a presidential candidate against Joaquín Balaguer, a moderate who had been serving as president when the dictator General Rafael Molina Trujillo was assassinated in 1961. Balaguer was living in exile in New York at the time that the 1965 uprising began. In a record turnout on June 1, 1966, more than 1.3 million Dominican voters chose Balaguer as president by a decisive margin over Bosch and the third candidate, Dr. Rafael Bonnelly (also a former president). Balaguer received 57 percent of the votes and a substantial majority in both houses of the congress. OAS observers from 18 countries were on hand to watch the elections, which were described by them as "an outstanding act of democratic purity."

In his memoirs, President Johnson acknowledged that he was troubled at first by criticism from Latin America after the U.S. intervention. "I was concerned," he said, "that the argument over the Dominican Republic might disrupt or slow down our cooperation in the Alliance for Progress. That did not happen. Indeed, as political events unfolded in the Dominican Republic, Latin Americans— including some of our most severe critics—came to realize that our emergency actions were for the best."

At the United Nations, Secretary-general U Thant noted that the dual intervention of the world organization and the OAS raised "some special and unfamiliar problems" and "led inevitably to difficulties in relationships." He dealt with the problem more specifically in a speech before the Annual Conference of Non-governmental Organizations in New York on May 27, 1965. Thant sounded a warning of future dangers if regional organizations should expand their functions to include enforcement actions. "If the Organization of American States is recognized as competent to take certain enforcement actions in a particular country in its own region," he said, "then we have to admit that the Organization of African Unity is also competent to take certain defensive action by way of enforcement in its region. The same considerations naturally apply to the League of Arab States, if the League decides to take certain enforcement actions in its region." He did not mention the communist countries, which were organized under the Warsaw Pact; but his warning proved to be prophetic in the case of Czechoslovakia three years later.[4]

The Czechoslovak crisis of August 1968 had no clear-cut starting point. The people had long been restive. Many resented efforts to break their cultural ties with the West. Others were angered by communist repressions, bureaucratic ineptness, and a deteriorating economy. The unrest assumed proportions of a political upheaval by mid–1967 when students began demonstrating against poor housing and other inadequate facilities at the universities, and police retaliated with harsh measures. Up to the end of 1967 the difficulties were internal, but Moscow was beginning to show signs of nervousness. Basically, what the people wanted was more freedom, and the old Stalinist regime under President Antonín Novotný was trying—under pressure from Moscow—to hold the line. Czech-oslovakia's strained relations with Moscow took a critical turn with the decision of the Czech Communist party leadership on January 5, 1968, to replace Novotný with Alexander Dubček as first secretary. It soon became apparent that Dubček's "Action Program" to liberalize the rigid communist controls had placed Czech-oslovakia on a collision course with the Soviet Union. Reforms envisaged in the Action Program included the restoration of personal liberties, a lifting of censorship, guaranteed freedom of speech, and curbs on the power of the security apparatus to interfere with private lives. Economically, the program called for wage and price reforms and decentralization of management to break the stran-glehold of bureaucracy.

While the Dubček government did want to remain allied with Moscow, it also wanted better relations with the West—particularly with its neighbor, West Germany. The rest of the communist bloc was dismayed by the "revisionist" policies of Dubček. Conservatives in the Kremlin feared that, if the reforms succeeded in Czechoslovakia, demands for the same concessions would soon be heard in the Soviet Union and other communist countries.

In Washington, President Johnson watched the developments with growing anxiety. Johnson later said that he and his advisors could see the possibility of Soviet military intervention to halt the reforms if negotiations failed. There was no feeling, however, that the United States could or should resist such action by force. "The Czechs themselves," Johnson said, "had indicated they did not plan to resist military force, and that they would not welcome any response from the West. . . . We hoped that increasing world criticism, combined with the confidence a great power like the Soviet Union should have, would convince Moscow not to crush the modest liberalism among the Czechs."[5]

Dubček refused to bow to the pressure, including such transparent threats as Warsaw Pact military maneuvers being conducted first along the Czech borders late in May and then actually inside Czechoslovakia. The Soviet Union de-manded that the Czech leaders go to Moscow for an emergency meeting with other Soviet bloc countries. Dubček refused, but offered to take part if the meeting were held on Czech soil. Surprisingly, the Soviets not only agreed but decided to send their top leaders—Leonid Brezhnev, Alexei Kosygin, and Nikolai Podgorny—who traveled by special train to the tiny village of Cierna. The Czech delegation was headed by First Secretary Dubček and President Ludvik Svoboda. Leaders of the two countries met for four days without reaching any substantive agreement. This meeting was followed two days later by another in Bratislava, where the Czech delegation met with Soviet leaders and representatives of four other Warsaw Pact members. The results were the same: no agreement. The Soviets had to return to Moscow empty-handed, faced with the difficult problem of deciding whether to give in or to crush the Czech rebellion by force.

In the early morning hours of August 20, soldiers of the Soviet Union, East Germany, Poland, Bulgaria, and Hungary moved across the borders into Czechoslovakia from several directions. By dawn 70,000 heavily armed troops—with tanks and modern weapons—held firm control of the country. Soviet officers burst into Communist party headquarters in Prague, arrested the leaders, and took them to Moscow for "negotiations." The Soviet press mounted a propaganda campaign designed to convince the world and the Soviet people that the troops had intervened at the request of the Czech government. In an unusual move, Soviet Ambassador Anatoly Dobrynin called at the White House a few hours after the invasion and informed President Johnson of Moscow's decision. He too claimed that the Warsaw Pact countries acted at the request of the Czech leaders to help meet the situation "created by a conspiracy of the external and internal forces of aggression against the existing social order in Czechoslovakia." Dobrynin told the president that he hoped the "current events should not harm Soviet–American relations, to the development of which the Soviet government as before attaches the greatest importance."

The situation was brought before the United Nations the next day when the representatives of Canada, Denmark, France, Paraguay, and the United States requested an immediate meeting of the Security Council to consider the invasion. Without waiting for the council meeting, which took place later that day, U Thant appealed to the invading countries to "exercise the utmost restraints." Through a press spokesman, the secretary-general called the invasion "another serious blow to the concepts of international order and morality" and "a grave setback to the East–West détente which seemed to be re-emerging in recent months." The Security Council held five meetings on the question between August 21 and August 24. The opening meeting produced a dramatic clash between the Soviet delegate and the representative of Czechoslovakia— the Soviet claiming that the invasion took place at the request of the Prague government, and the Czech insisting that the foreign troops entered the country without the knowledge or consent of the government. The Soviet delegate strongly opposed any U.N. discussion, on grounds that the events in Czechoslovakia were exclusively a matter of concern for the Czech people and the states in the communist bloc. The Soviet position—later described in more explicit terms—was that any questions arising between communist countries could and must be settled by those countries without "foreign interference." This, the Soviet Union contended, was within the provisions of the U.N. Charter concerning individual and collective self-defense and the provisions on regional arrangements for the maintenance of international peace and security.[6]

The majority of the Security Council rejected this argument and pressed for a vote on a resolution condemning the "armed intervention" in Czechoslovakia and calling for the immediate withdrawal of all foreign troops. The vote was ten in favor, two against, and three abstentions. The negative votes were cast by the Soviet Union and Hungary—two of the invading countries. The abstentions were from India, Algeria, and Pakistan. The Soviet vote being a veto, the resolution was dead. By this time President Svoboda and party chief Dubček, who were under arrest in Moscow, had capitulated to Soviet demands that they form a new government minus "counter-revolutionaries" and committed to resuming censorship and halting all resistance to Soviet dictates. Consideration of the Czech question by the United Nations formally ended when the Prague government—now firmly under Soviet control—requested that the item be withdrawn from the Security Council agenda. In September, Soviet tanks began withdrawing from the center of Prague, and Dubček appealed to the people to bow to superior power. "Reflect on the times in which we live," he urged. "We must proceed with realities." Although the Soviet troops had pulled out of Prague, they remained in the country on a more or less permanent basis.[7]

While the question was no longer before the United Nations, Thant continued to voice his concern over the use of force against Czechoslovakia and its possible effects on East–West relations. As Thant told correspondents at a luncheon on September 19,

I am very much afraid that there will be an intensification of the Cold War during the coming months as a result of the developments in Czechoslovakia. Whatever the motives might have been for the action taken by the Soviet Union and its Warsaw Pact allies, I cannot help observing that the action has produced a feeling of disquiet and insecurity in the world at large which, I am afraid, will continue for quite some time.[8]

In the introduction to his 1968 annual report dated September 24, the secretary-general discussed the Czechoslovak events at some length. While speaking out against the Soviet Union, he used the occasion to condemn unilateral military interventions generally and made an appeal for both superpowers to abandon what he referred to as the outmoded and dangerous "strong-arm methods common in the thirties." He said, in part:

It is certainly a frightening commentary on the ominous state of world affairs that one super-state or the other can become exercised to the point of resorting to military action because of the liberalizing of a regime in a small country like Czechoslovakia or because of an internal upheaval in another small state, such as the Dominican Republic. In both cases the action taken was regarded by those who took it as necessary self-protection without any thought of territorial acquisition. . . . It is, however, a dismal outlook for the small and militarily weak states of the world—as an overwhelming majority of states are—if they can hope to control their own affairs only in so far as they can do nothing to displease their neighbors.[9]

21

Trouble in Africa: Southern Rhodesia and Biafra

The last half of the 1960s was equally as difficult for the United Nations as the initial half of the decade. The troublesome Congo problem had been liquidated. But the organization was deeply involved in Cyprus; India and Pakistan were fighting again over Kashmir; the United States had sent marines into the Dominican Republic; the Soviet bloc had invaded Czechoslovakia; the Six-Day War had rocked the Middle East; and the Vietnam War was casting a shadow over everything. As if these problems were not enough, the United Nations was confronted with new crises in Africa—particularly in Southern Rhodesia and Nigeria. Although these crises were overshadowed by some of the others, they were significant for the United Nations in that they contributed to the understanding of what the organization could and could not do. They also showed that, even 20 years after the San Francisco Conference, the public and the media expected things beyond the capabilities of the organization.

Of all Britain's African colonies, Southern Rhodesia turned out to be the biggest problem during the great decolonization explosion of the 1960s. One by one—beginning with Ghana in 1957–a dozen British-ruled territories had attained independence by 1968. Southern Rhodesia's white-dominated government had declared its independence unilaterally on November 11, 1965, but Britain's Labor government denounced the act as rebellion and took the issue to the U.N. Security Council. This was the beginning of a controversy that involved Britain, the United Nations, and most of the African governments until 1980 when the territory officially became independent and was admitted to the United Nations under its new name—Zimbabwe.

Southern Rhodesia became a full British colony in 1923 following amendments to the 1889 charter of the British South African Company, which had been organized by Cecil Rhodes to exploit the territory's mineral resources. The colony was granted self-government—but not independence—after its white residents rejected union with South Africa. In 1953 Britain decided to pool the resources of Southern Rhodesia with the protectorate of Nyasaland and Northern Rhodesia to form the Federation of Rhodesia and Nyasaland, but the federation collapsed in 1963 as a result of increasing African nationalism. Many black African leaders were beginning to rebel against domination by the white minority. In 1964 Nyasaland and Northern Rhodesia attained independence under black-dominated governments and assumed new names—Malawi and Zambia.

In Southern Rhodesia it was a different story. In April 1964 white extremists ousted Prime Minister Winston Field and replaced him with his deputy, Ian Smith—a 46-year-old cattle rancher—who immediately launched a vigorous and highly publicized campaign to win independence, through negotiations if possible. One of the Southern Rhodesian government's first acts under Smith was to ban the two African nationalist parties and place their leaders under detention. Despite the constitution of 1961, which provided for a technical nonracist franchise, stringent legislation was adopted aimed at perpetuation of the white minority's control over the colony's 4.5 million blacks. The African leaders continued to urge Britain to hold out for a "one man, one vote" system as a condition for independence; but Smith's Rhodesian Front was just as determined to maintain white control of the government, even though the colony's total white poplation was only 230,000. During the election campaign of May 1964, posters proclaimed that Ian Smith would "never hand Rhodesia over"— meaning hand it over to a majority African government. Smith won the most overwhelming victory in Rhodesian history. Armed with this mandate, the prime minister decided that the time had come for a showdown. On October 1 he told the nation that he was flying to London for a final effort to negotiate independence. He arrived on October 3, and within five days the talks were hopelessly deadlocked. A communiqué said: "Despite intensive discussions, no means have been found of reconciling the opposing views. No further meeting has been arranged."

Britain had insisted: (1) a guarantee that Africans would have unimpeded progress toward majority rule, (2) no retrogressive amendments to the constitution, and (3) immediate improvement of the political status of Africans and progress toward ending racial discrimination. Smith told a news conference that the British government could not understand that the large majority of Rhodesia's black population was too primitive and uneducated to make political decisions. "We would rather go down fighting than crawling on our knees," he said.

The stage was set for implementation of Smith's threat to declare the independence unilaterally. In an effort to "avert a tragedy," British Prime Minister Harold Wilson flew to Salisbury on October 25. He had warned a year earlier that the British government would regard a unilateral declaration of independence (UDI) as an open act of defiance and rebellion, and that it would be treasonable to take steps toward effecting it. Neither that warning nor Wilson's last-minute efforts deterred Smith.

On November 11 he read his declaration of independence on national radio—the first such unilateral declaration by a British colony since the United States broke with Britain in 1776. "We have struck a blow for the preservation of justice, civilization and Christianity," Smith said, "and in the spirit of this belief, we have this day assumed our sovereign independence. God bless you all."

London reacted quickly. The British high commissioner was withdrawn. The British governor, Sir Humphrey Gibbs, was ordered to remain at his post as a symbol of lawful British rule—but Smith took away his telephone, his Rolls Royce, and much of his staff. Wilson made it clear that force would not be used against the Rhodesian government, but Britain did order severe sanctions: suspension from commonwealth preference areas, prohibition of arms exports to Rhodesia, removal from the sterling bloc, and—hardest blow of all—purchases of Rhodesian tobacco were banned. Despite these moves, some African states broke diplomatic relations with Britain because they felt that more forceful action was required. These included Tanzania, Ghana, the United Arab Republic, Guinea, Mali, Congo (Brazzaville), Algeria, Sudan, and Mauritania.

Britain had moved immediately to take the Rhodesian dispute to the U.N. Security Council. The council quickly condemned Smith's action, and called on Britain to take all necessary action—including the use of force— to put an end to the illegal government. Britain continued to hope that economic sanctions would do the job. The council voted to support the voluntary British sanctions, and called on all U.N. members to "do their utmost" to break off all relations with Southern Rhodesia. Speaking for the United States, Ambassador Arthur Goldberg urged all members to "close ranks" behind Britian and "make effective the measures it has taken." On December 17 Britain added an oil embargo to the sanctions already ordered. At the same time, it launched an oil airlift to Zambia, where oil supplies had been cut off by Smith as a response to the British embargo.[1]

It was not long before the British realized that they had miscalculated. They had believed that the Smith regime would collapse in a matter of weeks as a result of the economic squeeze; but, due mainly to the support of Portugal and South Africa, life went on—not as comfortably as before, but well enough to keep the Smith government in business. In an effort to exert more pressure, the Security Council voted on December 16, 1966, to make the sanctions mandatory. This was the first time in the United Nations' history that mandatory sanctions had been imposed. It turned out that the new action was no more effective than the voluntary sanctions, and for the same reasons: the refusal of South Africa and Portugal to comply, plus substantial clandestine trade with other countries. Broader sanctions were voted in 1968, but these too failed to bring down the Smith regime.

The United States supported the British by initiating a number of steps as part of the sanctions program. U.S. measures included: (1) ordering an arms embargo; (2) refusing to accept Southern Rhodesia's 1965 sugar quota, which was then on the high seas; (3) cancelling Southern Rhodesia's diplomatic representation in the British embassy; (4) requesting all U.S. importers of lithium, chromite, and asbestos to find alternate sources; and (5) discouraging U.S. travel in Southern Rhodesia by requiring U.S. citizens to have valid British visas.

Ignoring all the pressure, Smith submitted to the white minority voters in 1969 a new constitution providing for racially separated election rolls—thus allowing only a small number of African representatives in the legislature. The constitution was approved in a referendum on June 20, along with a plan to end all ties with the British Commonwealth and to establish a republic. In a statement on June 21, U.N. Secretary-general Thant condemned the referendum as a "deplorable step in the wrong direction." He discussed the question extensively in the introduction to his 1969 annual report, in which he described the new constitution as one of a series of "ominous developments" aggravating the existing threat to peace. The constitution, he said, "can have no validity whatsoever."

Thant frankly acknowledged that the mandatory sanctions had failed. "The primary responsibility for this impasse," he said, "rests with the governments of South Africa and Portugal which, in defiance of the decision of the Security Council, have continued to maintain close economic, trade and other relations with the illegal regime and to accord transit and other facilities through territories under their control for trade betwen Southern Rhodesia and its overseas principals."[2]

Thant also acknowledged that many U.N. members—especially the African governments—were unhappy with Britain's reluctance to use force to suppress the rebellion. He told a news conference that the United Nations as a whole felt that "further stronger measures are necessary on the part of the British government." The disappointment of the Africans was graphically demonstrated when 24 delegations walked out of the General Assembly as British Prime Minister Wilson rose to ask for "more time and patience" in putting down the rebellion. Some of the African states took matters into their own hands by assisting militant nationalist groups inside Southern Rhodesia and by organizing guerrillas in neighboring Mozambique and Zambia for raids across the borders. By mid–1978 an estimated 6,000 soldiers and civilians had been killed in skirmishes in Southern Rhodesia.

The controversy headed toward its end when Southern Rhodesia held its first universal-franchise election on April 21, 1979, and Bishop Abel Mjzorewa's United African National Council gained a majority in the Parliament. A British cease-fire was accepted by all parties on December 5; it had been 14 years since Smith's unilateral declaration of independence. The United Nations' prestige was definitely not enhanced by the Southern Rhodesian experience. The failure of the mandatory sanctions—the organization's biggest enforcement tool outside the use of armed force—raised serious doubts as to its effectiveness as a deterrent.

One of the most tragic events during the 1960s was the civil war in Nigeria, which broke out on May 30, 1967, when the Eastern Region seceded from the former British territory and proclaimed itself the Republic of Biafra. Despite the incredible human suffering, the United Nations could play only a limited role because of the internal character of the conflict. Under Article 2, paragraph 7, of the U.N. Charter, the organization has no jurisdiction over the internal problems of states. There had been exceptions, however, in cases where intervention was requested by the government concerned. This was the case—for example—in Southern Rhodesia, Cyprus, and the Congo. But when civil war broke out in Nigeria, the Lagos government not only did not seek U.N. assistance; it firmly rejected offers of such help except for humanitarian aid. The United Nations' inability to play a peace-keeping role—like its sidelines role in the Vietnam War—proved to be a difficult one to explain to the public, and another blow to its prestige.

At the outset of the war, U Thant wrote to General Yakubu Gowon—head of the military government of Nigeria—and offered his good offices for the purposes of negotiating a settlement, but the offer was not accepted. The secretary-general's offer was repeated later on, as were similar offers from other international figures—with the same result. The secretary-general discussed the problem personally with General Gowon during a brief visit to Lagos in September 1967 while en route to Kinshasa for a meeting of the heads of state and government of the Organization of African Unity (OAU). As Thant said later, he "deeply regretted" his inability "as secretary-general to help directly in forestalling the horrors of war in Nigeria."

Fighting began in July, five weeks after Lieutenant Colonel Odumegwu Ojukwu and the elders of the Ibo tribe declared Biafra independent. The new nation (named for the Bight of Biafra, the easternmost reach of the Gulf of Guinea) claimed all lands east of the Niger River and south of the Benue—an area slightly smaller than the state of South Carolina.

The Lagos government did not take the secession too seriously at first. It looked on the task of subduing the rebels as nothing more than a police action; but disillusionment came quickly. Biafran forces led by Ojukwu—a bearded graduate of Oxford University—offered a surprisingly strong resistance, and things were going badly for the federal forces until Britain began sending in arms and supplies to its commonwealth partner. The Soviet Union also lent its support to General Gowon with shipments of jet fighter planes and bombs. The tide turned early in 1968. By November, Biafra had shriveled to 2,000 landlocked square miles, choked with six million people—nearly half of them refugees. By that time the Biafran case was hopeless, despite last-minute support by French

President de Gaulle. The war had become mostly a blockade of the beseiged Biafrans, and it was simply a question of how long they could hold out.

During the months of fighting, Thant kept in close touch with Gowon on the humanitarian aspects of the war and was represented in Nigeria first by Nils-Goran Gussing and later by Said-Uddin Khan. These representatives served a twofold purpose: (1) to assist in the distribution of relief supplies, and (2) to keep the secretary-general informed of developments. The relief supplies were being channeled through the International Committee of the Red Cross. The dimensions of the disaster had become visible to the world when photographs began to appear showing hollow-eyed children with pipe-stem arms and legs. No one knew how many had died or were dying. Some reports from Biafra said that from 6,000 to 12,000 children were dying every day. The Biafrans pleaded for an airlift of supplies; but Gowon said, "We will shoot down planes flying over Nigerian territory." Gowon offered to open corridors for the transport of food by truck, but the Biafrans refused to accept food sent overland through Nigeria—fearing that the food might be poisoned. The Red Cross did manage to get some food in by flying under cover of darkness, but thousands continued to starve because of the stalemate. By November 25, planes flying on an irregular schedule were bringing the Biafrans 100 tons of food daily. The need was estimated at 1,000–2,000 tons daily.

As for the role of the international community in seeking a settlement of the conflict, the main effort was in the hands of a six-nation committee established by the OAU and headed by Emperor Haile Selassie of Ethiopia. The committee went to Nigeria after the Kinshasa meeting in September, but left empty-handed. Another peace effort was made by the secretary-general of the British Commonwealth, Arnold Smith. He did succeed in bringing about a meeting of the two parties in Uganda, but this too ended without positive results. Nigeria insisted on what amounted to unconditional surrender and a return to the 12-state federation. Biafra stood firm for complete sovereignty. Its forces were prepared to go into the bush for a long-term guerrilla resistance, if necessary. Ojukwu felt that he was fighting for the existence of the Ibos. "The only reason we are alive today," he said, "is because we have rifles in our hand. But, for that, the massacre would be complete."

At a press conference on January 18, 1968, U Thant was asked a question that was being raised with increasing frequency in the media, just as the press and the public were asking about Vietnam: "Do you see anything that the United Nations will or can do in Biafra?" The secretary-general replied,

The question of Nigeria and Biafra is before the Organization of African Unity. I attended the last session of the OAU conference in Kinshasa last September. The matter was brought to the attention of the OAU by the members themselves. The OAU has taken certain steps toward a settlement of that problem. The OAU has formed a committee. The committee is actively involved with the question. And since the regional organization is actively in the problem, I do not think it will be useful or even desirable for the United Nations to be involved.[3]

At a luncheon of the United Nations Correspondents Association on June 18 of that year, the secretary-general was asked again—after the collapse of Arnold Smith's efforts at the Uganda meeting—whether the United Nations might now play a useful role. Once more Thant replied,

I do not believe that the United Nations will be in a position to play a useful role in the very tragic situation in the Federal Republic of Nigeria. But I have been in correspondence with the head of state, General Gowon, for some time and General Gowon has very kindly kept me posted on the developments. On this occasion I can only express my very deep concern about the situation in Nigeria resulting in death and destruction, and I would very much hope that the parties concerned will get together and discuss their common problems in a mutual spirit of cooperation and accommodation, so that these talks can lead to an enduring peace in that unfortunate country.[4]

One thing that got Thant into trouble with the media and public opinion was his open support of the Nigerian government. In this he followed the lead of the OAU, which at the Kinshasa meeting had recognized "the sovereign and territorial integrity of Nigeria" and pledged "faith in the federal government." Thant said that his own policy was guided primarily—if not exclusively—by the OAU decision. When it came to the controversy over how food should be supplied to the beleaguered Biafrans, Thant took the side of the federal government. He appealed to Colonel Ojukwu on July 11 to take advantage of General Gowon's offer for an overland corridor, and urged Ojukwu to "cooperate more fully with the international community in this genuine endeavor to ameliorate the miserable plight of the peoples in that region." Thant sent a message to Gowon saying he was "encouraged to hope that" his proposal would help solve the problem.

The war came to a sudden end on January 15, 1970, and the Republic of Biafra ceased to exist. At that time Thant happened to be paying a visit to a number of states in Africa. As late as January 4, the secretary-general was asked at a press conference in Dakar whether or not there was any way he could contribute to a settlement of the conflict. Thant explained—as he had done many times—that he believed the best approach was to leave the matter in the hands of the OAU, which had only recently sent new peace proposals to both sides. He appealed to Ojukwu to accept the proposals "for the sake of a greater Nigeria, a more prosperous Nigeria and for the sake of African unity and for the sake of a more disciplined international organization." At a press conference in Accra, Thant said that certain individuals and certain newspapers had been advocating U.N. intervention for more than two years, but that not a single member state had seen fit to bring the matter before either the Security Council or the General Assembly. If any state had rasied the issue, he said, neither body would have inscribed the question on its agenda because it was generally agreed that this was an internal matter outside the competence of the United Nations. By the time Thant reached Lomé, Togo, on January 12, it was obvious that the end was near. The Biafran headquarters at Owerri had been taken over by federal forces, and Ojukwu had fled to the Ivory Coast. In a statement at Lomé, Thant said that he had sent an appeal asking Gowon to exercise restraint in dealing with the civilian population in Biafra.[5]

Although Lagos had not been on Thant's itinerary, he quickly revised it to accept an invitation from General Gowon. Thant was pleased to have an opportunity to talk with the Nigerian leader as well as with Said-Uddin Khan, the secretary-general's personal representative, and Henrik Beer, secretary-general of the League of Red Cross Societies—who were involved in the distribution of relief supplies. Thant decided, however, to stay only one day rather than cancel a scheduled meeting with French President Georges Pompidou in Paris. This added fuel to the criticism that the supporters of Biafra had already been directing at him. The secretary-general's critics were accusing him of being indifferent to the civilian suffering and of being biased in favor of the federal government. They now said that he should have taken time to visit the war-ravaged areas of the Eastern Region. To make matters worse, the mass media distributed throughout the world garbled versions of a statement that he issued before his departure from Lagos. In this statement, Thant quoted Dr. Beer as saying that, during a tour of the afflicted area, he saw no evidence of violence or ill-treatment of the civilian population by federal troops. The widely published version omitted any reference to Dr. Beer and attributed the assessment of the situation to Thant himself. On the basis of these reports, Thant was severely criticized in the press—especially in Europe. He was particularly upset because many newspapers brought up the question of his Burmese origin, and asserted that a European would have acted differently. This was not the first time that this issue had surfaced. In one instance, it had been raised after he ordered the withdrawal of the U.N. Emergency Force from Egypt. Obviously angered by what seemed to him to be a campaign to discredit him personally, Thant asserted that no secretary-general—whether Afro–Asian, European, or Latin American—would have even been invited to Lagos if that person's attitude had been contrary to the OAU or to the attitude of the Nigerian government. He was puzzled by the bias in Europe and the United States toward Biafra. "It is interesting to note," Thant said, "the divergence of attitude and the divergence of approach to this problem by the African leaders and by a substantial section of the European press." He said that African leaders were "amazed to find that a very substantial section of the European press and mass media blamed the side which accepted" the OAU peace proposals and praised the side which rejected them. "African leaders put the blame for the civil war on Colonel Ojukwu," Thant said. "One African leader even went to the extent of saying that Colonel Ojukwu had gambled with hundreds of thousands of African lives to serve his political ends. But a substantial section of the European press and mass media put the blame on the Federal Government of Nigeria."[6]

Without drawing any specific conclusions, Thant noted that the same public relations firm that worked for Ojukwu had worked for Moise Tshombe in the Congo ten years earlier:

You know the volume of criticism leveled at the United Nations and the then secretary-general, Dag Hammarskjöld. . . . That was, to my knowledge, more or less the same as the volume of criticism leveled at the United Nations and myself by a very substantial section of the Western European press—and of course a substantial section of the press in this country [the United States] also. It is very interesting to compare the two. The European mass media and the mass media of this country was solidly with Tshombe, and a similar situation has prevailed in the past two and a half years. I do not know why a very substantial section of the Western European mass media seems to be solidly with Colonal Ojukwu. . . . I must say it has something to do with false assumptions or distorted facts.

22

The Six-Day War in the Middle East

The Middle East enjoyed a period of relative quiet from the time of the Lebanese crisis in 1958 until 1967. There was never any real peace, however, or any prospect of real peace. The fears, suspicions, and animosities that had characterized Jewish–Arab relations since the partition of Palestine had never diminished. The peace, such as it was, was maintained primarily by U.N. peacekeeping machinery—the mixed armistice commissions, the United Nations Truce Supervision Organization (UNTSO), and the U.N. Emergency Force (UNEF). During Dag Hammarskjöld's final years as secretary-general and U Thant's first term, there were numerous incidents along the Israeli–Syrian and Israeli–Jordanian borders, but the Israeli–Egyptian border had remained quiet because of the buffer provided by UNEF (the so-called glass curtain). Both Thant and Hammarskjöld frequently mentioned the Middle East as a potentially explosive problem, but it was actually the most trouble-free area in the world during those years. It is notable that Secretary-general Thant never found reason to visit the Middle East, although he visited Europe, Asia, Africa, and Latin America during this period.

The situation began to change early in 1967. Developments along the Israeli–Syrian border were especially disturbing to U.N. officials in the area. Reports to Thant from General Odd Bull of Norway—chief of staff of UNTSO—told of large-scale buildups of heavy arms, armored vehicles, and military personnel in the area of the Demilitarized Zone, both in Syria and Israel. The secretary-general was concerned sufficiently to inform members of the Security Council of the threat and to send urgent appeals to the Syrian and Israeli governments "to restrain your military forces from any action which might result in an armed clash." He also directed the UNTSO chief of staff to take every step possible to halt the military buildups. General Bull did succeed in bringing representatives of the two countries together for three meetings of the Israeli–Syrian Mixed Armistice Commission. The agenda called for discussions on the issue of agricultural cultivation arrangements in the border areas. The talks bogged down over broader issues, however, and collapsed without even getting to the original agenda. The atmosphere was too tense for any sort of constructive discussions. Chances for further meetings were dashed by a major military clash on April 7. It appeared that this might explode into a full-scale war when it was followed by an air battle between Syrian and Israeli jets in which six Syrian fighter planes were shot down. These clashes did not spark a war; but they did result in an acceleration of the ongoing military mobilization in Syria and Israel, and were followed by mobilization of the armed forces in Jordan and Egypt, as well.

During the 60 days between April 7 and June 5, 1967, the situation continued to go downhill. A number of factors contributed to the increasing tension. Among these were the border raids by El Fatah–an Arab terrorist organization– and Israel's retaliatory counterattacks. Another factor was the wave of intemperate and belligerent utterances by officials on both sides. In these circumstances, the crucial developments that occurred in mid-May were not unexpected. The seriousness of the situation became apparent on May 22 when Gamal Abdel Nasser, president of the United Arab Republic, declared in a speech to the Egyptian armed forces, that Israel was concentrating forces on Syria's borders and that he would support Syria "from the very moment" of any Israeli attack. Nasser said further that Egyptian forces had begun moving "in the direction of Sinai to take up normal positions." "We had no plan before May 13," he said, "because we believed Israel would not dare attack any Arab country." Israeli Premier Levi Eshkol told the Knesset (the Israeli parliament) on May 23 that Egyptian forces in the Sinai Peninsula had more than doubled within a short time. Eshkol declared that "the status quo must be restored on both sides of the border." He denied that Israeli forces were concentrating on the Syrian border and declared that Israel had no intention of attacking anyone. "We do not intend launching an attack," Eshkol said. "I want to say this to the Arab states and especially to Egypt and Syria, although I have said it time and time again."

The United Nations was concerned by this threat of imminent war. It was especially worried about the safety of the UNEF units manning observation posts along the Israeli–Egyptian border. By this time their position had become precarious. They were in Egypt to observe and report on possible border violations, not to resist large-scale attacks from either side. On May 16—a week before the statements by Nasser and Eshkol—the UNEF commander, Major General Indar Jit Rikhye of India, was handed a letter from the UAR chief of staff informing him that UAR troops were moving into the Sinai and requesting the immediate withdrawal of U.N. forces from the area. Rikhye replied that he had no authority to withdraw the U.N. forces, but that he would transmit the request to the U.N. secretary-general immediately. He did so; and, on the same day, Thant replied with a request for clarification of the withdrawal request. In his reply, the secretary-general said, in part:

If it was the intention of the government of the United Arab Republic to withdraw the consent which it gave in 1956 for the stationing of UNEF on the territory of the United Arab Republic and in Gaza, it was, of course, entitled to do so. Since, however, the basis of the presence of UNEF was an agreement made directly between President Nasser and Dag Hammarskjöld as secretary-general of the United Nations, any request for the withdrawal of UNEF must come directly to the secretary-general from the goverment of the United Arab Republic. On receipt of such a request, the secretary-general would order the withdrawal of the UNEF troops from Gaza and Sinai, simultaneously informing the General Assembly of what he was doing and why.

Before he received a response, Thant found that the situation had already gone out of control. In a rapid series of reports from General Rikhye on May 17, the secretary-general was informed that:

—Thirty soldiers of the UAR army had occupied El Sabha in the Sinai Peninsula and had deployed in the immediate vicinity of the UNEF observation post there.

—Three UAR armored cars were located near the Yugoslav camp at El Sabha, and detachments of 15 soldiers each had taken up positions north and south of the Yugoslav camp at El Amr.

—UAR troops had occupied the UNEF observation post at El Sabha and the Yugoslav camps at El Quisaini and El Sabha, and were now behind the positions of the UAR army.

—General Mohammed Fawzy, chief of staff of the UAR armed forces, had requested the withdrawal of Yugoslav detachments in the Sinai within 24 hours and the withdrawal of the UNEF detachment from Sharm el-Sheikh within 48 hours.

—A sizable detachment of UAR troops was moving into the UNEF area at Kuntilla.

In Thant's opinion, the decision to withdraw UNEF had been taken out of his hands. Not only had the usefulness of the buffer been eliminated, but the safety of the U.N. troops was endangered. Thant notified the permanent U.N. representative of the UAR that UNEF could not remain in the field under these conditions. In other words, he said, UNEF could not be asked "to stand aside in order to become a silent and helpless witness to an armed confrontation between two parties." Thant added that, if the orders to the UAR troops were maintained, "the secretary-general will have no choice but to order the withdrawal of UNEF from Gaza and Sinai as expeditiously as possible."

Thant quickly called a meeting of the UNEF Advisory Committee at U.N. headquarters to hear a report on these developments. He was still awaiting a formal request from Nasser to withdraw UNEF, he said, but if such a request were received he would comply "since it is the legitimate prerogative of the United Arab Republic to make such a request." The permanent representative of Canada, George Ignatieff, urged Thant to inform the General Assembly immediately without awaiting a formal request for the withdrawal. However, the secretary-general insisted that this was his decision alone to make. The seven-nation Advisory Committee was divided over procedure. José Sette Camara of Brazil and Hans Tabor of Denmark backed Ignatieff's position, while the representatives of India and Yugoslavia favored immediate compliance. "If the government of the United Arab Republic requests the removal of UNEF," declared Indian Ambassador Gopalaswami Parthasarathi, "we have to abide by the request. The General Assembly in this case has no authority to deal with the matter."

At noon the next day—May 18—the UAR ambassador handed to the secretary-general the formal request signed by Foreign Minister Mahmoud Riad. Thant informed Ambassador el-Kony that "the force will be withdrawn," but under protest. Although he was complying with the request, Thant said, he had "serious misgivings about it for, as I have said each year in my annual report to the General Assembly, I believe this force has been an important factor in maintaining relative quiet in the area of its deployment during the past ten years and that the withdrawal may have grave implications for peace." Despite his misgivings, the secretary-general issued the order for the withdrawal to begin immediately.

Two days after he issued the order, Thant announced that he would fly to Cairo to confer with officials of the UAR and with UNEF commanders. While en route, he learned that the UAR had decided to impose a blockade on shipping through the Strait of Tiran, which was Israel's gateway to the Red Sea through the Gulf of Aqaba. By the time Thant arrived, UAR forces had occupied Sharm el-Sheikh. In a report to the Security Council, the secretary-general said that the UAR action "created a new situation." In fact, it virtually assured a confrontation with Israel, which had declared that it would regard the closing of the Strait of Tiran to Israeli ships as a casus belli. In announcing the blockade, Nasser had said, "The Aqaba Gulf constitutes our Egyptian territorial waters. Under no circumstances will we allow the Israeli flag to pass through Aqaba Gulf."

Thant told the Security Council that he had "called to the attention of the United Arab Republic the dangerous consequences" of the blockade and expressed his deep concern to Nasser, but the Egyptian leader had refused to back down. Thant told the council:

I greatly fear that a clash between the United Arab Republic and Israel over this issue, in the present circumstances, will inevitably set off a general conflict in the Near East. In my view a peaceful outcome to the present crisis will depend upon a breathing spell which will allow tension to subside from its present explosive level. I therefore urge all the parties concerned to exercise special restraint, to forego belligerence and to avoid all other actions which could increase tensions, to allow the Council to deal with the underlying causes of the present crisis and to seek solutions.[1]

The "breathing spell' might have delayed the clash temporarily, but it was too late to head off the threatened war. On June 3—two days before the armed conflict began—Israel's representative told the Security Council that the crisis had been precipitated without warning on May 16 when the UAR requested the withdrawal of UNEF and moved its own forces into the positions held by U.N. forces in the Sinai. The Israeli representative added that "the secretary-general tried to prevent the crisis from getting out of hand. He failed. It was not his fault."

At 8 a.m. (Israeli time) on Monday, June 5, a message flashed to Israeli airfields, asserting that "The Egyptian army is moving against our people." It told the already alerted pilots to

Fly on. Attack the enemy. Pursue him to ruination. Draw his fangs. Scatter him in the wilderness, so that the people of Israel may live in peace in our land and the future generations be secured.

At the United Nations, diplomats disagreed as to who struck the first blow. At 3:10 a.m. (New York time), the United Nations was notified that the Arabs had attacked Israel. Twenty minutes later, another telephone call said that Israeli had attacked the Arabs. The question was academic. Lightning Israeli air attacks were underway within minutes against airfields and radar bases in Syria, Jordan, Iraq, and Egypt. The Israeli strategy was to strike quickly, catch the enemy planes on the ground, baffle and elude the radar screen, and thus eliminate any Arab threat from the air. By noon—four hours after the signal to attack—Israeli Brigadier Mordechai Mod reported that his jets had destroyed more than 400 Arab planes either in the air or on the ground at 25 airfields. His losses amounted to 19 Israeli aircraft—all lost over Egypt. The surprise attack broke the back of Arab air power, stripped the Arab troops in the open desert of air cover, and gave Israel almost complete control of the skies. Israel was virtually free to strike Arab troops, tanks, and fortifications unmolested.

As the Israeli warplanes swept the skies, Israeli ground forces moved simultaneously against Egypt, Syria, and Jordan. In the Sinai, within hours of the battle's start, Israeli troops broke through initial Egyptian resistance, smashed into Khan Yunis, drove on to Rafah, and headed up the road to Gaza where 200,000 Palestinian Arabs were reinforcing the Egyptian troops. The fighting was fierce; but, by nightfall, the Israelis had taken the Gaza Strip and gone on to El Arish. So swift was the advance that paratroops scheduled to land in support at El Arish were reassigned to other objectives. The southern and middle thrusts into Egypt were pushed forward with equal speed. By Tuesday, encirclement of the Egyptian forces was complete, and the Egyptian retreat line severed. The Egyptians tried repeatedly to break out, but without success. At the gateways to the Suez Canal, there were five major battles on Thursday, June 8—involving some 1,000 tanks. All ended in defeat for the Egyptians. In four days, Israel controlled all of the Sinai Peninsula.

In the east, the Israelis' target was Jerusalem. They hoped to take it and press on to the Jordan River. Any hope that the Holy City would be spared the ravages of war quickly vanished. The seasoned soldiers of the Arab Legion fought courageously to hold the Old City sector, but Israeli troops—advancing from both the north and the south—inched forward building by building down the winding streets. Within 48 hours, the entire city was in Israeli hands. The Jordanians were rapidly driven back to the East Bank of the Jordan. During the fighting in Jerusalem, Government House—although supposedly inviolable as headquarters of UNTSO—was first entered by Jordanian troops and later occupied by Israel. U Thant protested strongly to the Israeli government and to King Hussein of Jordan. In Gaza, meanwhile, UNEF headquarters came under direct Israeli artillery fire during the night of June 5. A UNEF convoy south of Khan Yunis was strafed by Israeli aircraft, although the vehicle—like all UNEF vehicles—was painted white. Three Indian soldiers were killed in this attack; and three others, in the Gaza attack.

From the time the fighting began on June 5, the Security Council was in almost continuous session in New York. Four cease-fire resolutions were adopted by the council between June 6 and June 11. On one day alone, the secretary-general made ten oral statements on the developing situation.[2]

Jordan agreed to a cease-fire on June 7. Egypt agreed on June 8; Israel on June 9. The fighting on the Syrian front also ceased briefly, but erupted again on June 10. It was not until June 11 that the secretary-general was able to announce to the Security Council that the Six-Day War had ended.[3]

Although the gunfire had stopped, the verbal battle continued. Soviet leader Alexei Kosygin charged that Israel "bears the full responsibility for unleashing the war." Israeli Foreign Minister Abba Eban replied that the Arab states "methodically prepared and mounted an aggressive assault designed to bring about Israel's immediate and total destruction." The Arabs and their allies demanded that Israel be condemned as an aggressor and forced to withdraw from the conquered territories. "We know, of course," said King Hussein, "that world sympathy for the Jews created Israel in the first place. But world sympathy for a tragic past does not permit condoning aggressive acts on the part of those who were once victims of aggression." President Lyndon Johnson urged negotiations between Israel and the Arabs as the best approach to a stable peace. Israel was willing to negotiate, but asserted that it did not intend to abandon all the territory it had won. Premier Eshkol told the Knesset: "We are entitled to determine what are the true and vital interests of our country and how they should be secured. The position that existed until now shall never again return."

One thing that would not be given up was the Old City part of Jerusalem. On June 28 Israel officially merged the Old City and the Israeli sector—thereby ending the separation that had existed since the 1948 war. The U.N. General Assembly denounced the unification, and a number of nations protested individually; but Israel stood firm. It did agree that the religious shrines of Christians,

Jews, and Muslims would be protected from desecration and that free access would be guaranteed to members of the different religions.

The withdrawal of UNEF, which had been ordered on May 18, was not completed until June 17 after the war had come and gone. Secretary-general Thant was sensitive to the criticism directed at him and felt that he must defend his actions. He did so in a number of official reports and public statements. Criticism came from all directions—including Washington, where President Johnson accused Thant of acting with undue haste and with failing to bring the Security Council and the General Assembly into the decision on withdrawal of UNEF. Other critics contended that Nasser had counted on Thant playing for time or agreeing to some sort of partial withdrawal. One of these was Anthony Nutting, former British minister of state for foreign affairs.[4]

One of the most severe attacks came from Abba Eban. In a speech in the General Assembly on June 19, the Israeli foreign minister said,

It is often said that the United Nations procedures are painfully slow. This one, in our view, was disastrously swift. Its effect was to make Sinai safe for belligerency from North to South; to create a sudden disruption of the local security balance; and to leave an international maritime interest exposed to almost certain threat. I will not say anything of the compulsions which may have led to these steps; I speak only of consequences. I have already said that Israel's attitude to the peace-keeping functions of the United Nations has been traumatically affected by this experience. What is the use of a fire brigade which vanishes from the scene as soon as the first smoke and flames appear? Is it surprising that we are resolved never again to allow a vital Israeli interest and our very security to rest on such a fragile foundation?[5]

In a statement on May 23, President Johnson said, "We are dismayed at the hurried withdrawal of the United Nations Emergency Force from Gaza and Sinai after more than ten years of steadfast and effective service in keeping the peace, without action by either the General Assembly or the Security Cuncil of the United Nations. We continue to regard the presence of the United Nations in the area as a matter of fundamental importance. We intend to support its continuance with all possible vigor." Johnson had additional comments in his memoirs, published in 1971. Referring to the initial Egyptian request on May 16 for the withdrawal of UNEF, the president said, "In action that shocked me then, and that still puzzles me, Secretary-general U Thant announced that U.N. forces could not remain in Sinai without Egyptian approval. Even the Egyptians were surprised. Nasser's ambassador in Washington, Dr. Mostafa Kamel, told me that his government had hoped that U Thant would play for time. But he did not, and tension increased."[6]

Another severe critic was George Lord Brown, who was British foreign secretary during the Six-Day War. In his memoirs, as published in the London Sunday *Times* of October 25, 1970, Lord Brown called Thant's action "extraordinary." He came close to charging Thant with direct responsibility for starting the war. Here is the key passage from his comment as it appeared in the Sunday *Times* (this entire passage was omitted when Lord Brown's memoirs appeared in book form):

To everybody's surprise and, as we know now, certainly to President Nasser's, the secretary-general promptly recalled the force. I shall never understand how he was advised to come to this ill-considered and, I fell absolutely sure, totally unnecessary and unexpected decision. Certainly at that moment, if at no other, the need for a very different character at the head of this vital organization, already so weakened by big power conflicts and the growth of the so-called Afro–Asian group, became very apparent. . . . The withdrawal of the U.N. Force at once created tension and prompted the Egyptian closure, to Israeli shipping, of the Strait of Tiran, leading to the Israeli port of Eilath on the Gulf of Aqaba. That put us firmly under notice that either we, in the United Nations, carried out what we said we would do after the previous war and let Israel see that she could put her trust in the United Nations, or that the Israelis would act for themselves with their pre-emptive strike.[7]

In his official reports, Thant denied that he had acted with undue haste or without adequate consultations. He contended that he took the only feasible course in dealing with Nasser's demand. In a document entitled "Notes on Withdrawal of UNEF," Thant declared that he had "only three possible courses of action, namely, to comply with the request, to reject the request or deliberately to delay the request. In the considered opinion of the secretary-general the latter two courses . . . would have served no purpose other than to worsen an already explosive situation and might have had disastrous results as regards the safety of the United Nations Force." In reply to the charge that he should have appealed to Nasser to reconsider the request, Thant declared that he had been made "well aware of the high state of emotions and tension in Cairo and in the UNEF area and had the best possible reasons to be convinced that . . . any appeal by him for a reversal of this decision would most certainly be rebuffed." He had, in fact, been advised by Foreign Minister Riad not to make such an appeal. Thant also said that continuation of UNEF operations would have been impossible after the UAR withdrew its consent, because the force had begun to disintegrate as soon as Nasser's request was made. This was a reference to the decision of India and Yugoslavia to withdraw their contingents, which totaled almost one-half of the 3,378 troops in UNEF at the time.[8]

Nasser himself said in a May 22 speech that the secretary-general had no choice but to comply with the request:

It is obvious that UNEF entered Egypt with our approval and therefore cannot continue except with our approval. . . . A campaign is also being mounted against the United Nations secretary-general because he made a faithful and honest decision and could not surrender to the pressure being brought to bear upon him by the United States, Britain and Canada to make UNEF an instrument for implementing imperialism's plans. It is quite natural—and I say this frankly—that had UNEF ignored its basic mission and turned to achieving the end of imperialism, we would have regarded it as a hostile force and forcibly disarmed it. We are definitely capable of doing such a job.

Thant maintained that his critics failed to accept the concept that a peace-keeping force such as UNEF could not enter a country or remain without the consent of the host country. He pointed out that this principle was specifically recognized by the General Assembly in the case of UNEF. In 1956 Egypt had given its consent for the stationing of UNEF in Gaza and Sinai, but Israel had refused. Thant said that Egypt as a sovereign state had the right to withdraw its consent, just as Israel as a sovereign state had exercised it right to refuse the stationing of UNEF on its side of the border. Prime Minister David Ben-Gurion had laid down this policy on November 7, 1956, in these words: "Israel will not consent under any circumstances, that a foreign force—called whatever it may—take up positions whether on Israeli soil or in any area held by Israel."

Thant called attention to this stance in his reply to Eban's speech of June 19. Thant said,

Despite the intent of the General Assembly resolution that United Nations troops should be stationed on both sides of the line, Israel has always firmly refused to accept them on Israeli territory on the valid grounds of national sovereignty. There was, of course, national sovereignty on the other side of the line as well. There can be no doubt that it would have been a helpful factor of considerable importance if Israel had at any time accepted the deployment of the United Nations Emergency Force also on its side of the line. I may report in this connection that prior to receiving the United Arab Republic request for withdrawal and prior to giving my reply to it, I had raised with the permanent representative of Israel to the United Nations the possibility of stationing elements of the United Nations Emergency Force on the Israeli side of the line. I was told that the idea was completely unacceptable to Israel.

The Middle East problem continued to be debated in the United Nations throughout the summer and fall of 1967. The Fifth Emergency Session of the General Assembly ran from June 17 through July 5 and from July 12 through July 21, but the members were so divided that no significant action could be taken. Thant acknowledged that there was disenchantment with the United Nations following the Six-Day War and that the situation bordered on hostility in some quarters. The Arabs, he said, felt that the United Nations had not done enough, and Israel felt that the organization was no longer needed and was in the way. Despite this attitude, Thant proposed that the United Nations send a special representative to the Middle East to work on such unresolved issues as Israeli troop withdrawals, national security, innocent passage of ships through the Red Sea and the Suez Canal, and the future of the one million Palestinian refugees. "I am bound to express my fear," he said, "that, if again, no effort is exerted and no progress is made towards removing the root causes of conflict, within a few years at the most there will be ineluctably a new eruption of war."[9]

The secretary-general's proposal for a special Middle East representative was finally approved by the Security Council in November as part of the resolution that became widely known as Resolution 242. This measure laid down a set of principles intended as a blueprint for a "just and lasting peace." These principles included:

1. withdrawal of Israeli troops from all territory occupied during the Six-Day War;
2. termination of claims or states of belligerency, and respect for and acknowledgment of the sovereignty, territorial integrity, and political independence of every state in the area and their right to live in peace with secure and recognized boundaries free from the threats of force;
3. guarantee of free navigation through international waterways in the area; and
4. settlement of the refugee problem.[10]

On November 23—the day after adoption of the resolution—Thant notified the Security Council that he had named Gunnar Jarring of Sweden as special representative.

23

Nationalist China Out— Red China In

As a founding member of the League of Nations and a major Allied Power in World War II, it was assumed that China would play a leading role in the creation of the United Nations and eventually in the operations of the new organization. Long before the end of the war, in fact, China became involved in the discussions that laid the foundations for the United Nations. China was a signatory of the Moscow Declaration of General Security on October 30, 1943—which called for the establishment of a "general international organization" at the earliest practicable date. It was also an active participant in the Dumbarton Oaks conversations, the Bretton Woods Conference, and other meetings aimed at the establishment of postwar international organizations.

Thus, it came about naturally that Generalissimo Chiang Kai-shek joined Franklin D. Roosevelt, Winston Churchill, and Joseph Stalin as sponsors of the San Francisco Conference in 1945 and that China emerged as one of the five permanent members of the U.N. Security Council when the charter was finally approved. When the new organization came into being, China took its place as the predominant nation of Asia. Its future role as a leading power in the United Nations seemed assured.

The world organization had barely begun to function, however, when it was confronted by unanticipated developments in Asia, which—like the Cold War— were to have a profound effect on its operations and lead to two decades of controversy. By the end of 1949—just four years after the birth of the United Nations—Chiang and his Nationalist armies had been swept from Mainland China to the island of Taiwan, where the Nationalists were to remain as rulers of China in name only.

The so-called China question first came to the United Nations on November 18, 1949, in the form of a cable from Chou En-lai, foreign minister of the new People's Republic of China, declaring that the Nationalist delegation had no right to speak for the Chinese people. This was the first of a series of developments that escalated over the next few months into a major U.N. crisis.

Despite the weaknesses of Chiang's regime, the United States had little choice but to support it in the United Nations. The Truman administration was under strong pressure from the powerful China lobby led by Senators Robert Taft and William Knowland, and by the emerging McCarran–Jenner–McCarthy forces— which were accusing the State Department of being soft on communism. There was also a conviction among some Washington officials—which proved to be unfounded—that Chinese and Soviet communism would form a unified front against the West. The Soviet stand in the Security Council seemed to confirm this belief.

Soviet Ambassador Jacov Malik threw his support behind the Chinese communists with a declaration that his delegation would not recognize the Nationalists as representatives of China. Chou sent a second cable to members of the council, demanding the expulsion of the "Kuomintang" group. Malik announced that the Soviet Union would boycott the Security Council unless Peking was seated. But the council rejected a Soviet resolution calling for the replacement of the Nationalists by Peking representatives. The vote—six against, three in favor, and two abstaining—triggered a chain of Soviet walkouts, beginning with the council itself and spreading to one U.N. organ after another until it became almost a total boycott. Before leaving the council chamber, Malik declared that the U.S.S.R. would not recognize as legal any Security Council decisions adopted with the participation of the Kuomintang representatives.[1]

"January 13 was a dark day for the United Nations," Secretary-general Trygve Lie said in his memoirs. "Pessimism among the ten remaining representatives was obvious. . . . The United Nations was being pushed to the wall at a time when its existence hinged on holding fast to every vestige of strength and authority."[2]

The Soviet boycott was still in effect on June 25, 1950, when North Korean troops attacked South Korea. In the absence of the Soviet delegation, the Security Council quickly adopted a resolution directing the North Korean authorities to withdraw their troops to the 38th parallel and calling on all members "to render every assistance to the United Nations in the execution" of the resolution. It also called on the members "to refrain from giving assistance to the North Korean authorities." Observers along the battlefront had already reported that the North Koreans were using Soviet-made weapons as well as huge Soviet tanks. The Soviets certainly would have vetoed the resolution if they had not been boycotting the meeting. In the long run, it would have made little difference. On the basis of the resolution, President Truman announced immediately that the United States had dispatched air and sea forces to assist the South Korean government. A later resolution on July 7 gave the United

States responsibility for directing a Unified Command under the U.N. flag. Within a month, 15 countries besides the United States and South Korea had combat forces under General of the Armies Douglas MacArthur.

By this time Malik had resumed his seat in the Security Council, and the Soviet boycott of other U.N. organs and been terminated. Under the system of alphabetical rotation, the Soviet delegate became president of the council for the month of August. Malik ruled immediately that the Chinese Nationalist delegation could not sit at the table. This began a month-long procedural wrangle, which virtually paralyzed the Council. Malik's ruling on the Chinese Nationalists was reversed by a vote of eight to three, with only India and Yugoslavia joining him. The council later rejected a Soviet proposal for formal discussion of "recognition of the representatives of the People's Republic of China."[3]

Although the initial battleground was the Security Council, the Chinese representation question shifted to the General Assembly in the fall of 1950. It had already become known that Chinese troops had entered the Korean War. Peking called them "volunteers," but no one doubted that Red China was in the war. On November 10, six member nations submitted a resolution to the Security Council, calling on Peking to withdraw its forces from Korea. Britain proposed that the Chinese communist regime be invited to take part in the discussions, but Peking refused. Within days it had become obvious that the Chinese was intervening with massive forces. Defeat of the U.N. forces seemed imminent. On December 5, Trygve Lie declared in a speech that "the peace of the world is in the gravest danger only five years after the end of the Second World War and the establishment of the United Nations."[4]

It was at this time that Peking filed a complaint with the Security Council, charging the United States with "armed invasion of Taiwan." Of course, it was ridiculous to say that the United States had invaded Taiwan. At the beginning of the Korean War, not only did the United States have no military forces on Taiwan, but the White House had declared that the United States would not provide military assistance to the Nationalists or use U.S. armed forces in any way to interfere in the Chinese civil war. However, U.S. relations with Taiwan underwent a change on June 25, with the communist attack on South Korea. President Truman ordered the U.S. Seventh Fleet to seal off Taiwan from the conflict. It was this change in U.S. policy that led to the Peking complaint of "armed invasion of Taiwan."

Although the Chinese communist regime had rejected a U.N. invitation to send representatives to New York to discuss a Korean cease-fire, it decided to send a delegation a few weeks later to press the charges against the United States. The delegation, which was headed by General Wu Hsui-chuan, arrived at the end of November. This was the first and only Peking delegation to appear at U.N. headquarters during all the long controversy over Chinese representation. Both Secretary-general Lie and a number of U.N. delegates decided that the presence of the Chinese communists offered an opportunity to negotiate a

Korean cease-fire. Wu, however, took the rigid position that he was in New York only to press charges against the United States. Lie told him in private talks that, if the Chinese "volunteers" and the North Koreans would agree to a cease-fire, Peking would have a better chance of getting into the United Nations—but that this could not be a condition for the cease-fire. The peace efforts broke down when Wu insisted that the only negotiations could be on the Soviet terms—simultaneous talks on a cease-fire, Peking's seating in the United Nations, and a settlement of Taiwan's future. Wu's delegation left on December 19, effectively ending all direct contact with the United Nations for the next two decades. Lie said later, "I have often wondered which, if any, change in the course of events might have occurred had some degree of direct liaison been maintained, so as to avoid the sifting of all communications through indirect channels."

As early as March 1950, Lie had become personally involved in the controversy by circulating a legal memorandum, which declared that, when two governments contend for the same seat, "the question at issue should be which of the two governments is in a position to employ the resources and direct the people of the state in fulfillment of the obligations of membership." Lie argued that an inquiry should be made as to "whether the new government exercises effective authority within the territory of the state and is habitually obeyed by the bulk of the population." If the answer was in the affirmative, he said, that government should be given the right to represent China. It was obvious that the Nationalist regime—with authority over some 19 million Taiwanese—could not legitimately claim to rule the 800 million Chinese on the mainland. Lie was subjected to a barrage of attacks from Nationalist officials, as well as a segment of the U.S. press.[5]

Beginning with the 1951 session, the Chinese representation question returned each year. A pattern was set at that session when the assembly's General Committee approved a Thai proposal to postpone discussion of the question. Soviet Deputy Foreign Minister Andrei Vyshinsky moved in the plenary meeting to overrule the decision and place the issue on the agenda. U.S. Secretary of State Dean Acheson objected to discussing the question "at the very time when its [Peking's] international conduct was so low that it would take considerable improvement to raise it to the level of barbarism." The Soviet proposal was rejected by a vote of 37 to 11 with four abstentions. Each year from then until 1960, the United States led a parliamentary fight to postpone action and thus to prevent the issue from coming to a decisive vote on its merits. Beginning in 1961 the vote was on the question of expelling Nationalist China and seating Peking. Only in 1964 was there no vote—because of the Article 19 voting crisis, which caused the assembly to shelve all controversial issues. The voting on China was close only in 1965 when it was tied 47 to 47 with 20 abstaining, and in 1970 when Peking finally gained a 51–49 majority. In each case, however, the General Assembly had decided in advance that a two-thirds majority was needed.[6]

A peculiar facet in the battle over the China seat was the fact that the Peking government made little effort on its own behalf after its initial 1949 and 1950 moves. For the most part, it depended entirely on friendly countries to carry the ball. In the beginning the Soviet Union led the fight. Then it was India. After Red China's attack on India in 1962, the lead shifted to Albania. One of the best-known personalities involved in the fight was India's V. K. Krishna Menon, who was often critical of the United States and was sometimes accused of being procommunist. It was during the China debate in 1956 that he tangled with former Senator William Knowland, then a member of the U.S. delegation. Knowland said he was shocked that Menon had apparently become the "floor leader of the Soviet drive to bring Communist China into the United Nations." Menon shot back that shock was a state of mind and anyone suffering from it should see a doctor. He called on Chief U.S. Delegate Henry Cabot Lodge to disavow Knowland's statement. Lodge ignored the request.

During the years after 1950, the Peking regime was openly hostile to the United Nations. In fact, Red China seemed to go out of its way to show its disdain for U.N. objectives, such as U.N. Charter provisions against the use of force to settle disputes. Apart from its military intervention in Korea and its support of Ho Chi Minh's North Vietnam forces, Mainland China had invaded and occupied Tibet and had backed an unsuccessful coup by Indonesian communists. Early in 1955 Secretary-General Dag Hammarskjöld did get permission to go to Peking to discuss the possible release of some U.S. fliers held prisoner since the Korean War; but U Thant was rebuffed when he put out feelers in 1965 about a possible Peking visit to discuss a Vietnam cease-fire. Thant told a news conference that he had asked Algerian President Ben Bella to sound out the Chinese communists on Vietnam peace steps, but the word came back that Peking had ruled out any U.N. role. "In the face of Peking's reaction," Thant said, "I do not see any point in discussing the possibility of my visit to Peking."

Peking's hostility toward the United Nations was one of the reasons that the world organization was bypassed by the big powers in calling the 1954 Geneva Conference on Korea and Southeast Asia. Neither the Chinese communist regime nor any of the other communist participants in the Vietnam and Korean wars were members of the United Nations or wanted anything to do with the organization. The United States had not recognized the Peking government but Secretary of State John Foster Dulles agreed with Britain, France, and the Soviet Union on the necessity for including all the combatants in the Geneva discussions. Dulles was determined, however, to resist any Soviet attempts to have the Peking delegation receive equal status with the "Big Four." Before leaving Washington he stressed that U.S. agreement with inviting Peking to participate "does not imply our diplomatic recognition of Red China." As he said, "It is not a Big Five conference. The Soviet Union tried to make it that, but gave in before the combined opposition of France, Great Britain and the United States."[7]

Regardless of diplomatic status, Chou En-lai lost no time in establishing himself as a key figure at the conference. Making his debut in the world forum, he demanded that all foreign governments get their troops out of Asia and leave the continent's problems to Asians. Chou also called for: (1) an end to the U.S. "occupation" of Taiwan; (2) an end to the rearming of West Germany; (3) adoption of the Soviet Security Alliance for Europe; (4) world reduction of armaments; and (5) a ban on atomic, hydrogen, and other mass destruction weapons. Notable was the omission of any mention of the United Nations.

Although Chou participated in both the Korean and Southeast Asia phases of the conference, the United States carefully avoided any direct contact with him outside the meeting room. In an incident during one of the social hours, the charismatic Chou embarrassed a member of the U.S. delegation by walking up to him and extending his hand for a handshake. The U.S. delegate, Assistant Secretary of State Walter Robertson, had to decide quickly whether to shake hands or openly rebuff the smiling Chinese foreign minister. He shook hands. These social hours were closed to the press, and the incident would have passed without notice had not an amused diplomat reported it to a newspaper correspondent. When Robertson learned of the leak—not world shaking in importance, but personally embarrassing—he appealed to the correspondent to stop publication. It was too late. The item was already in print.

The Soviet Union and the People's Republic of China presented a solid front at the Geneva Conference in support of the North Vietnamese and the North Koreans. There were no signs yet that the communist world would soon be divided in a bitter name-calling conflict that led them to the brink of war. As early as 1958, evidence of the growing friction between the communist giants began to appear; but it was not until 1960 that the quarrel moved into full public view. Differences in ideology were part of the problem, but also Peking was unhappy about the meagerness of Soviet economic and military assistance. After an open break at the international meeting of communists in Bucharest in 1960, the Soviet Union tore up hundreds of agreements, withdrew Soviet experts working in China, and cut off the supply of important items of equipment. On its side, the Peking regime cancelled agreements calling for the delivery of rare metals to the Soviet Union. The feud was intensified in 1966 by the internal turmoil in China during the Great Proletarian Cultural Revolution. Red Guards—obviously with official blessing—harassed Soviet diplomats and proclaimed lasting Chinese hatred for the Soviet "revisionists." A huge poster plastered on the fence of the Soviet embassy declared that someday "we shall cut the skin off you, we shall tear out your guts, we shall burn your corpses and disperse your ashes to the winds." Moscow replied that Chairman Mao Tse-tung's regime was not communist or socialist, but a simple military dictatorship. In April 1969, Moscow broadcast a tabulation showing—it said—that the Peking regime had slaughtered 26 million persons in 20 years. It was about this time that a serious military clash occurred on the disputed far-east boundary of the U.S.S.R. A wider conflict was averted when Soviet Premier Alexei Kosygin flew to Peking and agreed with Chou to settle the dispute by negotiations. By this time Soviet–Chinese trade had virtually dried up.[8]

What effect did all this have on the China representation question in the United Nations? It meant that the Soviet Union, which had once boycotted U.N. organs on Peking's behalf, no longer took an active role in pressing for the seating of the Chinese communists. The Soviets did vote in favor of the Chinese communists, but that was all. India had stopped leading the fight for Peking, but was also still voting for its representation. It was now left to maverick Albania to push for the seating of Peking. The rift in the communist ranks did, however, lead the United States to rethink its position. In 1967 President Richard M. Nixon wrote in the important quarterly *Foreign Affairs*: "We simply cannot afford to leave China forever outside the family of nations." In 1970 Nixon declared that the Chinese communists "should not remain isolated from the international community." From that time on, the main U.S. problem was what to do about its friend and ally, Nationalist China. It was this quandary that gave birth to the Two Chinas policy, which was rejected by both Taiwan and Peking and was liked by almost no one. By this time, it was clear that the United States would lose its 22-year battle on China representation.

The real clincher was Nixon's decision to visit Peking. Many countries that had stuck with the United States in the past on the China issue decided the time had come to look to their own relations with Peking. The main test in the 1971 General Assembly session was on a U.S.-sponsored resolution that would have invoked the two-thirds rule. This was defeated by a vote of 55 in favor, 59 against, and 15 abstaining. A few minutes later the assembly approved an Albanian resolution expelling the Nationalists and seating Peking. Even before the vote, however, the long conflict ended when Nationalist Foreign Minister Chow Shu-kai led his delegation from the blue-and-gold assembly chamber after a dramatic farewell blast. "To deny the Republic of China its rightful position in the United Nations," he told a news conference, "is to violate the charter and negate its noble and sacred principles and purposes upon which the United Nations was founded. We have been very patient. The U.N. has deteriorated. It is no longer the organization that was founded in 1945. It is a circus."[9]

The vote itself touched off a jubilant demonstration among pro-Peking delegates—which, indeed, bore some resemblance to a circus and which incensed some U.S. politicans, including Nixon himself. Tanzanian delegates dressed in their colorful national garb danced a jig in the aisles, while Algerians and Albanians stood and embraced each other or raised their hands in a victory salute. As viewed on U.S. television, the whole scene was especially shocking because of its anti-U.S. overtones. Senator Barry Goldwater of Arizona called on the United States to pull out of the United Nations and banish its headquarters to "some place like Moscow or Peking." And Senate Majority Leader Hugh Scott of Pennsylvania spoke derisively of "hot pants principalities" that had opposed the United States. Nixon's press secretary, Ron Ziegler, denounced "the shocking demonstration and undisguised glee among some delegates following the Assembly vote."

On November 15—three weeks after the U.S. defeat—Peking finally took the Chinese seat in the General Assembly. Chinese experts agreed that the delegation was top flight, and that its composition reflected a desire to play an active role. At its head was Deputy Foreign Minister Chiao Kuan-hua—one of Peking's most experienced diplomats. As permanent U.N. representative was round-faced Huang Hua, who had been standing by as ambassador to Canada during the crucial 1971 developments. After a welcoming ceremony that lasted five and a half hours and included speeches from 56 delegates, Chiao took the rostrum for his acceptance speech. Much to the surprise of diplomats who had predicted a low-key approach, the Chinese delegate launched an attack on the "super powers." Although it hit the Soviet Union to some extent, this tirade was aimed mainly at the United States. Chiao accused the United States of aggression in Taiwan, Vietnam, Cambodia, and Laos and demanded that U.S. forces be withdrawn from all these areas.[10] U.S. Ambassador George Bush responded by issuing a White House–approved statement calling it "empty cannons of rhetoric."[11]

What surprised many diplomats was the exchange that developed in the next weeks between the Chinese and the Soviets. The two countries transferred their ideological conflict to the U.N. meeting rooms, and aired their differences before a worldwide audience. The ensuing name-calling match was reminiscent of the worst days of the Cold War. The split in the communist world was never more evident than during the debate in the Security Council on the India–Pakistan War. It was odd to find the Soviet Union supporting India and wielding the veto three times while China supported Pakistan and lined up with the United States and the council majority in pushing for a cease-fire resolution. Even that early, it had become clear that Peking would follow its own policies and would not be just another element in a monolithic communist bloc.

24

The United Nations' Frustrating Battle with South Africa

No single problem has been more frustrating for the United Nations from its inception than the continued conflict with the Republic of South Africa over the territory of South-West Africa and over the policy of apartheid. Despite more than four decades of effort, the United Nations has made absolutely no progress in solving either of these problems. Resolution after resolution has been adopted, hundreds of hours of debate have taken place, punitive measures have been taken, and the International Court of Justice has made rulings; but—as U Thant once observed—all these efforts have "met a solid wall of defiance." Along the way, South Africa has shown its contempt for the United Nations numerous times, one notable example being its flouting of the mandatory sanctions against Southern Rhodesia.

The status of South-West Africa—a League of Nations mandate administered by South Africa—came under discussion in the United Nations in 1946 when Prime Minister Jan Christiaan Smuts proposed incorporation of the 317,887-square-mile territory into South Africa. The General Assembly rejected the proposal and demanded that South-West Africa be placed under the U.N. trusteeship system, as other League mandates had been. Smuts refused. This was the beginning of the long feud between South Africa and the United Nations. With the rise of independent countries in southern Africa and their membership in the United Nations, the issue became increasingly critical.

Even as early as 1953 when Trygve Lie was leaving office, the secretary-general listed South Africa's challenge as one of several "entrenched disagreements," which were likely to plague the organization in the future. "The South African problems of the status and treatment of Indian minorities and the fate of South West Africa," he said, "have consistently beset the United Nations and the South African policy of apartheid, or separation of races, threatens to become a third." Actually, South Africa's Nationalist party—militant advocate of apartheid—had come to power in 1948 and pushed through Parliament the Group Area Act, which empowered the government to designate areas throughout the country for the exclusive residence of one or another racial groups. The party's position on apartheid had been explained bluntly and simply in a campaign pamphlet, foreshadowing the legislation that would follow during the years to come. "Either we must follow the course of equality," the pamphlet said, "which will eventually mean national suicide for the white race or we must take the course of separation."

The concern of the United Nations—even before the flood of new African members—was reflected in the 1950 session of the General Assembly, which established a three-member commission to "study the racial situation in the Union of South Africa." The commission reported back in 1953 that "the doctrine of racial differentiation and superiority on which the apartheid policy is based is scientifically false, extremely dangerous to internal peace and international relations." It was in 1950 also that the International Court of Justice delivered an advisory opinion on South-West Africa, holding that the League mandate remained in force and that South Africa was obliged to submit to U.N. supervision over the administration of the territory. The South African government ignored the court ruling as well as action by the General Assembly accepting the advisory opinion as binding.

At the 1966 session of the assembly, 54 African and Asian countries introduced a resolution proposing that the United Nations take over the administration of South-West Africa and prepare it for independence, regardless of South Africa's stand. Up to that time, some 75 resolutions had been adopted on the subject of South-West Africa in the preceding 21 years, but without positive results. The new proposal provided for the creation of a 14-member Ad Hoc Committee, which would recommend practical means for the takeover. The General Assembly adopted the resolution on October 27. The Ad Hoc Committee was directed to give a report to a special session of the assembly as soon as possible, but not later than April 1967.[1]

When the special session was convened on April 21, the committee reported that it had been unable to agree on how to accomplish the takeover. On May 19, however, the assembly adopted a resolution setting up an 11-nation Council for South-West Africa to administer the territory until it attained independence. This council was to be based in South-West Africa and was directed to "enter immediately into contact with the authorities of the Republic of South Africa to lay down procedures . . . for the transfer of the territory with the least possible upheaval." The assembly members seemed to assume that South Africa would somehow agree to the takeover. Without consulting South Africa, the General Assembly had changed the name of the territory to Namibia and set June 1968 as the target date for independence. The resolution was approved by a vote of

85 to 2 with 30 abstentions. As usual, the negative votes had been cast by South Africa and Portugal. During the debate, South Africa had contended that the assembly's action terminating the mandate and all related actions were illegal. South African officials made it clear that they would not cooperate in any way with the newly created council. Not only did they refuse to deal with the council; they announced a policy of closer integration of the territory into South Africa.[2]

One surprising development during this phase of the dispute was the line taken by the Soviet Union. The Soviets deplored the whole idea of a U.N. interim administration, and demanded immediate independence for South-West Africa. The African nations did not take the demand seriously. They felt that this was a political ploy, since they were convinced that immediate independence was out of the question. One effect of the Soviet stand was to force the Africans to shelve a tentative plan to create a U.N. police force for use against South Africa. The Soviet Union argued that any enforcement action necessary could be taken through the Organization of African Unity (OAU). While the Africans were upset by the Soviet attitude, they were also unhappy over the reluctance of the United States and Britain to back a showdown with South Africa. The attitude of the Western powers was one of "Let's be patient" and "Let's study the whole question."

Despite the attention given to the South African problem by the United Nations, it was not until an event on March 21, 1960, that the world was made aware of the true gravity of the situation. This was the Sharpsville massacre in which 69 Africans were killed and 178 wounded when police opened fire on a crowd of demonstrators. The demonstration was part of a protest against the government's passbook laws, under which black Africans over the age of 16 were required to carry elaborate "reference books" with the person's life history. A crowd variously estimated at between 5,000 and 20,000 had gathered outside the fence surrounding the police station at Sharpsville, 30 miles south of Johannesburg. On the other side of the fence were some 300 police armed with rifles and machine guns and supported by four Saracen tanks. Nothing happened for several hours, but suddenly the police opened fire. Within less than a minute, 700 rounds of ammunition were poured into an unarmed crowd. What triggered the attack was never known—or, at least, never disclosed. The government tried to justify it by presenting testimony at a formal investigation to the effect that the crowd was ugly and threatening.

The massacre brought the U.N. Security Council into the apartheid dispute for the first time. Until then, U.N. efforts had been confined to the General Assembly, the Human Rights Commission, and various special groups set up by the assembly. At the request of 29 Asian and African states, the Security Council took up the Sharpsville incident immediately.[3]

On April 1 the council adopted a resolution deploring the racial policies and actions of the South African government, and called for an end of apartheid. The resolution declared that the situation, "if continued, might endanger international peace and security." This phrase was significant, since it made the distinction between the domestic affairs of a country—which were outside the jurisdiction of the United Nations—and a situation that was within the competence of the organization. The council's resolution requested Secretary-general Hammarskjöld "in consultation with the government of the Union of South Africa, to make such arrangements as would adequately help in upholding the purposes and principles of the charter." The vote was nine to zero, with Britain and France abstaining on grounds that the action constituted an intervention in the internal affairs of South Africa—as the Pretoria government maintained.[4]

Hammarskjöld met in London on May 13 and 14 with South African Foreign Minister Eric Louw. Agreement was reached on plans for the secretary-general to conduct further consultations in Pretoria, on the understanding that the talks would "not require prior recognition from the Union government of the United Nations" jurisdiction.[5]

Hammarskjöld planned to visit South Africa in July; but he had to postpone his trip because of the Congo crisis, which was involving the United Nations at that time. The secretary-general did visit South Africa early in 1961 in an effort to find a way out of the problem, but his talks with Prime Minister Hendrik Verwoerd got nowhere. Hammarskjöld took some comfort in the fact that he was at least received by the South African leader, but he saw no reason for further direct talks unless there appeared to be a chance that "such consultations might yield results." Hammarskjöld added that "Consultations are not and cannot be an end in themselves."

There was a period during the 1950s and early 1960s when South Africa seemed to be heading toward total withdrawal from the increasingly hostile world. In 1955, for example, the South Africans withdrew from the U.N. Educational, Scientific, and Cultural Organization (UNESCO) because of mounting criticism in that agency; and in 1956 it decided to maintain only a token representation at U.N. headquarters until the General Assembly discontinued "interfering" in the Union's domestic affairs. In an all-white referendum in 1960, voters approved the establishment of the Republic of South Africa. This meant a break with the British Crown, although not yet with the Commonwealth. However, it did withdraw from the Commonwealth in 1961, after African members of that group began pressing for its expulsion. The Addis Ababa Conference of African States went further by calling on all African countries to sever diplomatic relations with South Africa, close their seaports to South African ships, boycott South African goods, and refuse landing and passage rights to South African aircraft.[6]

Evidently the Pretoria government had second thoughts about isolating itself. In 1958 it ended its token representation at the United Nations, restored its full delegation, and began fighting back at its critics. Foreign Minister Louw attended the 1961 session of the General Assembly and caused an uproar by delivering a speech defending South Africa's apartheid policies. African delegates tried to shout him down and demanded that his remarks be expunged from the records. They failed to get sufficient support for such an unprecedented move, but the assembly did approve a censure motion—the first of its kind in U.N. history—by a vote of 67 to 1 with 20 abstentions.

By this time it was obvious that a negotiated settlement had become impossible. The black Africans were becoming more militant, and the South African government was adopting an increasingly hard line. The hand of the authorities was strengthened by elections in 1953, 1958, and 1961 that gave the Nationalist party bigger and bigger majorities in Parliament.

The General Assembly decided that it, too, must look to stronger measures to halt the deterioration of the situation. In 1962 it voted a series of nonbinding economic and political sanctions, requesting member states to: (1) terminate or refrain from establishing diplomatic relations with South Africa; (2) close ports to all vessels flying South Africa's flag; (3) prohibit their ships from entering South African ports; (4) boycott all South African goods, and refrain from exporting goods—including arms and ammunition—to South Africa; and (5) refuse landing and passage facilities to all aircraft belonging to South Africa. The sanctions were doomed at the outset, when none of South Africa's major trading partners voted for the resolution. Failure of the action was soon confirmed when reports showed that few countries were fully complying.

In August 1963 the Security Council took a limited step toward sanctions by voting 9–0 for an arms embargo. Although this was not mandatory, Britain and France again abstained. The resolution "solemnly" called on all states to "cease forthwith the sale and shipment of arms, ammunition of all types, and military vehicles to South Africa." The United States immediately announced that it would comply. Britain followed later, as did a substantial number of other countries. This—like the assembly action and that of the African states—proved to be ineffective. Nevertheless, the council continued to grapple with the problem. In December 1963 it established a special task force headed by Alva Myrdal of Sweden to "examine methods of resolving the present situation through full, peaceful and orderly application of human rights and fundamental freedoms to all the inhabitants of the territory as a whole, regardless of race, color or creed, and to consider what part the United Nations might play in the achievement of that end." The task force made two major recommendations: (1) that all the people of South Africa be permitted to decide the future of the country in a fully representative national assembly; and (2) that a practical and technical study of the logistics of sanctions be authorized. The council approved these recommendations. The logistical study, however, was not very helpful. After a year of work, the experts found that sanctions might be sucessful if universally applied and if adequate enforcement machinery were established. It did not seem likely that either of these conditions could be met in the case of South Africa.[7]

In Pretoria the government was resorting to the harshest sort of measures to control the militant black nationalists. In 1962 sabotage was added to the list of capital offenses. The South African authorities were particularly concerned by the stepped-up activities of Spear of the Nation—the action arm of the African National Congress (ANC), engaging in sabotage and other violence against property. In July 1963 the secret police raided a house in Rivonia (a section of Johannesburg), and rounded up 17 alleged leaders of Spear of the Nation—including Nelson Mandela, the so-called Black Pimpernel of the African underground. At this point, the U.N. Security Council intervened in an effort to head off the wave of executions in South Africa. During 1963–64— according to U.N. figures—257 Africans were condemned to death, and 164 of them actually hanged. The Security Council urged South Africa to renounce the death penalty for anti-apartheid acts and to grant amnesty to all political prisoners. Two days after the council's appeal, all but one of the Rivonia prisoners—including Mandela—were sentenced to life imprisonment.

It was also in 1964 that U Thant intervened on behalf of three black men facing execution for anti-apartheid acts. Noting resolutions of the Security Council, the General Assembly, and the U.N. Special Committee on Apartheid—all urging the release of political prisoners—Thant sent a memorandum to South Africa's U.N. ambassador, Matthys I. Botha, in which he said, "I wish to request you to convey my urgent and earnest appeal to your government to spare the lives of those facing execution or death sentences for acts arising from their opposition to the government's racial policies, so as to prevent an aggravation of the situation and to facilitate peaceful efforts to resolve the situation."[8] The secretary-general received an angry rebuke from Ambassador Botha for his efforts. Botha told Thant that the South African government felt "compelled to give expression to unqualified disappoveal" of his intervention. He demanded that Thant "respect the principle of nonintervention in the judicial processes of an independent state."[9]

The tug of war went on. In 1967 the South African government adopted a Terrorism Act, which laid down penalties ranging from five years imprisonment to capital punishment for various activities defined as terrorism. It also provided for indefinite detention—without trial—of suspects accused of withholding information about acts of terrorism. Among the first to be tried under the Terrorism Act were 37 Bantus from South-West Africa who were accused of guerrilla activities. Under the new law, the accused were required to prove their innocence. Once again the Security Council, the General Assembly, and the Human Rights Commission intervened with a demand for release of the prisoners. And once again their appeals were ignored. All the accused were given long prison terms—19 of them, life imprisonment.[10]

In his 1970 annual report, U Thant reviewed the quarter-century of futile U.N. efforts to solve the South African problem. It was "with a heavy heart," Thant said, that he told the story of the organization's failure through the years:

It is disheartening to note all the efforts made by the organization over the years have not yet resulted in alleviating the situation which prevails in southern Africa. Disregarding the appeals and demands of the Security Council, South Africa has evolved a system of government which is entirely inconsistent with the purposes and principles of the charter of the United Nations and the Universal Declaration of Human Rights. The enforcement of increasingly ruthless and inhuman measures of racial segregation has heightened racial bitterness in the country and created an explosive situation. By suppressing the legitimate opposition to apartheid and by resorting to extreme repressive measures, which are clearly in violation of the principles of the rule of law, the government of South Africa has closed all avenues of peaceful change in the country. The leaders of the oppressed people of South Africa have expressed their determination to resort to violent methods in order to redress the situation and achieve their inalienable rights and freedom. The situation, as it now exists, constitutes a threat to international peace and security. Moreover, by extending the policies of apartheid to the international territory of Namibia and by encouraging the other white-minority regimes in southern Africa to defy U.N. resolutions, South Africa has clearly shown its determination to challenge the authority of the organization in the region.

"The General Assembly, aware of the seriousness of the situation, has prescribed the enforcement of sanctions against South Africa. The Security Council has recommended that the government of South Africa should either hold referendums among all the peoples of South Africa with a view to determining a new policy likely to ensure human rights and freedoms for all or face sanctions by the international community. What is needed above all is the political will on the part of the member states to take effective measures which would induce South Africa to renounce its policies.[11]

The explosive situation referred to by Thant finally erupted in June 1976, in what history would call the "Soweto uprising"—one of the worst racial upheavals in South African history. By the time it was over at least 176 persons—all but two of them blacks—were dead, and another 1,139 people were injured. Some 1,300 were under arrest. The clash began between police and students protesting the compulsory use of the Afrikaans language in black schools on a 50–50 basis with English. The blacks regarded Afrikaans as the language of their oppressors. The initial clash on June 16 grew into a week of violence as enraged black students roamed the 26 square miles of the township—burning, looting, and shouting black power slogans. They attacked cars, buses, schools, administration buildings, liquor stores, libraries, and clinics, and hurled rocks at police patrols trying to restore order. The rioting spread from Soweto—the largest township in South Africa—to other townships around Pretoria and Johannesburg. The government called in thousands of police—many armed with automatic rifles—and put army reservists on a standby alert. Rioters were bombarded with tear gas from helicopters. The townships were sealed off by roadblocks. Prime Minister John Vorster warned the nation: "We will not be intimidated and we will maintain order at all costs." Police were authorized to use "every available means" to put down the rioting.

Order was finally restored, but trouble erupted again two months later when Zulu migrants in Soweto resisted a strike call by black militants. More than 30 blacks were killed in the August clashes. Another 70 blacks died in December in intertribal fighting outside Capetown.

The Soweto upheaval was the forerunner of future bloody confrontations between the black Africans and the police—which occurred periodically over the next decade. On June 16, 1986, for example, millions of blacks throughout the country marched to mark the tenth anniversary of the Soweto uprising. Four days earlier the government had declared a nationwide state of emergency, giving almost unlimited powers to the security forces.[12]

The 1970s and 1980s also saw continued conflict over South-West Africa— or Namibia, as it was called by the United Nations. A new element was added when guerrilla fighters organized by the Marxist South-West Africa Organization (SWAPO) began receiving their training in Angola from that country's Cuban-backed troops. The presence of the guerrillas added to the tension in South-West Africa, where the political situation was in a state of confusion. In June 1971 the International Court of Justice handed down another advisory opinion— this one declaring that South Africa was occupying Namibia illegally. This did not prevent South Africa from going ahead with elections in 1978—without U.N. supervision—for a constituent assembly in South-West Africa. The decision was ignored by the major black parties, which stayed away from the polling places. The United Nations regarded the elections as illegal—as expected—and went ahead drafting plans of its own to be unveiled in 1980. The U.N. plans called for a cease-fire and for a demilitarized zone 31 miles deep on each side of the Namibian borders with Angola and Zambia, to be patrolled by U.N. peace forces guarding against guerrilla action. Impartial elections would be held in 1982. South Africa and SWAPO agreed in principle to the proposed cease-fire and elections, but South Africa insisted on the withdrawal of Cuban forces from Angola as a precondition to Namibia's independence. The prospects for peace vanished in January 1983 when South Africa dissolved the Namibian National Assembly and resumed direct control of the territory. The world got still another shock when South Africa sent its troops into neighboring Zambia, Zimbabwe, and Botswana to strike at suspected guerrilla strongholds.

As the U.N. confrontation with South Africa entered its fifth decade, a solution seemed even more remote. Sanctions—including those imposed unilaterally by the United States—had not had any appreciable effect on South Africa's policies. U.S.-based corporations that pulled out of South Africa had been replaced by South African owners—many of whom terminated the U.S.-required social reforms that had been in place. In the 1987 white-only election, the racially moderate Progressive Federal party was replaced as the official opposition party in Parliament by the pro-apartheid Conservative party. As a result, President P. W. Botha faced criticism not for moving too slowly to abolish apartheid, but for moving too quickly.

All this raises the question of what—if anything—can be done by the United Nations or by its individual members to end this situation that the world has deplored and denounced for so many years. As early as 1966, U Thant was saying that the problem could be solved only by enforcement action. Nobody then or during the following two dcades has been able to get big power support for the use of force against the Pretoria government. As a matter of fact, the big powers were never able to agree on the much milder step of imposing mandatory sanctions against South Africa. The failure of U.N. action could eventually lead to an alternate solution—one that many fear and dread: an armed uprising of the black majority, with the help of sympathetic African countries. This would mean civil war and a possible bloodbath for the white minority.

POSTSCRIPT

As this was written, the long controversy over Namibia (South-West Africa) finally appeared to be approaching its end. As part of an agreement that included the withdrawal of Cuban and South African military forces from Angola, the Pretoria government promised to pull out of Namibia by mid–1989 if Cuban forces leave Angola by that time. Withdrawal of South African troops from the former League of Nations mandate was scheduled for November 1, 1988 and independence elections were planned for June 1, 1989.

25

Round Four: The Yom Kippur War

Almost immediately after the end of the Six-Day War in the Middle East, events began moving in the direction of another armed conflict, perhaps bigger and more devastating than any of the previous three. Efforts of U.N. special envoy Gunnar Jarring were making little or no progress toward resolving the issues left pending after the 1967 cease-fire.[1]

The whole Middle East was in a state of ferment. Two years after the end of the Six-Day War, U Thant was frankly predicting that, failing some early progress toward a settlement, the Middle East "will recede steadily into a new dark age of violence, disruption and destruction." In the introduction to his 1969 annual report, the secretary-general wrote;

War actually is being waged throughout the area, short only of battles between large bodies of troops. Patrol and guerrilla activities have become common, as have raids by land and sea and at times by air, bombardments of suspected centers of guerrilla activities and explosive charges on roads and in civilian structures.[2]

In addition to the breakdown of law and order in the area, there were international developments adding fuel to the fire. One of them was a new treaty of friendship between Egypt and the Soviet Union under which the Soviets would go on supplying Egypt with weapons and training facilities "with a view to strengthening its capacity to eliminate the consequences of the [Israeli] aggression." The treaty also provided for urgent consultations in the event of a renewed threat of war. Addressing the Knesset in Jerusalem, Prime Minister Golda Meir described the treaty as giving to the Soviet Union control over Egyptian policies.

She called on the United States to supply Israel with more planes and sophisticated equipment to counter Soviet arms shipments to Egypt.

Another development was an erosion of Arab unity. Because of its crackdown on Palestine guerrillas, Jordan was at odds with almost all the other Arab states; and Libya's Muammar al-Gaddafi called publicly for the assassination of King Hussein. Sudan had broken off diplomatic relations with Iraq after the Iraqi government had prematurely recognized precommunist rebels who briefly overthrew Premier Gaafer al-Nimeiry. Iraq also was still engaged in a long-time feud with Syria.

The suspended peace talks were resumed at U.N. headquarters in January 1971 under the auspices of Jarring. He met separately with the representatives of Israel, Egypt, and Jordan and—at the request of Israel—flew to Jerusalem for discussions with Prime Minister Meir and Foreign Minister Abba Eban. The talks disclosed no substantial movement toward agreement. On February 8—in an effort to break the deadlock—Jarring submitted an aide-mémoire asking the parties to make prior commitments to him on the key questions of Israeli troop withdrawal and acceptance of a peace agreement by Egypt and Jordan. The Egyptian government formally accepted the proposal on February 15; but Israel reacted angrily, asserting that Jarring had exceeded his terms of reference by proposing the withdrawal of Israeli troops to the former international boundary between Egypt and the British mandate of Palestine. This—the Israelis said— went even further than the November 22, 1967, resolution calling for withdrawal to the lines that existed prior to the Six-Day War. Israel told Jarring that it would not agree to the former international boundary or to the 1967 boundary, but that it would undertake to withdraw "to recognized and agreed boundaries to be established in a peace agreement." Thant had worked with Jarring on the aide-mémoire, and had fully approved its contents before its submission to the parties. Plainly disappointed by Israel's response, he made a personal appeal to the Israeli government to reconsider its position and "respond favorably." Instead, Israel refused to take part in further peace talks on the basis of the aide-mémoire. Jarring let the matter drop and returned to his post as Swedish ambassador to Moscow.[3]

At a press conference in Geneva on April 29, the secretary-general said that he and Jarring had reviewed the situation and agreed there "is at present no real basis for Ambassador Jarring's immediate return to New York."[4]

During this press conference and at a later one in Boston on May 27, Secretary-general Thant supported Jarring's February 8 initiative. He said that the Big Four powers also felt Jarring "was strictly within his mandate in taking that initiative," and "I fully endorse that position."[5]

Shortly after this deadlock developed, Egyptian War Minister Lieutenant General Muhammed Sadek was named commander of all Egyptian and Syrian troops facing Israel. Sadek told his troops that "The battle is coming sooner than you imagine." Egyptian President Anwar el-Sadat donned an army uniform, assumed direct command of the armed forces, and moved his office to military headquarters. On November 11, Sadat told the National Assembly that Egypt would take part in no further diplomatic negotiations until Israel committed itself to withdrawing from occupied Arab lands. Israel stuck to its previous position that it would withdraw to "secure and recognized borders" only when these had been worked out as part of a peace agreement. Israel had already taken the position that some of the occupied territory would not be the subject of negotiations. These included the Golan Heights, the Old City of Jerusalem, and Sharm el-Sheikh, which commanded the entrance to the Red Sea.[6]

At U.N. headquarters, representatives of the United States, Britain, France, and the Soviet Union continued the consultations that they had begun after the 1967 cease-fire, but still they had not succeeded in producing a formula for easing the tension. The United States—acting on its own—did manage to get a cease-fire agreement between Egypt and Israel in the Suez sector in 1970. This was connected with the negotiations being carried on by Secretary of State William Rogers for the clearing and reopening of the canal to shipping. In the introduction to his 1971 annual report, U Thant took note of the limited cease-fire, and said;

It is not possible to predict how long this quiet will last, but there can be little doubt that, if the present impasse in the search for a peaceful settlement persists, new fighting will break out sooner or later. Since the parties have taken advantage of the present lull to strengthen their military capabilities, it is only too likely that the new round of fighting will be more violent and dangerous than the previous ones, and there is always the danger that it may not be possible to limit it to the present antagonists and to the confines of the Middle East. I see no other way to forestall such a disastrous eventuality than by intensifying the search for a peaceful and agreed settlement.[7]

In July 1972 hopes for a settlement glimmered briefly when President Sadat ordered Soviet "military advisers"—estimated at from 10,000 to 15,000—to leave Egypt. Sadat charged that Moscow was an "over-cautious" ally who would not provide his country with advanced aircraft and missiles needed for another war with Israel. The swift departure of the Soviets was especially significant because it was seen as decreasing the danger of the big powers' being drawn into a new war. Israeli Prime Minister Meir seized the Soviet expulsion as an opportune moment to call on Sadat for a meeting with her as "equals," to make peace. During a speech in the Knesset, she said, "It would seem that this hour in the history of Egypt can, indeed should, be the appropriate hour for change and if it is truly the hour for change let it not be missed."

Sadat did not accept the bid. He repeated his long-standing objections to direct talks without an Israeli commitment to withdraw from occupied territories. Hopes for a settlement received a devastating blow a few weeks later when Arab terrorists struck the Summer Olympics in Munich in one of the most shocking and bloody raids the world had yet witnessed. The toll was 11 Israelis, five of the Arab commandos, and a German policeman killed. Revenge came three days later when warplanes from bases all over Israel made simultaneous strikes at ten different Arab guerrilla bases inside Syria and Lebanon. The Lebanese government reported 16 civilians dead and more than 50 wounded. Syria said that casualties there exceeded 150, and demanded condemnation of Israel by the U.N. Security Council. When the council met on September 10 to approve a resolution calling for the cessation of all military operations in the Middle East—but without referring to the terrorist attacks that had provoked the air strikes—the United States cast its second veto in the history of the United Nations. Arab commentators said that the veto gave Israel the green light to strike again. As a matter of fact, Israel had become accustomed long before that to ignoring U.N. resolutions that it considered to be one sided. Prime Minister Meir said that Israel had "no choice but to strike at terrorist organizations wherever our long arm can reach them," without waiting for an attack.

In what amounted to an undeclared war between Israel and the Arab commandos, the wave of violence continued to escalate in 1973 not only in the Middle East, but in Europe and elsewhere. There was a Palestinian attempt to bomb the Israeli ambassador's residence in Cyprus; the Israeli assassination of three Palestinian guerrillas in downtown Beirut; the slaying of an Israeli military attaché outside his suburban Washington, D.C., home; an attack on an El Al Airlines office in Athens by a Palestinian, who was chased into a hotel where he held 17 hostages; the interception of an Iraqi airliner by Israeli jets, which forced it to land near Haifa (where the Israelis discovered that the radical Palestinian they were looking for had decided not to take the flight. There were Palestinian shoot-outs at the airports in Athens and Rome—which killed 35 and wounded scores of others. And there were scores of hijackings—mostly of airliners, but one of a train carrying Jewish immigrants en route to Austria from the Soviet Union. All this was bound to drag the parties sooner or later into all-out war. The outcome became even more certain after a three-hour Syrian–Israeli dogfight on September 13 over the Mediterranean Sea. This was the biggest air battle between Arabs and Israelis since the Six-Day War. Syria said that it shot down five Israeli planes and lost eight of its own. Israel said that it had downed 13 Syrian jets and lost one of its own.

The war came on October 6—the Jewish fast of Yom Kippur—when Egypt and Syria struck at Israel from two sides by land and by air. It was the fourth time that the Arabs and Israelis had gone to war since Israel's independence. Behind the attack was the deep bitterness over the Sinai Peninsula and the Golan Heights—which were stripped from Egypt and Syria in 1967—and a desire to wipe out the humiliation that the Arabs had suffered in the Six-Day War. This time, during the first hours, the Arabs definitely had the advantage. The Egyptians threw 11 bridges across the Suez Canal, and Egyptian tanks by the thousands crossed into the Israeli-held Sinai. On the Golan Heights, the Syrians attacked with 1,000 tanks. Arab broadcasts in Beirut said that 100 Israeli planes had been shot down. The Israeli command acknowledged that Syrian forces had made "a number of ground advances."[8]

While Jordan, Iraq, Algeria, Tunisia, Morocco, and Libya prepared to join the Arab forces, U.S. President Richard Nixon and Soviet Leader Leonid Brezh-nev exchanged private messages. If the messages were aimed at ending the fighting, they produced no apparent results. On October 8—two days after the first Arab strikes—Israel counterattacked. Skyhawks and Phantoms knocked out all the Egyptian bridges over the Suez Canal. In 30 hours of fighting—Israeli officials announced—most of Egypt's armor and infantry had been destroyed or driven back. Israeli fighter-bombers struck Syria's five major military airfields. On the ground, Israeli tanks and self-propelled artillery concentrated on the three wedges that Syrian forces had driven into Israeli lines on the Golan Heights. Lieutenant General David Elazar, Israel's chief of staff, said that, by nightfall on October 8, "we managed to push almost all of them back to the [1967] cease-fire line." He numbered Syrian tanks destroyed at "many hundreds."

No one looked for a quick victory. Under an umbrella of Soviet-built SAMS on the west bank of the Suez, Egypt pumped fresh tanks and men across the canal. They reported advancing nine miles into the Sinai, wiping out an entire Israeli unit. The Egyptians had crossed the canal with about 600 tanks, and the Israelis said that about 300 of them were still operational. On the Golan Heights, the Israelis had pushed the major Syrian advances back, but had failed to sweep the heights clean. In a religious holiday address, Golda Meir said that she had no doubt the war would end in an Israeli victory, but—she said—"this may take more than six days."

At this point the Israeli command reached a major strategy decision, which called for a temporary holding operation in the Sinai to permit an all-out assault on Syria as the immediate priority. On October 11—the sixth day of the war—the attack on the Golan Heights began by air and land. By October 13 the Israelis had advanced to within 18 miles of Damascus, and consolidated their lines.

As the fighting continued, both the Soviet Union and the United States began stepping up military aid to their allies. The Soviets started resupplying Syria and Egypt with thousands of tons of equipment from supply centers in Hungary. The United States, in turn, began preparing to ship F–4 Phantoms and A–4 Skyhawks to replace the aircraft that the Israelis had lost. The Arab countries responded to the U.S. moves by cutting oil exports to the United States. Within days Qatar, Kuwait, Bahrain, Dubai, Abu Dhabi, and Libya had embargoed all their oil exports to the United States.

The delayed Israeli attack on the Egyptian front began in the predawn hours of October 16. East of the Suez Canal, the Egyptians and Israelis had assembled forces described by Israeli Major General Haim Herzog as bigger than the com-bined forces at El-Alamein in World War II. Through a wedge they had driven into the Egyptian positions on the east bank of the Suez, the Israelis pushed more and more tanks across the canal. As the Israeli bridgehead expanded, four Arab foreign ministers brought a general peace proposal to President Nixon in Washington, and Soviet Premier Kosygin met in Cairo with President Sadat. On October 20 Secretary of State Henry Kissinger flew to Moscow. He met with Soviet Leader Brezhnev as soon as he arrived and again the following day for four hours. The war became a race to gain the best possible positions before an expected U.S.–Soviet cease-fire move could bear fruit.

Late on Sunday, October 21, the Soviet Union and the United States announced that they had agreed to submit to the U.N. Security Council a joint resolution for an end of the hostilities. At their request, the council met at 10 P.M. that same day. U.S. Ambassador John Scali said, "We believe this council, in exercising its primary responsibilities in the field of peace and security, can make a major contribution to this end by adopting this resolution promptly." Soviet Ambassador Jacov Malik also urged quick action. "Time will not wait," Malik said. Just before 1 A.M. on October 22, the council approved the cease-fire appeal by a vote of 14 to 0, with the People's Republic of China not voting.[9]

The resolution said: "All parties to the present fighting [must] cease all firing and terminate all military activity immediately, no later than 12 hours after the moment of the adoption of this decision, in the positions they now occupy." Prime Minister Meir met with her cabinet all night, but the deciding factor in her decision was a personal appeal from President Nixon. "At a time when Israel was more dependent than ever on the United States," she said, "we were hardly in a position to say no." At 7 A.M. Israel accepted the truce, and Egypt followed at 2:30 P.M. Syria finally agreed to the cease-fire, although reluctantly.

The truce almost collapsed when fighting broke out anew in part of Israel's bridgehead in Egypt. The Soviet Union warned Israel of "grave consequences" unless the fighting stopped. By dawn on October 24, Israel had driven all the way south to the Gulf of Suez—isolating the Egyptian Third Army on the west bank of the canal. The 20,000 Egyptians, who were cut off from food and water as well as fuel for their 200 tanks, tried in vain to fight their way out. At the urgent request of the Security Council, Israeli Defense Minister Moshe Dayan proposed a new cease-fire to begin at 7 A.M. the next day, and Egypt accepted.

Egyptian President Sadat asked the Soviet Union and the United States to send military contingents into the Middle East to supervise the cease-fire, but Nixon rejected the proposal. As night fell, Brezhnev sent to Nixon a private message described by Senator Henry M. Jackson as "brutal, rough." Although the State Department denied it, *Time* magazine said that the note "threatened the destruction of the State of Israel." The next day Nixon ordered a worldwide "precautionary alert" of all U.S. forces. In midafternoon, the Security Council voted to establish a U.N. emergency force—similar to the one liquidated in 1967—to supervise the cease-fire. The council specifically excluded troops from the superpowers. Both the Soviet Union and the United States voted for the resolution. Nixon said that the crisis had been the worst since the Cuban missile confrontation in 1962. He said he believed that the Soviet Union had planned to send "a very substantial force" into the Middle East. In his note—Nixon said—Brezhnev was "very firm and left very little to the imagination as to what he intended. And my response was also very firm and left little to the imagination of how we would react."

As the United Nations installed its peace-keeping force between the Israelis and the Egyptians in the Sinai Peninsula, the United States and the Soviet Union gradually removed their forces from the state of alert. Under pressure from Washington, the Israelis permitted a U.N. truck convoy to reach the trapped Egyptian Third Army with medical supplies, food, and water. In an effort to bolster the cease-fire, Egyptian Foreign Minister Ismail Fahmi and—later—Israeli Prime Minister Meir conferred with President Nixon in Washington. Secretary of State Kissinger made a whirlwind visit to Morocco, Tunisia, Egypt, Jordan, and Saudi Arabia, while Assistant Secretary of State Joseph Sisco visited Tel Aviv. They got agreements from both sides on a number of crucial issues, including the following:

—Mutual discussion of a return to positions held at the time of the first U.N. cease-fire, and mutual disengagement of forces

—Food, water, and medicine for the town of Suez, and evacuation of all wounded civilians

—Nonmilitary supplies for the trapped Egyptian Third Army

—U.S. checkpoints on the Suez–Cairo road, and the exchange of prisoners of war—which numbered 241 Israelis in Egypt and 8,301 Egyptians in Israel.[10]

It was not until July 1974 that disengagement of the Israelis and the Arabs was completed, after a delayed Syrian–Israeli accord. Much of the credit went to Kissinger, whose tireless shuttle diplomacy finally brought agreement on terms for a Golan Heights settlement. The accord was signed on May 31 by Israeli and Syrian generals, meeting in Geneva. On June 1 the International Red Cross began exchanging Israeli and Syrian prisoners of war. Opposing armies pulled back into designated zones on each side of the buffer strip, which would contain 1,250 U.N. peace-keeping troops. As part of the truce agreement, Israel surrendered 154 square miles of Syrian territory taken during the Yom Kippur War and 30 square miles captured during the Six-Day War. Kissinger's search for peace had taken him to Jerusalem 16 times, to Damascus 13 times, and on side trips to Cairo, Nicosia, Alexandria, Amman, Riyadh, and Algiers—a total of 24,230 miles. Among the troublesome questions left unresolved was the matter of what to do about the Palestinian guerrillas who continued to shatter the peace with terrorist raids on Israel.

26

Tempest around the Persian Gulf

One of the world's major trouble spots during the 1980s was the Persian Gulf area, where Iran and Iraq were locked in a continuing war and Iran's political and spiritual leader—the Ayatollah Ruhollah Khomeini—was sounding strident calls for an Islamic revolution. As Jeane Kirkpatrick, U.S. ambassador to the United Nations from 1981 to 1985, has said, "Not since Adolf Hitler has one prophet of violence been the center of so much concern and activity." The crisis in the Persian Gulf is deep rooted, growing originally out of the split in Islam in the late seventh century. Khomeini is leader of the Shiite faction, while a majority of Iran's conservative Arab neighbors belong to the Sunnis. The crisis has grown in intensity because of Khomeini's threat of a Holy War to free Muslims of "the infidel yoke." He has vowed that Iranians would eat dust before abandoning their revolutionary aims. One of his objectives has been to oust the royal family in Saudi Arabia—which he liked to call the "lackeys" of the United States. The ayatollah's attacks on the United States, in fact, were often more violent than his thrusts at neighboring countries. This, too, added to the tension in international relations, and produced a serious threat to peace.

The situation in Iran was relatively quiet until 1978 when widespread demonstrations by conservative Muslims forced Shah Mohammed Reza Pahlavi to declare martial law in 12 cities and later to appoint a military government. Continued violence caused the shah to flee the country on January 16, 1979, after designating Prime Minister Shahpur Bakhtian to head a regency council in his absence. Khomeini was still in exile in Paris at the time, but he named a provisional government to prepare for his return to Iran. The 80-year-old ayatollah made his triumphal return on February 1, 1979, after his supporters had routed Iran's elite imperial guard and forced the resignation of Prime Minister Bakhtian.

There is no question but that the ayatollah had his domestic problems during those first months, but no one could have anticipated the event that occurred on November 4, 1979, just nine months after his return to Teheran. During the rash of mass demonstrations that were common occurrences during those months, a group of radicals seized the U.S. Embassy and held its occupants as hostages—a total of 62 Americans. The Iranian group vowed to remain in the embassy until the deposed shah was returned to Iran to face trial for his "crimes" against the people. It so happened that the shah had just arrived in the United States from Mexico to receive medical treatment for reported gallstone and cancer illness. It seems doubtful that the seizure of the embassy was planned by the government—or even had its blessing in the beginning—but it was quickly exploited as a way to strike at the United States for its friendly relations with the shah. One of the ayatollah's top aides, Ali Akbar Hashimi Rafsanjani—who later became speaker of the parliament—explained it this way:

We never had any intention to move against the embassy. But the ex-dictator's arrival in the United States pushed the people over the deep end. When the attack on the embassy came, it took place so quickly and decisively that, frankly, all we could do was express our support ex post facto. Even if we had tried to stop them, we would have failed.

Regardless of whether the seizure was planned, it quickly won government support. The radical group in charge released 13 of the hostages; but Khomeini repeatedly threatened that the remaining 49 would be tried as spies and possibly executed if the United States did not turn over the shah, who was in a New York hospital. The White House warned that "The consequences of harm to any single hostage will be extremely grave." It added that, while it was seeking a peaceful settlement, "other remedies are available." The White House statement explained that the other remedies were "explicitly recognized in the charter of the United Nations." This was a reference to Articles 42 and 51. Article 42 empowers the Security Council to authorize action by "air, sea and land forces" of member nations to restore peace and security. Article 51 recognizes the right to individual or collective self-defense if an armed attack occurs against a member before the Security Council has time to respond. Seizure of the U.S. Embassy— it was asserted—could be regarded as an attack on the United States itself. In a bravado response to the threat, Khomeini said, "Why should we be afraid? We consider martyrdom a great honor."[1]

This was the beginning of a tug-of-war that was to continue for many months. Efforts for a solution turned toward the United Nations. At the request of the United States, Secretary-general Kurt Waldheim called an urgent meeting of the Security Council. The council met, but adjourned for four days to permit a representative of Iran the opportunity to fly to New York. However, Iran's Revolutionary Council voted to boycott the debate. Khomeini denounced the meeting as having been dictated by the United States. The council went ahead despite the boycott; and speaker after speaker, including the representative of the Soviet Union, condemned Iran for holding the Americans. By a vote of 15 to 0, the council adopted a resolution demanding the immediate release of the hostages. The Iranian response was unexpectedly mild. Foreign Minister Sadegh Ghotbzadeh complained that the resolution did not deal with Iran's demand for the return of the shah, but called it a "step forward." He did not agree to release the hostages.[2]

The United States tried—but failed—to get the Security Council to denounce Iran for its threat to put the hostages on trial as spies. The other council members, who noted that the Iranians had ignored the earlier appeal to free the hostages, doubted that such a statement would do any good. President Jimmy Carter wanted to get U.N. sanctions, but found U.S. allies cool to the idea. He did go on national television to declare that "Iran stands in arrogant defiance of the world community."[3]

Meanwhile, quiet diplomatic efforts were being made to find a peaceful solution. Carter's special emissary, Ramsay Clark, flew to Teheran, but gave up after Khomeini refused to see him. The Palestine Liberation Organization (PLO) also failed in an effort to act as mediator. Secretary-general Waldheim journeyed to Teheran after putting out private feelers to Iran's U.N. representative. They all recognized that Iran's conditions for releasing the hostages left little room for bargaining. President Carter had made it clear that he would not consider turning the shah over to the Iranian government. On the other hand, Iranian President Abolhassan Benisadr insisted on: (1) a U.S. admission of guilt for its support of the shah, (2) recognition of Iran's rights to seize the shah and his assets, and (3) a pledge of noninterference in Iran's affairs. Ali Rafsanjani said in an interview that Iranians might be willing to settle for less than the return of the shah. What they wanted, he said, was an acknowledgment that there was sufficient evidence to warrant an investigation into criminal charges against the shah.

This was the situation when Waldheim went to Teheran on January 3, 1980— two months after seizure of the hostages. His visit did not produce the release of the Americans, but it did lead to an agreement for a U.N. "fact-finding" mission to hear grievances of the Iranian leaders against the shah. This was far short of Iran's demand for a commission to investigate past U.S. "crimes" in Iran—which had been vigorously opposed by the United States. However, it was hoped that agreement to the limited U.N. inquiry might bring release of the hostages.[4]

It did not—and President Banisadr firmly denied that there was any connection between the U.N. commission and the detention of the Americans. By this time, the shah had ended his 54-day stay in the United States. He flew to

Panama, after the Mexican government refused him permission to return there. Later he went to Egypt at the invitation of his long-time friend, Anwar Sadat, and remained there until his death on July 27.

By that time, a number of important developments had taken place. The United States broke diplomatic relations with Iran on April 7. Again Khomeini was defiant. "We take this break in relations as a good omen," he said. "Iranians have forced an oppressive super-power to terminate its pillage here. The nation is justified in celebrating the advent of victory." The five-member U.N. fact-finding commission did hold a series of hearings in Teheran, but it packed up and left after Khomeini reneged on an agreement to allow commission members to visit the hostages.

On April 22 President Carter entered the White House briefing room to announce a new tough U.S. policy. Declaring that the United States had made every effort to gain release of the hostages "on honorable, peaceful and humanitarian terms," Carter said that the Iranian government "can no longer escape full responsibility by hiding behind the militants in the embassy." He said that Iranian diplomats and military officials would be expelled from the United States, all U.S. exports to Iran would be prohibited, some of the $8 billion in Iranian assets already frozen would be used to help settle U.S. claims against Iran, and visas would not be issued or renewed for Iranians to visit the United States. "The steps I have ordered today," Carter concluded, "are those that are necessary now. Other actions may be necessary if the steps do not produce the prompt release of the hostages." The Iranian militants responded by threatening to kill the hostages if the United States took any military action against Iran. Carter's statement also touched off a new wave of demonstrations in Iran, where millions marched and shouted anti-American slogans.[5]

The steps announced by Carter were, in fact, a prelude to military action. On April 25—three days after his statement—the president told the nation that a military raid to rescue the hostages had been aborted, leaving the burned bodies of eight U.S. servicemen behind in the Iranian desert. The raid was almost universally regarded as a blunder and a humiliating failure for the president. It raised questions not only of judgment, but of the capabilities of the U.S. Sea Stallion helicopters that had attempted the rescue. In Iran, Khomeini crowed over the bungled rescue attempt, and Iran haggled over return of the bodies left behind. No action was taken against the hostages, despite the threats; but their whereabouts was now a closely guarded secret, to thwart any future rescue attempt.[6]

While the hostage drama was unfolding in Iran, Iraqi strongman Saddam Hussein was watching with more than casual interest from Baghdad. He had just strengthened himself politically by a bloody purge of his associates, and the time seemed perfect to challenge Iran—his perennial enemy. In the predawn hours of September 23, 1980, six Iraqi divisions roared across the border into Iran, mainly into the oil-rich southern province of Khuzistan. Hussein was in for a bitter disappointment. His armies were unable to sustain the early gains.

The war that Iraq had hoped to win in three days was still going on in 1987, with no end in sight. Both sides took heavy losses and—after seven years—were feeling serious economic pressures because of reduced oil prices. U.S. sources estimated that Iran had lost 250,000 dead and nearly 500,000 wounded; Iraq, 100,000 dead and 150,000 wounded.[7]

Hussein's goal appeared to be twofold: to take control of the disputed border territories, including full control of the Shatt-al-Arab border estuary; and to bring down the Shiite Muslim regime of Khomeini. Hussein had been seeking a cease-fire and peace talks since 1982, but the ayatollah steadfastly rejected efforts by the United Nations and by some neighboring countries to mediate. There could be no peace, Khomeini insisted, until Hussein was removed from power.

When the initial attack took place in 1979, the United States tried to follow a hands-off policy, since its relations with Iraq were strained and it was still in the midst of its conflict with Iran over the hostages. President Carter's early reaction was that the war might convince the Iranians "they were part of the international community" and thus induce them to release the hostages. That did not happen. Instead, the Iranians introduced a new problem by threatening to close the Strait of Hormuz to oil shipments from neighboring Arab countries—including Kuwait, Bahrain, and the United Arab Emirates. Carter announced that the United States would intervene to keep the Persian Gulf route open. This brought an unexpected reaction from the Soviet Union. The United States was accused by the Soviet news agency, Tass, of making "preparations for armed interference" in the area. Secretary of State Edmund Muskie warned that the situation "could escalate to the point where the unthinkable hostilities may take place"—meaning, presumably, a U.S.–Soviet confrontation. Fortunately, however, Iran did not attempt to close the Strait of Hormuz, after all, and oil traffic continued without interruption.

Muskie said that the United States would welcome a U.N. Security Council call for a cease-fire, but he did not request a council meeting. His aides said that, if the United States appeared to be leading the peace efforts, both Iran and Iraq would reject them. The council did meet at the request of Norway and Mexico, but the session ended in some confusion as members quarreled over the proper role of the council itself. Eventually the council adopted a number of cease-fire resolutions, and Iran ignored all of them.[8]

After 14 months of apparently hopeless stalemate, word finally came that release of the U.S. hostages was imminent. On Sunday morning (U.S. time), January 19, 1981, Behzad Nabavi—Iran's chief hostage negotiator—announced: "The government of the Islamic Republic of Iran and the United States finally reached agreement on resolving the issue of the hostages today." The first reaction in Washington was cautious. Vice-president Walter Mondale said, "We're very, very close, but we do not yet have an agreement." Nabavi explained that "trivial details" still remained to be worked out. A State Department official said that the timing was still undecided, "but for all practical purposes there is agreement."[9]

These developments came some 48 hours before the end of Carter's term as president, and it was assumed that he would be on hand to welcome the hostages before leaving office. On a top secret document in Teheran, Prime Minister Muhammed Ali Raja'i wrote, "Transfer scheduled for Tuesday morning Teheran time." That would be Monday night in the United States. Elaborate preparations had been made. A team of Algerian doctors had been flown to Teheran to examine the hostages. Some $2.2 billion in frozen Iranian gold and currency had been transferred from New York to London so it could be turned over to Iran as part of the agreement within minutes after the release of the hostages. A 30-member U.S. hostage recovery team including former Secretary of State Cyrus Vance was ready to fly to West Germany to meet the hostages at a U.S. military hospital. Everything went according to plan, except for one thing. It was not Carter, but Ronald Reagan, who greeted the released hostages. Whether the Iranians delayed the release in a deliberate effort to embarrass Carter was never known; but, in any event, the release came on January 21—after Reagan's inauguration. The event touched off a nationwide wave of celebration and thanksgiving, and ended a sad chapter in U.S. experience.

In 1987 the crisis in the Persian Gulf again became intense when Khomeini announced a new decision to close the Strait of Hormuz to shipping, and the United States responded by authorizing Kuwaiti oil tankers to fly the U.S. flag and to sail with U.S. naval escorts. The United States also took the initiative in lining up support for a new U.N. peace effort to end the Iran–Iraq War. The Security Council was called into session at the request of the United States and the Soviet Union after Secretary of State George Shultz made a whirlwind visit to the various capitals, including Moscow and Beijing (Peking). A joint U.S.–Soviet resolution adopted unanimously on July 20, 1987, demanded that Iran and Iraq observe an immediate cease-fire—ending all military action on land, at sea, and in the air—and withdraw their forces to internationally recognized borders. It authorized U.N. Secretary-general Javier Perez de Cuellar to send observers to supervise the cease-fire and withdrawals. Shultz called the resolution a "historic step," and noted that compliance was mandatory under applicable provisions of the U.N. Charter. As expected, Iraq announced its acceptance of the cease-fire. Iran did not reject it outright, but continued to insist on the ouster of Hussein as a condition for peace.[10]

On July 31—11 days after the Security Council action—the Persian Gulf area was shaken by a bloody riot at Mecca in Saudi Arabia, where thousands of Muslims gather each year for the annual *hajj* (pilgrimage). The hajj period has always been a problem for Saudi Arabian security authorities. Every year, at least 40 people are trampled to death, and others die of heatstroke and disease. In 1979 a group of Saudi fundamentalists seized the Grand Mosque and held it in violent seige for several days. The Ayatollah Khomeini's office broadcast a charge that the action was instigated by the United States. "The Moslems must . . . expect this sort of dirty act by American imperialism and international Zionism," the statement said. The Iranian allegations touched off a wave of anti-American demonstrations in Pakistan, Bangladesh, India, Turkey, and other countries with Muslim populations. The U.S. embassy in Pakistan was burned.

The 1987 riot was even more serious because an estimated 400 were killed, including 275 Iranians. Iranian officials declared immediately that the clashes were the result of yet another "American plot," although they offered no evidence of U.S. involvement or motivation. President Sayed Ali Khameini said in Teheran that there was "no doubt the U.S. shoulders the responsibility for it. Of course, the Saudi government is also responsible because it was carried out through the Saudis and their police." Saudi Arabian officials denied that police had fired on the crowds, and insisted that the victims had been trampled under the feet of the two million pilgrims when they stampeded. It was generally agreed that the 150,000 Iranian pilgrims—the largest group ever sent from that country—touched off the riot by waving controversial banners and turning the pilgrimage into a Shiite propaganda show. They had been fired up by messages from the ayatollah condemning those who claimed "the pilgrimage is a place of worship, not a battlefield." Khomeini said that the pilgrims should "go from Holy hajj to Holy war" by bathing themselves in blood and martyrdom to seek "deliverance from infidels." He urged his followers to "break America's teeth in its mouth." When the riot was over, Iranian Prime Minister Mir Hossein Mousavi said that Iran would mobilize its resources to avenge what he called the "massacre of the pilgrims." The Iranian government called for a "Day of Hatred for America."[11]

In addition to the shipping conflict in the Persian Gulf, a major factor in the new "Hate America" frenzy was the congressional hearings on the U.S. arms-for-hostages deal with Iran. These dealings had first been disclosed in November 1986. The fresh airing of the scandals was deeply embarrassing to Iran since it disclosed Khomeini's willingness to traffic with the Great Satan. The Khomeini regime apparently felt the need to demonstrate anew its hatred for the United States. One U.S. expert on Iran said, "They had to respond to redeem themselves both domestically and internationally." Other observers expressed the belief that President Reagan's tough attitude on Persian Gulf shipping may also have been influenced by embarrassment over the Iranian arms deal.

The United States and the neighboring Arab states were not the only ones having trouble with Iran. Its most serious dispute was with France, which severed diplomatic relations with Iran over its refusal to permit France to question an Iranian embassy official about his alleged links with bombing attacks in Paris in mid-July 1987. The official was Vahid Gordji, an embassy interpreter. French security police sealed off the Iranian embassy to prevent Gordji from leaving. In Teheran, the Iranian government responded by blocking roads leading to the French embassy.

As the summer of 1987 drew to an end, the crisis in the Persian Gulf continued to dominate the international scene. There were a few hopeful signs, however. Visitors to Teheran reported that the public fervor for mass demonstrations appeared to have cooled somewhat, perhaps signifying a moderation in government plicy. Another positive development was an unexpected statement by Foreign Minister Ali Akbar Velayati in mid-August that Iran would welcome a visit by U.N. Secretary-general Perez de Cuellar to discuss security in the Persian Gulf. Despite these developments, the continued seriousness of the situation was reflected in the world press. Under the title "Iran vs. the World," *Time* magazine made this the subject of a comprehensive cover story in its issue of August 17, 1987. "The greatest threat to Khomeini's Iran, *Time* said, "may finally come not from the battlefield but from the country's almost suicidal tendency to cut itself off from the rest of the world."[12]

No one—except possibly the Soviet Union—seemed to know how to deal with the ayatollah's unpredictable behavior.

POSTSCRIPT

After a year of effort, the U.N. secretary-general achieved a breakthrough in the Iraqi-Iranian war. With the agreement of both countries, he was able to arrange a cease-fire that took effect on August 20, 1988. Face-to-face talks in Geneva began on August 25 to implement the Security Council resolution adopted in July 1987. The U.N. sent a peace-force to the area to monitor the disengagement. One Iranian correspondent was close to tears as he watched the negotiators take their seats to begin the talks. "It is a sad moment," he said. "We fought for eight years and now we have to sit face to face and talk with these people." Iranian and Iraqi officials swapped charges of cease-fire violations after the truce began, but the situation remained quiet along the 700-mile frontier. The peace talks were open-ended. Secretary-general Perez de Cuellar said the process could take years, with each side deeply mistrustful of the other's intentions.

27

The Soviets Try to Tame Afghanistan

All the way back to antiquity, Afghanistan's history has been stormy at times—marked by numerous invasions and violent political upheavals. Foreign conquerors alternated rule with local emirs and kings until the eighteenth century when a united kingdom was established. The country finally became a republic in 1973 after a military coup. Five years later pro-Soviet leftists seized power and concluded an economic and military treaty with the Soviet Union. During the next year and a half, two regimes were overthrown and their leaders killed. As 1979 was nearing its end, the Soviets were having problems with a third leader—President Hafizullah Amin—who had turned out to be a more independent-minded nationalist than they wanted. On December 24, the Soviet Union made a last attempt to persuade Amin to cooperate, but he refused.

Other governments watched with alarm as Soviet forces massed on the borders of Afghanistan. U.S. Ambassador Thomas J. Watson, Jr., delivered several warnings to the Soviet Foreign Ministry. On Christmas Eve of 1979, the Soviets began to airlift their troops into Kabul, the Afghan capital. Between December 24 and December 27, at least 350 Soviet aircraft landed at Kabul International Airport and Bagram Air Base, 20 miles north of the capital. They brought in a full airborne division from near Moscow, and support troops from Turkestan. On December 27, Soviet troops stormed Darulaman Palace. Amin was captured and shot, along with some of his relatives. By December 28 the capital was entirely in Soviet hands. Amin was being denounced posthumously as "a man who was in the service of the CIA."[1]

When President Jimmy Carter used his hot line to send Soviet Leader Leonid Brezhnev a tough protest on December 28, Brezhnev claimed that the Soviets had ben invited by Amin to protect the country from an unidentified outside threat. Carter denounced this explanation as "completely inadequate and completely misleading."[2]

The second phase of the invasion took place between December 29 and December 31. One Soviet motorized division moved in from Kuskka in the Soviet Union to Kandahar; another streamed in from the Soviet city of Termez; and other Soviet units moved east from Kabul toward the Khyber Pass and into Paktia Province, a center of Muslim insurgence. By the end of December, the Soviet Union had 50,000 men in Afghanistan.[3]

Carter condemned the Soviet invasion as "a deliberate effort by a powerful atheistic government to subjugate an independent Islamic people," and said that "a Soviet occupied Afghanistan threatens both Iran and Pakistan and is a stepping stone to their possible control over much of the world's oil supplies." It was imperative, Carter insisted, that world leaders "make it clear to the Soviets that they cannot have taken this action to violate world peace . . . without paying serious political consequences."

After a Soviet veto blocked action by the U.N. Security Council, the United States and 50 other countries called for an emergency meeting of the General Assembly. On January 12, 1980, the assembly adopted a resolution calling for the immediate withdrawal of Soviet forces. The Soviet Union ignored the resolution, even though it reflected a general condemnation by Third World countries—including Egypt, Tunisia, and Sudan. Communist China was enraged by the invasion. Beijing's *People's Daily* declared that "escalation of the Afghanistan intervention will only result in the spread of the flames of armed rebellion into a conflagration and Moscow will get its fingers burned." This proved to be an accurate prediction. Eight years later the Soviets were still involved in a costly stalemate against guerrilla forces in a war reminiscent of the one that the United States fought in Vietnam. Even the Ayatollah Ruhollah Khomeini warned the Soviet ambassador to Iran, Vladimir Vinogradov, that the Soviet Union had made a serious mistake. An aide reported Khomeini as saying to the Soviet envoy that "Brezhnev was stepping into the Shah's shoes and was heading for the same catastrophe that befell the ex-dictator. He said the Soviets would come to grief if they remained in Afghanistan."[4]

President Carter not only called Ambassador Watson home from Moscow "for consultations," but announced a number of unilateral sanctions against the Soviet Union. Not even during the Soviet invasions of Hungary and Czechoslovakia had a U.S. ambassador been called home from the Soviet Union. The sanctions ordered by Carter included the cancellation of sales of grain and high tech equipment, curtailment of Soviet fishing privileges in U.S. waters, and restriction of the cultural exchange program. In addition, Carter announced that the United States "along with other countries will provide military equipment, food and other assistance" to help Pakistan defend its independence. This turned out to be especially significant. Not only did thousands of anti-Soviet refugees pour across the Afghanistan border—placing a heavy burden on

Pakistan—but Pakistan also became a base for Afghan guerrillas, who eventually were receiving millions of dollars a year in covert assistance from the United States and Arab countries.

The repercussions of the Soviet invasion were felt even in the world of sports. In his television speech, President Carter brought up the possibility of a U.S. boycott of the 1980 Summer Olympic Games. "Although the United States would prefer not to withdraw from the Olympic Games scheduled in Moscow this summer," the president said, "the Soviet Union must realize that its continued aggressive actions will endanger both the participation of athletes and the travel to Moscow by spectators who would normally wish to attend the games." Vice-president Walter Mondale suggested that the problem might be solved by transferring the Olympics to another city. The idea of either a boycott or a transfer of the games brought protests from some athletes, but Carter did eventually order a boycott of the games. The United States was joined in the boycott by 62 other countries. This did not end the dispute. The Soviet Union retaliated by boycotting the 1984 Olympics in Los Angeles, along with other Soviet bloc countries.[5]

Meanwhile, the fighting inside Afghanistan continued to drag along at an estimated cost of 200 Soviet troops dead or wounded each month. Western intelligence sources at Islamabad, Pakistan, expressed the belief that the Soviet Union had lost from 5,000 to 10,000 dead or wounded since 1979. In an attempt to reduce Soviet casualties, the Soviets worked with the Afghan regime to build up a surrogate army of loyal Afghan troops to face the guerrillas. This would permit Moscow to begin withdrawing some of the 120,000 Soviet troops who were tied down in Afghanistan by 1984.

The international community based its main hopes on U.N. mediation efforts, which began in 1982 shortly after Javier Perez de Cuellar assumed office as the organization's fifth secretary-general. He inherited the problem of Afghanistan along with the Iran–Iraq War and the perennial crises in the Middle East, Southeast Asia, Cyprus, and South Africa. One of his early initiatives was the appointment of his undersecretary for political affairs, Diego Cordovez, to act as mediator between Pakistan and the Soviet-dominated government of Afghanistan. After five years of shuffling between rooms at the United Nations' Geneva offices—meeting alternately with the foreign ministers of the two governments—no solution was in sight. Up to mid–1987 there had been no face-to-face meeting between the two foreign ministers. Iran—although an official party to the negotiations—continued to boycott them. Cordovez put forward a new set of proposals in 1986, but these dealt mainly with peripheral issues: a pledge by Afghanistan and Pakistan not to interfere in each other's affairs; international guarantees of Afghanistan's independence by the Soviet Union and the United States; and the return of the three million refugees who had fled from Afghanistan. The United States announced its willingness to act as a guarantor of a settlement that would involve Soviet troop withdrawal and an end to U.S. aid to the guerrillas. No agreement had been reached, however, on how to monitor the troop withdrawal and the cessation of U.S. aid. Pakistan expressed its readiness to allow outside monitoring on the border—under U.N. supervision—but demanded similar monitoring of Soviet troop withdrawals. The Soviets insisted on the end of all "interference" and "intervention" before troop withdrawal. They also opposed U.N. monitoring on the Pakistan border. At the end of 1987 the two sides remained far apart on the proposed timetable for Soviet troop withdrawal. Afghanistan wanted a four-year schedule, and Pakistan called for six months. This was one of the problems under discussion. One of the most crucial issues—and one that had not been seriously addressed—involved the composition of the Afghan goverment after the cessation of all outside intervention. Would the guerrillas, for example, lay down their arms if the communists continued to control Kabul? On the other hand, would the Soviets withdraw their forces without being assured of a friendly regime on their northern border?

Early in 1988 signs began to appear that the Soviet Union was ready to begin withdrawing their military forces, even if it meant leaving the government of Major General Najibullah to stand by itself against the guerrillas. After the many months of negotiations in Geneva, agreements were finally announced on April 14, 1988 on the Soviet pullout. The agreements included provisions that (1) the Soviet withdrawal would begin on May 15 and be concluded by the end of 1988 and (2) U.S. aid to the guerrillas would decrease as Soviet military supplies to the Kabul government was reduced.

The agreements were signed at U.N. headquarters in Geneva in the same room where France agreed in 1954 to pull out of Indo-China. Speaking during the ceremony, Secretary-general Perez de Ceullar said: "I am confident that the signatories of the agreements will abide fully by the letter and spirit of the text and that they will implement them in good faith." The United States and the Soviet Union agreed to serve as guarantors of the agreements. As this was written, the withdrawals were proceeding on schedule.

28

Guns Roar in the South Atlantic

The Falkland Islands hardly seem worth a war. They consist of some 200 scattered, rocky, inhospitable islands in the South Atlantic—many of them little more than dots on the map. Prevailing west winds are so fierce that the Falklands have no trees. There are no paved roads, newspapers, or television sets outside the capital, Port Stanley—population, 1,000. The entire population of the islands is less than 2,000—97 percent of British descent—whose principal occupation is sheep-raising. The islands have been a British dependency since 1833 when King William IV wrested them from Argentina. For 150 years both Britain and Argentina had claimed sovereignty over the islands—known to Argentines as the Malvinas—and both had insisted that the question of sovereignty was nonnegotiable.

After years of diplomatic jousting between the two countries, Argentine President Leopoldo Fortunato Galtieri took matters into his own hands and seized the virtually undefended islands by force. On April 2, 1982, Argentine troops overpowered the small garrison of Royal Marines guarding Port Stanley. On the following day, they seized South Georgia Island, 800 miles away—thus completing the occupation of the Falklands.

If President Galtieri thought this would finally end the dispute, he had miscalculated the response of Britian's "Iron Lady"—Prime Minister Margaret Thatcher. "We have to recover those islands," she said in a television interview as she ordered the British navy into action. On April 5—two days after the initial Argentine landing—the aircraft carriers *Invincible* and *Hermes* sailed from Portsmouth for the Falklands with Harrier aircraft and Sky King helicopters on board. One of the helicopter pilots was 22-year-old Prince Andrew. Once out in the Atlantic Ocean, the carriers were joined by destroyers, frigates, and support vessels until the fleet numbered close to 30. Running at night under blackout conditions, the largest British fleet since World War II ploughed through the seas toward the Falklands 7,800 miles away.

Meanwhile, Argentina's C–130 Hercules military transport planes roared back and forth—bringing troop reinforcements, food, ammunition, and trucks to bolster the invading forces. In London, British Defense Secretary John Nott warned that the Royal Navy would sink any Argentine vessel—whether warship or merchantman—within 200 miles of the islands. "We will shoot first," Nott said. The Argentines, in turn, said they would sink any British ship that came near either the mainland or the islands.

As the two sides plunged headlong toward almost certain war, diplomatic efforts were launched by the United States, the United Nations, and the Organization of American States to find a peaceful solution. Britain's foreign secretary, Lord Carrington, resigned because of his failure to anticipate and prevent the Argentine invasion. "The invasion of the Falkland islands has been a humiliating affront to this country," Lord Carrington said in his letter of resignation. Prime Minister Thatcher accepted his resignation and quickly replaced him with Francis Pym. She herself was under a strong Labor party attack for misjudging Argentina's intentions and failing to keep a naval squadron near the Falklands during the period of tension.

In New York, the U.N. Security Council was quickly convened. On April 3, the council adopted a resolution calling for a cessation of hostilities, the withdrawal of Argentine troops, and negotiations between the two parties. Thatcher responded that Britain would not negotiate until Argentina withdrew its forces. And Galtieri told a cheering crowd: "If the British want to come, let them come. We will take them on."[1]

The Reagan administration in the United States found itself caught in the middle, as it sought to maintain its traditional ties with Britain without endangering its improved relations with Argentina and alienating other Latin American countries. "It is a very difficult situation for the United States," President Reagan said, "Because we're friends with both the countries engaged in the dispute." The United States did support the Security Council resolution calling for the withdrawal of Argentine troops, but did not go as far as the British expected in lining up on their side. Despite Margaret Thatcher's declaration that she would not negotiate, Reagan sent Secretary of State Alexander Haig dashing off to London and Buenos Aires to seek a peaceful solution.[2]

British Ambassador Sir Nicholas Henderson told Haig: "If U.S. territory were occupied or assaulted, you wouldn't start negotiating until the military situation was restored. The U.S. did not sit down with Japan the day after Pearl Harbor." After a five-hour meeting with Haig, Prime Minister Thatcher was reported to have told the secretary of state: "Stop talking about American even-handedness and tell the junta to obey the Security Council resolution to withdraw its forces. Only after that happens will we be prepared to talk about the future of the islands." Dennis Healey, the Labor party's shadow foreign secretary, took the same line. "The time has come," Healey said, "when we must tell the U.S. that the attitude of even-handed broker is not quite enough." Thatcher told the House of Commons that "gentle persuasion is not going to make the Argentine government give up what it has seized by force. . . . Argentina is not only in defiance of Resolution 502 but has violated it further by reinforcing its troops in the islands."

Haig was not yet ready to give up his mediation efforts. He continued until the British fleet finally arrived within striking distance of the Falklands. On April 25 at dawn, Britain landed a Royal Marine commando company of 100 men on South Georgia Island. They met strong resistance, but secured the island after 24 hours of fighting. The Argentine government acknowledged a "disembarcation" of British troops on South Georgia, and called for help from its Latin American allies. On a one-day visit to Port Stanley, President Galtieri said, "The Argentine flag will continue to fly. All necessary defense measures have been taken."

The recapture of South Georgia as a staging area was the first step in a three-phase British strategy. The second step was a sea and air blockade of the Falklands, to be followed by bombing raids and a major ground assault on the Port Stanley area. The war was on in earnest when British bombers—flying from Ascension Island—opened the air attack on Port Stanley. On May 1 a terse communiqué from the British Defense Ministry said simply: "Early this morning British aircraft took action to enforce the total exclusion zone and to deny the Argentines use of the airport at Port Stanley." The opening attack was carried out by a long-range Vulcan bomber, which was refueled in the air and proceeded to drop 21 half-ton bombs on its target. The strike was followed by a raid conducted by carrier-based Sea Harrier jets armed with 1,000-pound bombs and cannon. In a separate strike, British jets attacked a grassy airstrip 50 miles away, near the settlement of Goose Green.

One of the last proposals made by Secretary of State Haig was for a nine-nation administration of the Falklands for a five-year period, during which Britain and Argentina would attempt to settle the question of sovereignty. The proposal was rejected by both sides. The British insisted that: (1) all Argentine troops must leave the Falklands prior to any negotiations, (2) there should be an "identifyably British" administration during the transitional period, and (3) the interests and wishes of the inhabitants must have top priority in negotiations over the future of the islands.

After the British began military operations against the islands, Haig finally acknowledged the failure of his peace efforts. He blamed Argentina, and announced that the United States was abandoning its formal stance of neutrality. The United States, he said, was joining 14 other western nations in economic sanctions against Argentina. He announced that the United States would suspend all military exports to Argentina, and suspend new Export–Import Bank credits and loan guarantees as well as loan guarantees of the U.S. Commodity

Credit Corporation. In addition, Haig said that the United States would provide "material support" for Britain, if requested to do so. He stressed, however, that there would be "no direct military involvement" in the Falklands.[3]

The British foreign secretary welcomed the U.S. declaration. "To have the world's most powerful state on our side," he said, "must make Argentina see that aggression does not pay."

Within minutes after Haig finished his statement, Argentina's foreign minister, Nicanor Costa Mendez, appeared at the United Nations to state that his country "is always willing" to comply with the Security Council resolution. He went on, however, to repeat previous declarations that Argentina's claim of sovereignty over the Falklands was nonnegotiable. British Foreign Secretary Pym said, "Let him put his money where his mouth is. All the junta has to do is officially apply for British permission for the troops to be withdrawn from the islands." Costa Mendez took his case to the OAS in Washington—where most of the Latin American countries were sympathetic to Argentina's claims of Falklands sovereignty. After a lengthy debate, the OAS adopted a resolution by a vote of 17–0 supporting Argentina on the sovereignty question but also demanding compliance with Security Council Resolution 502. The United States and three other countries abstained. Later on, at another emergency meeting, the OAS approved a second resolution by the same 17–0 vote condemning Britain's "unjustified and disproportionate armed attacks" and asking the United States to lift its economic and military sanctions. In another last-minute effort, the Security Council instructed Secretary-general Javier Perez de Cuellar "to negotiate mutually acceptable terms for a cease-fire." He made a determined effort, but gave up after three weeks. "The efforts in which I have been engaged," he said, "do not offer the present prospect of bringing about an end to the crisis nor, indeed, of preventing the intensification of the conflict."[4]

D-Day came on May 21. Instead of striking directly at Port Stanley and the main Argentine troop concentration, the British target was the Port Carlos area on the northeast corner of East Falklands, about 50 miles west of the capital. With blackened faces and heavy camouflage, British commandos sped silently toward the moonlit beaches in amphibian landing craft—much like the Allied assaults on countless beaches during World War II. Waves of Scorpion tanks hit the lightly defended shores and fanned out across the wind-whipped moors. The Argentine troops offered little resistance on the ground, but counterattacked with furious air assaults.

British Defense Secretary Nott announced that British forces had shot down 16 Argentine planes and four helicopters, while losing one Harrier jet and two helicopters. Also, he said, four British ships had been damaged, and one sunk. That was the frigate HMS *Ardent* with a loss of 20 dead or missing and 30 injured. Nott claimed that the landing was "a complete success," despite the damage to the fleet. During the operation, the British had put ashore 5,000 troops and established a major bridgehead of ten square miles. Nott said that the British planned to advance from the bridgehead "to place the occupying

Argentine troops under increasing harrassment while the Royal Navy tightens the blockade around the islands." By the end of the week, British troops were edging forward over swampy terrain deep into the interior.

This was the beginning of the second phase. While British forces advanced overland, other crack troops using helicopters descended 20 miles south of Darwin and—from there—launched an attack on the garrison of 600 Argentine troops guarding that settlement. After fierce fighting, the British captured both Darwin and Goose Green. Meanwhile, the British fleet was suffering heavy losses as a result of intense aerial attacks. Waves of Skyhawk bombers struck at the armada—sinking the frigate *Antelope*, the *Coventry*, and the merchant ship *Conveyor*. Loss of the *Conveyor* was particularly painful because it was carrying a large cargo of invasion equipment. The British had already lost the destroyer *Sheffield*, which had been sunk by an Exocet missile at a cost of 44 dead, missing, or wounded. On the other hand, the British had sunk the Argentine cruiser *General Belgrano*. There were only 800 survivors out of the *Belgrano*'s crew of 1,042.

A week after the breakout of the original bridgehead at Port Carlos, the Birtish had the main force of 7,000 Argentine troops hemmed in at Port Stanley. Some 9,000 British troops were encamped on the hills above the capital, ready to attack. The Argentine commander still showed no signs of surrendering. General Mario Benjamin Menendez said that his forces were eagerly awaiting the attack. "We should not only defeat them," Menendez said, "but we should do it in such a way that they will never again have the daring idea of attacking our soil."

The main attack came after a week's pause. It was preceded by a heavy artillery barrage from British warships and by a saturated bombing attack by Harrier jets on the Argentine garrison. Within hours after the start of the all-out attack, General Menendez asked for a temporary cease-fire. Major General John Jeremy Moore, the British commander, agreed to talk. The rival commanders met, and the surrender was arranged. That was June 14—74 days after the Argentine invasion.

In London, Prime Minister Thatcher said, "This is a great vindication of everything we have done. . . . What a night this has been. What a wonderful victory." Three days after the British triumph, Argentina's top generals ousted President Galtieri. He was replaced by another general, Interior Minister Alfredo Oscar Saint Jean. Galtieri said, "I am going because the army did not give me the political support to continue." His departure was hastened by massive public demonstrations outside the presidential palace—with the crowds chanting, "Galtieri to the wall." It was one of the worst displays of public discontent since 1976. Later, Galtieri was court-martialed and sentenced to 12 years imprisonment for military incompetence. Apparently, his main sin was not starting the war with Britain, but losing it. The war was not a major conflict, as wars go. But it did cost the British 255 lives; and the Argentines, 712.

Five years later, the debate on the future of the Falkland Islands was still going on at the United Nations, in the OAS, in London, and in Buenos Aires. The U.N. General Assembly each year adopted resolutions calling for negotiations, including the question of sovereignty. Public opinion polls in Britain also favored some sort of change in the status of the Falklands, but Margaret Thatcher refused to negotiate on sovereignty. Meanwhile, the British were paying a high price to keep the islands. Since the end of the 1982 war, it cost some $25 billion annually to maintain 3,500 troops in the Falklands, plus warships and warplanes at $2.6 billion. That comes to $1.4 million for each islander.

29

The United States
Invades Grenada

Since 1979 the United States had been watching political developments in the Caribbean state of Grenada with growing concern because of Cuban penetration. Prime Minister Eric Gairy was overthrown on March 13 of that year by Maurice Bishop, a charismatic leader of the leftist New Jewel Movement. Within three days a Cuban ship carrying Soviet weapons and ammunition had arrived in Grenada. From then on, Cuban influence grew steadily although Grenada remained a member of the British Commonwealth.

President Jimmy Carter took official notice of the situation by warning Prime Minister Bishop that his government could expect no more economic aid from the United States if it aligned itself with Cuba. Bishop protested against what he called U.S. interference. And, instead of bowing to Carter's threat, he announced that Fidel Castro would help Grenada build a new international airport, ostensibly to bolster the island's tourist trade.

Shortly after taking office in 1981, President Ronald Reagan told Bishop that his ties with the Cubans posed a threat to the peace of the region. As relations with the United States worsened, Grenada's links with the communists became more open. Deputy Prime Minister Bernard Coard had already visited Moscow in May 1980, and signed a treaty giving the Soviets permission to land their long-range TU–95 reconnaissance planes on the island when the new airport was completed.

In June 1983 Bishop traveled to Washington without any official invitation, apparently in an attempt to patch up U.S. relations. After cooling his heels for a while, Bishop finally met with National Security Advisor William Clark. What happened there was not disclosed; but, after his return to Grenada, the prime minister toned down his anti-American rhetoric and talked openly of beginning a dialogue with the United States. Cuba decided that he would have to go. It gave Bernard Coard the nod to take over the government. Coard not only ousted Bishop; he went further and placed him under house arrest on October 13. Bishop's supporters—several thousand strong—rushed the gates of the prime minister's residence on October 19, freed Bishop, and carried him to a rally in the center of the capital, St. George's. Bishop spoke briefly before the crowd moved on to Fort Rupert, headquarters of the Grenadian army. There— according to eyewitnesses—violence erupted, and a dozen people were killed. Bishop was blamed by his opponents, and he was promptly executed along with three other top officials and two union leaders. General Hudson Austin, a tough former prison guard, announced on Grenada radio that a 16-man military gov-ernment under his leadership had taken control. He ordered a 24-hour curfew, and warned that violators would be shot on sight.

That was the situation when, at the request of six of Grenada's worried Caribbean neighbors, the United States decided to intervene. With the declared purpose of protecting 1,000 U.S. students trapped on the island after the military coup, the United States launched a full-scale invasion during the predawn hours of October 25. In the original announcement of the invasion, President Reagan said that the primary consideration was the safety of the students at St. George's University School of Medicine.[1]

Secretary of State George Shultz also stressed this. "With the violent and uncertain atmosphere that certainly was present on Grenada," Shultz said, "the question is: should the president act to prevent Americans from being taken hostage? I think that if he waited and they were taken hostage or many were killed then you would be asking me that same question: why didn't you, in the light of this clearly violent situation, take some action to protect American citizens there?"[2]

Spearheading the invasion was a contingent of U.S. Navy Seals—trained in special seaborne operations—who slipped ashore under cover of darkness and crept up the hill overlooking the capital. From there they rushed toward Gov-ernment House, where the island's governor-general—British-appointed Paul Scroon—was being held under house arrest by the military junta. Driven back at first by gunfire from the house guards, the seals attacked again and took possession of the mansion.

Later in the predawn light, U.S. air forces struck at Grenada's two airports— one operational, and the other the international airport still under construction. The attack on Pearls Airport was led by some 400 marines aboard troop heli-copters from the amphibian assault ship *Guam*. A half-hour later, hundreds of U.S. Army Rangers parachuted onto the uncompleted airstrip at Point Salines on Grenada's southeastern tip. The marines met little opposition, but the rangers ran into heavy antiaircraft fire as their helicopters approached Point Salines. Much of the flak came from the barracks where Cuban workers were housed.

The Pentagon had expected to find 350 Cubans at the construction site; but instead, the Rangers faced 600 well-armed professionally trained soldiers. Despite the surprise resistance, the airstrip was secured within two hours. But the fighting was far from over. An additional 400 Cubans plus an unknown number of Grenadian soliders continued sniper and mortar fire.

U.S. students at the True Blue campus of the university were awakened by the sound of bomb blasts and gunfire, but were unaware that an invasion was in progress. They had no idea who was doing the bombing and shooting. Some students rolled under beds, and others jumped into bathtubs as bullets crashed into their rooms. The fighting around the university was mainly between U.S. forces and a small number of Cubans and Grenadian soldiers who had isolated the True Blue buildings from the Grande Anse campus. The medical school's chancellor, Charles Modica, was highly critical of the invasion. He contended that the students had not been in danger until the shooting started.

The invasion drew a wave of protests around the world. In London, Prime Minister Thatcher deplored the violation of Grenada's sovereignty. Despite the token participation of the six Caribbean neighbors of Grenada, many Latin American nations saw the invasion as a revival of gunboat diplomacy. A total of 400 troops had been provided by Antigua, Barbados, Dominica, Jamaica, St. Lucia, and St. Vincent; but the U.S. forces did the fighting. The U.N. General Assembly, which was in session at the time, voted 108 to 9 to denounce the U.S. action, but President Reagan dismissed the U.N. vote with a quip. "It did not upset my breakfast," he said. The international censure faded quickly. At an OAS meeting in Washington, not one delegate suggested any censure of the United States.[3]

The Reagan administration did encounter a barrage of criticism for its handling of press coverage. This was the first time in recent history that representatives of the press had not been included in the initial stages of a military action. The press did not accept the explanation of Defense Secretary Caspar Weinberger and General John Vessey, Jr., chairman of the Joint Chiefs of Staff, that the ban was necessary to preserve secrecy and for the safety of the press representatives themselves. The press had not only been excluded from the initial landings, but was not allowed on the island until two days after the invasion—when a small selected group was escorted around Grenada. The American Society of Newspaper Editors formally complained that the exclusion went "beyond the normal limits of military censorship." The executive editor of the Washington *Post*, Ben Bradlee, said, "As long as I have been in the business, the press has been on military landings right along with the troops."

The invasion had begun on a Tuesday. By late Thursday, Atlantic Fleet Commander Wesley McDonald reported that "all major military objectives in the island were secured." But on Friday, he acknowledged that "scattered points of resistance" remained "and fighting is still in progress." McDonald said that captured Cuban documents showed that as many as 1,000 Cubans had been in Grenada, but that only 638 were in the custody of U.S. forces. The captured records showed—McDonald said—that Castro had planned to send 341 officers and 4,000 soldiers to the island, in addition to those already there. By mid-November all resistance had ended. All U.S. combat forces were withdrawn by mid-December. General Austin was arrested, and the Cubans were sent home. Governor-general Scroon announced that an Advisory Council would govern until parliamentary elections could be held.

On December 3, 1984, the residents of Grenada lined up for their first free elections since 1976. Observers from the OAS described the balloting as "flawless." The voters decisively rejected the kind of political radicalism that had prompted the U.S. invasion 13 months earlier. The landslide winner—with 59 percent of the vote—was the centrist New National party led by Herbert Blaize, age 66, a conservative former head of the government. His party won 14 of the 15 seats in Grenada's new House of Representatives. A day after the election, he was sworn in as prime minister at a ceremony at York House, Grenada's government building. The big loser was the United Labor party led by Eric Gairy, the country's first prime minister after independence. Almost completely ignored by the voters was the Maurice Bishop Patriotic Movement—the remnants of the New Jewel Movement that had seized power from Gairy in 1979.

The Reagan administration was openly pleased with the election outcome. A State Department spokesman praised the islanders for concluding "a year-long process aimed at putting Grenada firmly back on a democratic path." "We look forward," he said, "to cooperating with a new government." U.S. officials insisted that Washington had maintained a hands-off policy during the election campaign, despite the continued presence of 225 U.S. servicemen in Grenada. Blaize asked Reagan and the other countries to extend until March 1985 the stay of their peace-keeping forces on the island while his government carried out a review of security requirements. Actually, it was not until June 11, 1986, that the last U.S. troops left except for a team of security specialists. A small contingent of Jamaican troops remained to assist at Richmond Prison.

30

The United Nations Enters Its Fifth Decade

The fires of war still burned brightly all around the horizon as the United Nations passed its fortieth anniversary. Despite the peace-keeping efforts of the organization, many of its members still preferred to use military force to deal with troublesome problems. Since 1948 seven peace-keeping forces and six military observer missions involving 400,000 soldiers had cost the United Nations more than $3.5 billion. More than 700 soldiers wearing the U.N. blue berets had died while serving the organization. In 1987, 10,000 troops from 23 nations were serving in three peace-keeping forces and two small observer missions. The United Nations' two largest peace-keeping forces—in South Lebanon and in Cyprus—were in the red by more than $400 million. The organization still had not found a way to finance its peace-keeping operations except through volunteer contributions. Both France and the Soviet bloc have refused to either pay peace-keeping assessments voted by the General Assembly or make voluntary contributions. And quite apart from this, the United Nations faced horrendous fiscal problems because of out-of-control spending by the 159-nation General Assembly. In September 1986 the organization's deficit was $462 million, and the U.S. Congress was threatening to withhold part of the U.S. assessment unless economies were put into effect and controls established.

The preceding pages record the story of some 20 violent conflicts ranging in size from the Korean and Vietnam wars to small skirmishes such as those in Bizerte and Grenada. In mid–1987 some of these were still being fought, or were in a state of suspension that could activate at any time into a new flare-up. A full-scale war was going on in the Persian Gulf area; the Greeks and Turks lived under an armed truce in Cyprus; the Soviets were engaged with guerrillas in Afghanistan; and the Middle East remained a powder keg. A little-noticed war in northcentral Africa found the former French territory of Chad pitted against Muammar al-Gaddafi's Libyan army. Chad—one of the world's poorest nations—was trying with the support of France and the United States to win back the 1,000-mile-long, 70-mile-wide Aouzou Strip along Chad's northern border, which had been annexed by Gaddafi in 1973. Despite the area's apparent lack of strategic or economic importance, France spent $500 million a day during 1983 in a military operation aimed at preventing Libya from taking over Chad. France continued to pour in military aid, and in 1987 U.S. President Reagan authorized a $25 million grant to Chad for emergency military aid. By 1987 Chad was reported to have destroyed more than a billion dollars worth of captured Libyan military equipment. Chad's President Hissene Habre said that he was ready to talk peace with Gaddafi, but the Libyan leader showed no signs of seeking peace. "What we do not accept," Habre said, "is Gaddafi occupying our country, training terrorists, coming at you from a neighboring country, continuing to send forces into the north."

In addition to these international conflicts, blood was being shed in internal strife in a dozen countries in Central America, Africa, Asia, and the Middle East. These included Nicaragua, El Salvador, Angola, Mozambique, Namibia, Cambodia, Sri Lanka, the Philippines, and Lebanon. Government-sponsored terrorism and the taking of hostages added to the turbulent situation and caused dangerous international friction. One glaring example was the U.S. bombing raid on Tripoli in retaliation for Gaddafi's alleged training and sponsorship of anti-U.S. terrorists. Although foreign participation was involved in some of the civil strife, the United Nations has generally regarded most cases as being primarily domestic problems, and therefore outside the organization's jurisdiction. It has intervened, however, when requested by the government concerned.

The problems of the 1970s and 1980s were much the same as the problems of the 1940s, 1950s, and 1960s. The United Nations has always had its hoppers full of complaints of aggression, threats to international peace, and simple disputes between nations. In some cases, the organization has been instrumental in preserving or restoring peace. In others—especially those involving the superpowers—it has found its efforts futile for one reason or another.

What about the future? It has been said—and undoubtedly it is true—that the United Nations will be as good as its members want it to be. One major problem is unwillingness of the members to back up U.N. decisions with force. The Security Council has been reluctant even to vote mandatory sanctions, much less to authorize the use of miltary force—which it has the power to do—to enforce its decisions when a country defies it. There is also the tendency of member nations to place self-interest above the general good. During the past 40 years, this tendency has not diminished, and it does not appear likely to do so.

How can the fires of war be extinguished when the nations of the world are spending $1.7 million a minute on weapons and making them available to terrorists, guerrillas, and irresponsible governments? This figure—a historic high—was published in 1986 in a study sponsored by the Arms Control Association, the Rockefeller Foundation, and other private groups. Critics of U.N. expenditures should be concerned that the total U.N. budget of $650 million a year is not a drop in the bucket when compared to arms production costs. Even more frightening than the spurt in arms production is the proliferation of nuclear weapons. While the United States and the Soviet Union were negotiating a reduction in their nuclear weapons, some nations were expanding their nuclear arsenals and others were rapidly achieving the capabilities to produce such weapons. Despite the 1968 treaty on nonproliferation signed by 120 countries, there is evidence that several countries may now have joined the nuclear club or have reached the threshhold of nucelar weapons capability. These include Israel, India, Pakistan, and possibly South Africa—although none of them admit to having the bomb. Perhaps it is worth noting that all four of these countries have been involved in violent conflicts and that their disputes remain unresolved, even though dormant at the moment. That is something for the United Nations to think about in its fifth decade. It could be worse. What if the Ayatollah Khomeini or Muammar al-Gaddafi got their hands on the bomb?

Notes

INTRODUCTION

1. Dag Hammarskjöld, "The Walls of Distrust," Address at Cambridge University, June 5, 1958. U.N. Press Release SG/684.
2. Adlai E. Stevenson, "Let None Mock Its Weakness," Speech before the American Association for the United Nations, San Francisco Chapter, October 23, 1961.
3. U Thant, Speech before the Annual Conference of Non-governmental Organizations, May 12, 1966. U.N. Press Release SG/504, Rev. 1.

CHAPTER 1

1. General Assembly Official Records, First Session, Part I, First Plenary Meeting, January 10, 1946.
2. Security Council Official Records, January 19, 1946.
3. Trygve Lie, *In the Cause of Peace* (New York: MacMillan, 1954), pp. 32–34.
4. Security Council Official Records, March 21, 1946.
5. General Assembly Official Records, First Plenary Meeting, Part II, October 23, 1946.

CHAPTER 2

1. Lie, *Cause of Peace*, pp. 55–60 and 107–124.
2. U.N. Headquarters Committee Official Records.
3. Dean Acheson, *Present at the Creation* (New York: Norton, 1969), pp. 111–112.

CHAPTER 3

1. U.S. Department of State Bulletin, Supplement 16, May 4, 1947, pp. 827–909.
2. Harry S. Truman, Message to Congress, Congressional Record 99–1999, March 12, 1947.
3. Lie, *Cause of Peace*, p. 104.
4. Acheson, *Present at Creation*, pp. 220–25.
5. Security Council Official Records, April 7, 1947.
6. U.N. Economic and Social Council, Official Records, 1947.

CHAPTER 4

1. Acheson, *Present at Creation*, pp. 176–82.
2. General Assembly Official Records, November 29, 1947.
3. Alfred Lilienthal, *What Price Israel?* (Washington, D.C.: Institute for Palestine Studies, 1969).
4. For Lie's views on the competence of the United Nations to enforce partition, see U.N. Palestine Commision Document A/Ac 21/13, February 9, 1948.
5. Joseph P. Lash, *Eleanor: The Years Alone* (New York: Norton, pp. 131–133).
6. On the reversal of U.S. position, see Lie, *Cause of Peace*, pp. 170–73 and 178–79.
7. Margaret, Truman, *Harry S. Truman* (New York: Morrow, 1973), pp. 388–89.
8. Andrew W. Cordier, Wilder Foote, and Max Harrelson, *The Public Papers of the Secretaries-general of the United Nations* (New York: Columbia University Press, 1969), Vol. 1, p. 2.

CHAPTER 5

1. Leland M. Goodrich, *Korea* (Westport, Conn.: Greenwood Press, 1956).
2. Dean Acheson, Speech before the National Press Club, January 12, 1949.
3. Charles W. Yost, *The Insecurity of Nations* (New York: Praeger, 1968), p. 146.
4. Trygve Lie, Speech in Chicago, September 8, 1950, U.N. Press Release SG/119.
5. General Assembly Official Records: On Lie's resignation plans, see November 10, 1952; on Lie's final statement, see April 7, 1953.
6. Security Council Official Records, June 25, June 27, and July 7, 1950.
7. Lie, *Cause of Peace*, pp. 329–30.
8. Ruth B. Russell, *The United Nations and the U.S. Security Policy* (New York: Columbia University Press).
9. Inis L. Claude, "The United Nations and the Use of Force," *International Conciliation.*

CHAPTER 6

1. Robert Murphy, *Diplomat among Warriors* (New York: Doubleday), pp. 313–23.
2. Security Council Official Records, October 25, 1948.
3. Joint Communication from Assembly President Herbert V. Evatt and Secretary-

general Trygve Lie Addressed to the Delegations of the Four Powers Signatory to Moscow Agreements, U.N. Press Release PSC/45, November 13, 1948.
  4. Acheson, *Present at Creation*, pp. 267–74.
  5. General Assembly Official Records, May 15, 1949.

CHAPTER 7

  1. Security Council Official Records, Supplements for 1948–49.
  2. Acheson, *Present at Creation*, p. 336.
  3. Security Council Official Records, January 1, 1949.
  4. Ibid., January 16, 1957.
  5. Ibid., March 30, 1951.
  6. U.N. Press Release SG/1095, December 7, 1961.
  7. Security Council Official Records, Supplement for July–August–September 1965, Documents S/6647, S/6651, S/6683, S/6686, S/6699, and S/6699 Add. 1.
  8. U.N. Monthly Chronicle 2 (August–September 1965): 17.
  9. U.N. Press Releases SG/SM359, SG/SM363, SG/SM364, September 15 and 16, 1965; and SG/SM431, January 11, 1966.
  10. *U.N. Monthly Chronicle* 8 (June, July, August–September, and November 1971).
  11. Henry Cabot Lodge, *The Storm Has Many Eyes* (New York: Norton, 1973), p. 151.
  12. Henry Kissinger, *White House Years* (Boston: Little, Brown, 1979), pp. 885–918.

CHAPTER 8

  1. Anthony Eden, *Full Circle* (Boston: Houghton, Mifflin, 1960), p. 588.
  2. Hugh Thomas, *Suez* (New York: Harper and Row), pp. 105–120.
  3. Security Council Official Records, Supplement for October–November–December, Documents S/3671, S/3675, and S/3679.
  4. Security Council Official Records, Meetings on October 30, October 31, and November 4, 1956.
  5. Brian Urquhart, *Hammarskjöld* (New York: Alfred Knopf, 1972), p. 174.
  6. Dwight David Eisenhower, *Waging Peace* (New York: Doubleday, 1965), pp. 52–53.
  7. General Assembly Official Records, First Emergency Session, November 2, 3, 4, 5, and 7, 1956.
  8. U.N. Press Release SG/519, November 7, 1956.
  9. U.N. Note to Correspondents No. 1447, November 12, 1956.
  10. Anthony Nutting, *No End of a Lesson* (New York: Potter, 1967), pp. 294, 296, and 304.
  11. Cordier, Foote, and Harrelson, *Public Papers*, vol. III (New York: Columbia University Press, 1973).

CHAPTER 9

  1. Hernane Tavares de Sa, *The Play within the Play* Alfred Knopf, p. 242.
  2. Murphy, *Diplomat* pp. 427–32.

3. Security Council Official Records, October 28, October 30, November 3, and November 4, 1956.

4. General Assembly, Second Emergency Session, Resolution 1004 (ES II), November 4, 1956.

5. Associated Press, November 3, 1956.

6. Eisenhower, *Waging Peace*, pp. 87–89.

7. General Assembly, Special Emergency Sessions, Resolutions 1005, 1006, and 1007 (ES II), November 9, 1956.

8. Ibid., Meetings on November 19, November 20, and November 21, 1956.

9. Ernest A. Gross, *The United Nations Structure for Peace* (New York: Harper and Brothers, 1962), p. 26.

CHAPTER 10

1. Dwight D. Eisenhower, *Mandate for Change* (New York: Doubleday), pp. 421–27.

2. *International Conciliation* 547 (March 1964): Inis L. Claude, "The O.A.S., the U.N. and the United States," 32.

3. Security Council Official Records, June 20 and June 25, 1954.

4. Urquhart, *Hammarskjöld*, pp. 88–94.

5. General Assembly Official Records, Supplement No. 1 (A/2663), 1954.

6. Security Council Official Records, Supplement for April–May–June 1958, Document S/4023, June 11, 1958.

7. U.N. Note to Correspondents No. 1821, June 12, 1958.

8. Eisenhower, *Waging Peace*, pp. 268–70.

9. Lodge, *Storm*, p. 138.

10. U.N. Press Release LEB/21, July 16, 1958.

11. Security Council Official Records, June 15, July 16, July 21, and July 22, 1958.

12. General Assembly Official Records, Third Emergency Session, August 8, August 13, and August 18, 1958.

13. General Assembly Resolution 1237 (ES-III).

CHAPTER 11

1. General Assembly Official Records, Committee IV, 1947 Session.

2. Trusteeship Council Official Records, 1948 Session.

3. Ibid., First Meeting, March 26, 1947.

CHAPTER 12

1. Claude, "O.A.S., U.N. and United States."

2. Lie, *Cause of Peace*, pp. 275–76.

3. John Foster Dulles, Speech at San Francisco Commemorative Session, 1955.

4. General Assembly Official Records, 1947 Session.

5. Ibid., September 20, 1950.

6. Lash, *Eleanor*, pp. 194–95.

7. U.N. Note to Correspondents No. 2176, June 2, 1960.

8. Arthur M. Schlesinger, Jr., *A Thousand Days* (Boston: Houghton, Mifflin, 1965), pp. 507–8.

9. Nikita Khrushchev, Speech on De-Colonization, General Assembly Official Records, 1960 Session.

10. On creation of a special committee, see General Assembly Official Records, 1961 Session.

CHAPTER 13

1. Security Council Official Records, July 14, July 22, and August 9, 1960.

2. Security Council Official Records, Supplements from July 1960 to March 1963, especially Documents S/4382, S/4426, S/4414, S/4417, S/4420, S/4571, S/4704, and S/4771.

3. General Assembly Official Records, September 23, September 26, October 3, and October 13, 1960.

4. Alexander Dallin, *The Soviet Union and the United Nations* (New York: Praeger, 1962), chs. 9, 10, and 11.

5. General Assembly Official Records, March 29 and following meetings through April 18, 1961.

6. U.N. Press Releases SG/1089, SG/1094, SG/1097, SG/1099, SG/1106, SG/1393, SG/1416, and SG/1420.

7. "Report on U.N. Military Disengagement," Security Council Official Records, Document S/5428, September 17, 1963.

8. Michael Harbottle, *The Blue Berets* Stackpole, (Harrisburg, PA: Stackpole Books, 1972), pp. 38–60.

CHAPTER 14

1. Security Council Official Records, Supplement for July–August–September 1961, Documents S/4874, S/4875, S/4885, S/4894, and Add. 1.

2. Security Council Official Records, July 22 and July 28, 1961.

3. General Assembly Official Records, Special Session, Resolution 1622 (S-III), August 25, 1961.

CHAPTER 15

1. Security Council Official Records, July 18, 1960.

2. Theodore Sorensen, *Kennedy* (New York: Harper and Row, 1965), pp. 205–6 (Kennedy–Nixon fourth TV debate), 294–309 (Bay of Pigs), and 667–718 (missile crisis).

3. Security Council Official Records, January 4 and January 5, 1961.

4. Schlesinger, *Thousand Days*, pp. 253–97.

5. General Assembly Official Records, April 21, 1961.

6. Security Council Official Records, February 22, 1962.

7. Security Council Official Records, October 22, October 24, and October 25 (Stevenson–Zorin clash), 1962.

8. U.N. Press Releases SG/1357, SG/1358, SG/1359, SG/1360, SG/1363, and SG/1368 Rev. 1.

9. Security Council Official Records, Supplement for January–February–March 1963, Documents S/5227 and S/5229.

CHAPTER 16

1. U.N. Press Releases SG/1098, SG/1116, SG/1118, and SG/1128, December 1961 through February 1, 1962.

2. U.N. Press Releases SG/1204, SG/1209, SG/1227, SG/1228, SG/1229, and SG/1233, May and June 1962.

3. General Assembly Official Records, Resolution 1752 (XVII), approved September 21, 1962.

4. U.N. Press Releases SG/1291 and SG/1330.

5. U.N. Note to Correspondents No. 2673.

6. Security Council Official Records, Supplement for April–May–June 1963, Document S/5298.

7. Security Council Official Records, Meetings on June 10 and June 11, 1963.

8. Security Council Official Records, Supplement for July–August–September 1963, Document S/5412; Supplement for October–November–December 1963, Document S/5447; and Supplement for July–August–September 1964, Document S/5927 Annex I.

9. Carl von Horn, *Soldiering for Peace* (New York: McKay, 1966), pp. 383–93.

10. For Thant's comment on von Horn resignation, see U.N. Correspondents Note No. 2798.

11. U.N. Press Releases SG/1559, SG/1563, SG/1566, and SG/1583, August–September 1963.

12. On Indonesia's withdrawal from U.N. membership, see U.N. Press Release SG/SM/212, January 1, 1965.

CHAPTER 17

1. Lodge, *Storm*, p. 151.

2. U.N. Note to Correspondents No. 2430, December 3, 1961.

3. Security Council Official Records, May 21, 1964.

4. Eric Sevareid, in *Look*, November 30, 1965.

5. U.N. Note to Correspondents No. 3075, February 24, 1965.

6. Lyndon B. Johnson, *The Vantage Point* (New York: Holt, Rinehart, and Winston, 1971), p. 395.

7. U.N. Press Releases SG/SM/524 and SG/SM/531, 1966.

8. *U.N. Monthly Chronicle* 3, (August–September 1966): 32–33.

9. U.N. Press Release SG/SM/543, July 30, 1966.

10. Security Council Official Records, Supplement for October–November–December 1966, Document S/7658; U.N. Press Release SG/SM/609 Rev. 1, November 11, 1966.

11. U.N. Press Release SG/SM/637, January 10, 1967; SG/SM/660, February 10, 1967; SG/SM/668, March 4, 1967; and SG/SM/673, March 15, 1967.

12. *U.N. Monthly Chronicle* 4 (April 1967).

13. Henry Kissinger, *White House Years* (Boston: Little, Brown, 1979), pp. 1471–73.

CHAPTER 18

1. Security Council Official Records, March 4, 1964.
2. Security Council Official Records, Supplement for January–February–March and July–August–September 1964, especially Documents S/5593, S/5593, Annex I, S/5593 Add. 1, and S/5600; also Supplement for October–November–December 1967, Document S/8286; Supplement for April–May–June 1969, Document S/9233, and October–November–December 1969, Document S/9521; and Supplement for October–November–December 1971, Document S/10401.
3. Harbottle, *Blue Berets*, pp. 66–88.

CHAPTER 19

1. Tavares de Sa, *Play Within Play*, pp. 22–36.
2. John S. Reshetar, Jr., *The Soviet Polity* (New York: Dodd, Mead), p. 517.
3. General Assembly Official Records, December 1, 1964.
4. Ibid., February 16 and February 18, 1965.

CHAPTER 20

1. Johnson, *Vantage Point*, pp. 187–205.
2. Security Council Official Records, May 14, June 11, and June 18, 1965.
3. U.N. Press Release SG/SM/309, May 18, 1965.
4. U.N. Note to Correspondents No. 3140.
5. Johnson, *Vantage Point*, pp. 486–89.
6. Security Council Official Records, August 21–24, 1968.
7. General Assembly Official Records, Supplement No. 1A (A/7201/Add1).
8. *U.N. Monthly Chronicle* 5 (August–September 1968).
9. Introduction to Thirty-Third Annual Report, September 24, 1968.

CHAPTER 21

1. Security Council Official Records, November 1965 and December 1966.
2. *U.N. Monthly Chronicle* 3 (May 1966).
3. *U.N. Monthly Chronicle* 5 (February 1968).
4. U.N. Press Releases SG/SM/998, July 13, and SG/SM/967, September 13, 1968; and SG/SM/1139, July 30, and SG/SM/1151, September 7, 1969.
5. U.N. Press Releases SG/T/277, January 12, SG/T/284, January 19, and SG/T/285, January 19, 1970.
6. *U.N. Monthly Chronicle* 7 (February–March 1970).

CHAPTER 22

1. Security Council Official Records, May 19 and May 26, 1967.
2. Security Council Official Records, June 5, June 7, and June 8, and June 9, 1967.
3. Security Council Official Records, Supplement for April–May–June 1967, Documents S/7930 and S/7930 Add 1.

4. Nutting, *Lesson.*

5. General Assembly Official Records, June 19 (Abba Eban's attack on Thant) and June 20 (Thant's reply).

6. Johnson, *Vantage Point*, pp. 290–304.

7. For Lord Brown's comment on the UNEF withdrawal, see London *Sunday Times*, October 25, 1970.

8. U.N. Press Release EMF/449 ("Notes on the Withdrawal of UNEF"), June 3, 1967.

9. General Assembly Official Records Document A/6672, July 12, 1967.

10. Security Council Official Records, November 9–22, 1967, Adoption of Resolution 242(1967).

CHAPTER 23

1. Security Council Official Records, January 13, 1950.

2. Lie, *Cause of Peace*, pp. 256–74 (on legal memorandum controversy).

3. Security Council Official Records, Supplement for January–February–March 1950, Document S/1466.

4. General Assembly Official Records, Resolutions No. 113 (II) and No. 187 (III).

5. U.N. Press Release, SG/61, March 10, 1950.

6. On the Acheson–Vyshinsky debate, see General Assembly Official Records, 1951.

7. Associated Press dispatches by the author on the 1954 Geneva Conference.

8. John Roderick, *What You Should Know about the People's Republic of China*, The Associated Press, pp. 55–56.

9. General Assembly Official Records, October 25, 1971.

10. *U.N. Monthly Chronicle* 8 (November 1971).

11. General Assembly Official Records, November 15, 1971.

CHAPTER 24

1. General Assembly Official Records, October 27, 1966.

2. General Assembly Official Records, Special Session, May 19, 1967; U.N. Press Release SG/SM/787, August 10, 1967.

3. Security Council Official Records, Supplement for April–May–June 1960, Document S/4305, April 19, 1960.

4. Security Council Official Records, April 1, 1960.

5. U.N. Press Release SG/918, May 15, 1960.

6. William R. Frye, *In Whitest Africa* (Englewood Cliffs, N.J.: Prentice-Hall): pp. 45–46 and 59–61.

7. Security Council Official Records, December 3, 1963.

8. U.N. Press Release SG/SM/473, March 24, 1966.

9. U.N. Press Release SG/SM/48, March 30, 1964.

10. U.N. Press Release SG/SM/641, January 17, 1967.

11. General Assembly Official Records, Supplement No. 1A (A/800/ Add. 1), Section VII, September 14, 1970.

12. General Assembly Official Records, Supplement No. 1A (A/600/ Add. 1), September 20, 1965.

CHAPTER 25

1. General Assembly Official Records, Supplement No. 1A (A/6701/Add. 1), September 15, 1967.

2. *U.N. Monthly Chronicle* 6 (February 1969).

3. Security Council Official Records, Supplement for July–August–September 1970, Document S/9902; and Supplement for January–February–March 1971, Document S/10070.

4. U.N. Press Release SG/T/347, April 29, 1971.

5. *U.N. Monthly Chronicle* 8 (June 1971).

6. U.N. Press Release SG/SM/1313, August 4, 1970.

7. General Assembly Official Records, Supplement No. 1A (A/8401/Add. 1), Part II, Section IV, September 17, 1971.

8. Details on the fighting are drawn from Associated Press Year Book for 1973.

9. Security Council Official Records, October 21, 1973.

10. Kissinger, *White House Years*, pp. 1276–89.

CHAPTER 26

1. Security Council Official Records, Supplement for October–November–December 1979.

2. Security Council Official Records, November 9, 1979 (resolution calling for release of hostages).

3. White House statement calling seizure of hostages an "outrage", November 11, 1979; White House statement warning against trial of hostages, November 15, 1979; Security Council Official Records, November 20, 1979; Secretary-general Waldheim's news conference, November 25, 1979; President Carter's nationally televised news conference, November 28, 1979.

4. Security Council Official Records, November 27 and December 4, 1979; General Assembly Official Records, December 17, 1979; Security Council Official Records, December 31, 1979 (resolution threatening Iran with economic sanctions and authorizing Waldheim to go to Teheran); Waldheim news conference, January 4, 1980.

5. President Carter's news conferences, February 13 and April 22, 1980.

6. White House statement on aborted rescue attempt, April 25, 1980.

7. On Iraqi attack against Iran, see the New York *Times*, September 23, 1980.

8. Security Council Official Records, September 23 and September 28, 1980; Supplement for July–August–September and October–November–December 1980.

9. On release of the hostages, see the New York *Times*, January 19 and January 21, 1981.

10. Security Council Official Records, July 20, 1987.

11. On the Mecca riots, see the New York *Times*, July 31, 1987.

12. *Time*, August 17, 1987.

CHAPTER 27

1. TASS dispatch on December 28, 1979, saying that the Afghan government had asked for urgent Soviet aid and that the U.S.S.R. "has met the request."

2. Message from Carter to Brezhnev on hot line warning that the Soviet action, if not "corrected, could have serious consequences to U.S.–Soviet relations," December 28, 1979; President Carter denounced Brezhnev response in TV interview on December 31, 1979.

3. December 30, 1979, Pravda dispatch acknowledging that the U.S.S.R. had sent a "limited" military contingent to Afghanistan in the face of "imperialist interference."

4. Security Council Official Records, January 7 and January 10, 1980 (Soviet Union vetoes resolution condemning invasion); General Assembly Official Records, January 12, 1980 (resolution condemning Soviet action).

5. In TV speech on January 4, 1980, Carter warned of possible boycott of summer Olympic games in Moscow; on "Meet the Press," NBC-TV, January 20, 1980, President Carter proposed that summer Olympics be removed from the Soviet Union, postponed, or cancelled.

CHAPTER 28

1. Security Council Official Records, April 3, June 2, June 3, and June 4, 1982 (resolution calling for cease-fire and negotiations vetoed by the United States and Britain).

2. President Reagan statement at news conference, April 5, 1982, saying that the Argentine–British controversy placed the United States in a "very difficult situation."

3. Statement by Secretary of State Alexander Haig on April 30, 1982.

4. OAS Official Records, April 28, 1982.

CHAPTER 29

1. President Reagan's news conference, October 25, 1983.

2. Secretary of State Shultz's news conference, October 25, 1983.

3. Security Council Official Records, October 28, 1983 (resolution condemning U.S. invasion vetoed by United States); General Assembly Official Records, November 2, 1983 (resolution condemning U.S. approved).

Selected Bibliography

Acheson, Dean. *Present at the Creation*. New York: Norton, 1969.

Byrnes, James F. *Speaking Frankly*. New York Harper and Brothers, 1947.

Claude, Inis L. "The O.A.S. the U.N. and the United States." *International Conciliation* 547 (March 1964).

———. "The United Nations and the Use of Force." *International Conciliation*.

Cordier, Andrew W., Foote, Wilder, and Harrelson, Max. *The Public Papers of the Secretaries-general of the United Nations*, 8 vol. New York: Columbia University Press, 1969–1977.

Dallin, Alexander. *The Soviet Union and the United Nations*. New York: Praeger, 1962.

———. "The Soviet View of the United Nations." In *Soviet Policies and Government*. Knopf.

Dayan, Moshe. *Diary of the Sinai Campaign*. New York: Weidenfeld and Nicolson, 1966.

Eden, Anthony. *Full Circle*. Boston: Houghton Mifflin, 1960.

Eisenhower, Dwight D. *Mandate for Change*. New York: Doubleday, 1963.

———. *Waging Peace*. New York: Doubleday, 1960.

Frye, William R. *In Whitest Africa*. Englewood Cliffs, N.J.: Prentice-Hall, 1968.

De Gaulle, Charles. *War Memoire*. New York: Simon and Schuster, 1971.

Gross, Ernest A. *The United Nations Structure for Peace*. New York: Harper and Brothers, 1962.

Harbottle, Michael. *The Blue Berets*. Harrisburg, PA: Stackpole Books, 1972.

Ismael, Tarec Y. *The Middle East in World Politics*. Syracuse, N.Y.: Syracuse University Press, 1974.

Johnson, Lyndon B. *The Vantage Point*. New York: Holt, Rinehart, and Winston, 1971.

Kelen, Emergy. *Hammarskjöld*. New York: Putnam, 1966.

Kissinger, Henry. *White House Years*. Boston: Little, Brown, 1979.

Kraslow, David, and Loory, Stuart H. *The Secret Search for Peace in Vietnam*. New York: Random House, 1968.

Lall, Arthur. *The U.N. and the Middle East*. New York: Columbia University Press, 1970.

Lash, Joseph P. *Dag Hammarskjöld: Custodian of the Brushfire Peace*. New York: Doubleday, 1961.

———. *Eleanor: The Years Alone*. New York: Morrow, 1972.

Lie, Trygve. *In the Cause of Peace*. New York: Macmillan, 1954.

Lilienthal, Alfred. *What Price Israel?* Washington, D.C.: Institute for Palestine Studies, 1969.

Lodge, Henry Cabot. *The Storm Has Many Eyes*. New York: Norton, 1973.

Love, Kenneth. *Suez*. New York: McGraw-Hill, 1969.

Murphy, Robert. *Diplomat among Warriors*. New York: Praeger, 1968.

Nutting, Anthony. *No End of a Lesson*. New York: Potter, 1967.

Oliver, Robert T. *Syngman Rhee, The Man behind the Myth*. New York: Dodd, Mead, 1954.

Paige, Glenn D. *The Korean Decision*. New York: Free Press, 1968.

Russell, Ruth B. *The United Nations and the U.S. Security Policy*. New York: Columbia University Press.

Schlesinger, Arthur M. Jr. *Thousand Days*. Boston: Houghton Mifflin, 1965.

Tavares de Sa, Hernane. *The Play within the Play*. New York: Alfred Knopf, 1966.

Thomas, Hugh. *Suez*, New York: Harper and Row, 1967.

Truman, Harry S. *Years of Decision*. New York: Doubleday, 1958.

Truman, Margaret. *Harry S. Truman*. New York: Morrow, 1973.

Urquhart, Brian. *Hammarskjöld*. New York: Alfred Knopf, 1972.

U.S. Department of State. *U.S. Policy in the Korean Crisis*. Washington, D.C.: U.S. Government Printing Office.

von Horn, Carl. *Soldiering for Peace*. New York: McKay, 1966.

Wadsworth, James J. *The Glass House*. New York: Praeger, 1966.

Walton, Richard J. *The Remnants of Power*. New York: Coward McCann, 1968.

Williams, G. Mennen. *Africa for the Africans*. Grand Rapids, Mich.: Eerdmans, 1969.

Yost, Charles W. *The Insecurity of Nations*. New York: Praeger, 1968.

Index

ABOUT THE AUTHOR

MAX HARRELSON was a reporter, correspondent, and editor for the Associated Press for 40 years—35 of them devoted to foreign affairs. He is a graduate of Ouachita Baptist University and Northwestern University, where he received a master's degree in journalism.

In 1939, Harrelson served as diplomatic correspondent in London, and afterward in Amsterdam, Copenhagen, Helsinki, Budapest, Athens, Belgrade, and Berne during the first years of World War II. After three years in the U.S. army, he joined the U.N. staff of the Associated Press in 1946 and served there for 26 years, including 22 years as Chief AP Correspondent. During that time he covered many top stories abroad. Among these were East–West summit conferences in Geneva and Paris, the Geneva Conference of 1954 on Southeast Asia and Korea, the Geneva conference on the reunification of Germany in 1959, NATO meetings in Ottawa and Paris, and part of the Vietnam peace talks in Paris in 1969. He also helped cover a Latin American trip of President Eisenhower and trips of Presidents Kennedy, Nixon, and Johnson to Canada. He covered a 1961 visit of Adlai Stevenson to ten South American countries as special emissary of President Kennedy, as well as visits of Queen Elizabeth II and Charles de Gaulle to Canada.

Harrelson was president of the U.N. Correspondents Association in 1955–56 and won the Deadline Club award for distinguished U.N. correspondence in 1962 and 1967. After his retirement from the Associated Press in 1972, he became a research associate for the Columbia University School of International Affairs, where he served as coeditor—along with Andrew W. Cordier and Wilder Foote—of *The Public Papers of the Secretaries-general of the United Nations*. He also assisted the late U.N. Secretary-general U Thant as a research assistant in preparing Thant's book, *View from the United Nations*. Max Harrelson now lives in Holiday, Florida, with his wife Louise. He has three children.